THIGH HIGH
Reiwa Hanamaru Academy

3

story & art by
Kotobuki

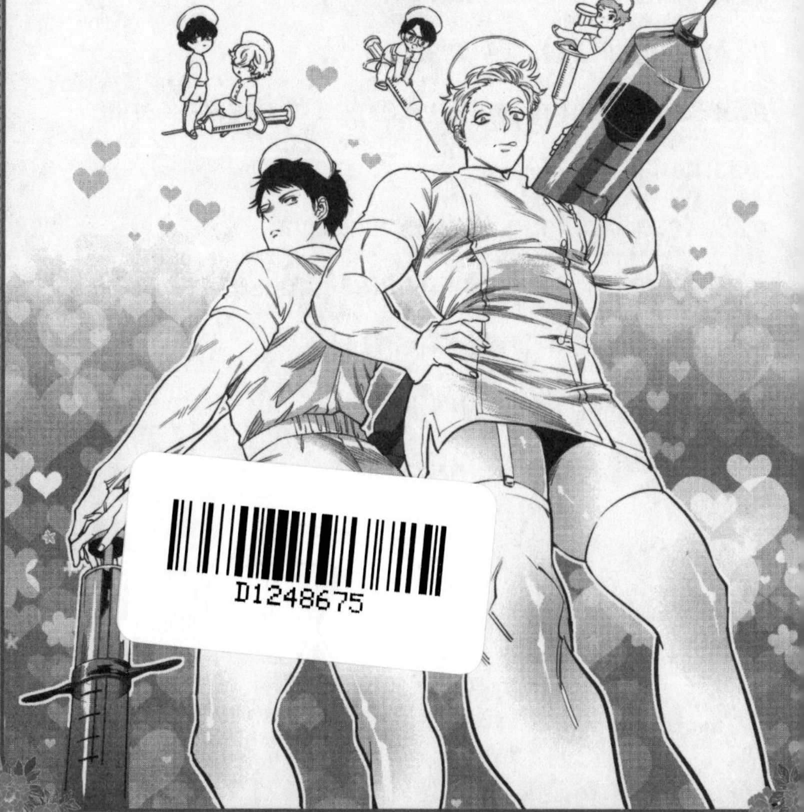

CONTENTS

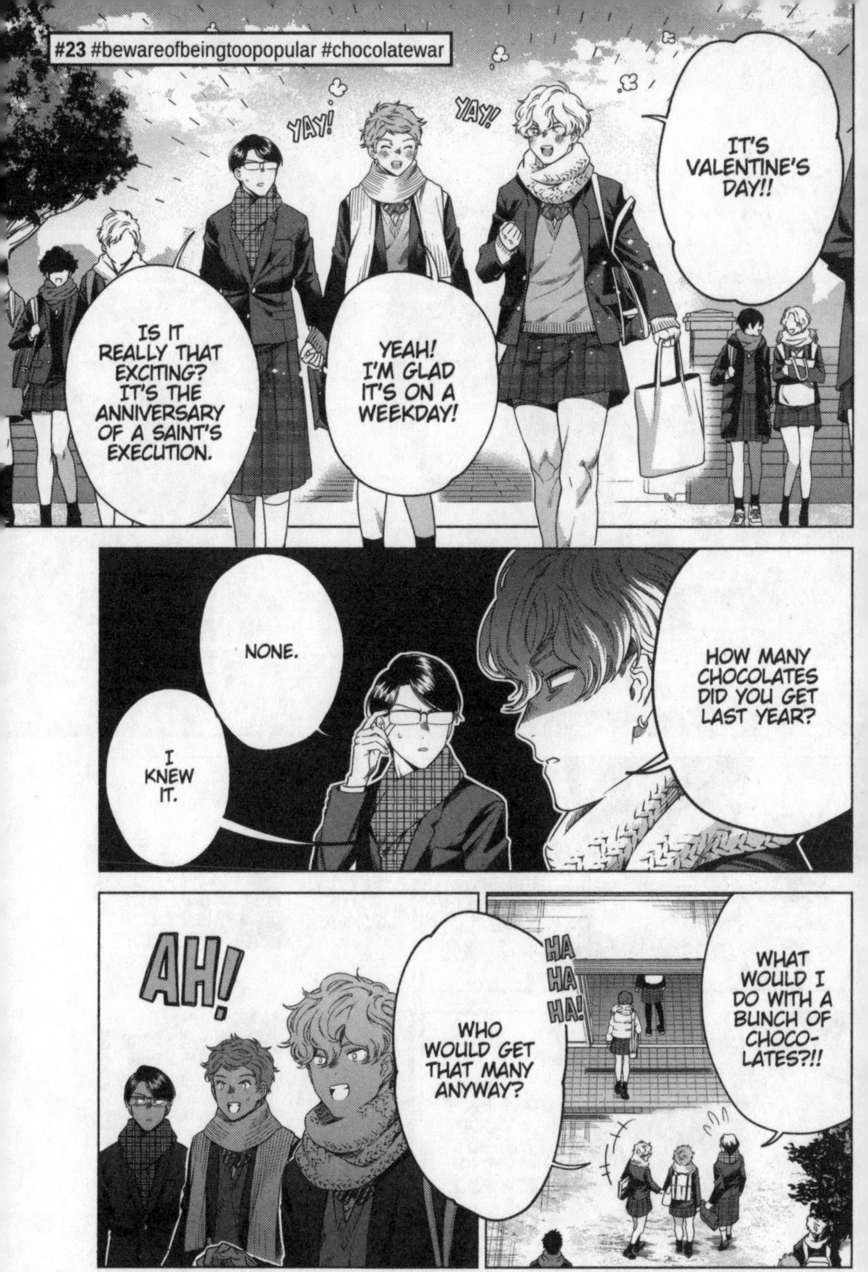
#23 #bewareofbeingtoopopular #chocolatewar
IT'S VALENTINE'S DAY!!
YAY!
YAY!
YEAH! I'M GLAD IT'S ON A WEEKDAY!
IS IT REALLY THAT EXCITING? IT'S THE ANNIVERSARY OF A SAINT'S EXECUTION.
HOW MANY CHOCOLATES DID YOU GET LAST YEAR?
NONE.
I KNEW IT.
WHAT WOULD I DO WITH A BUNCH OF CHOCO-LATES?!!
HA HA HA!
WHO WOULD GET THAT MANY ANYWAY?
AH!

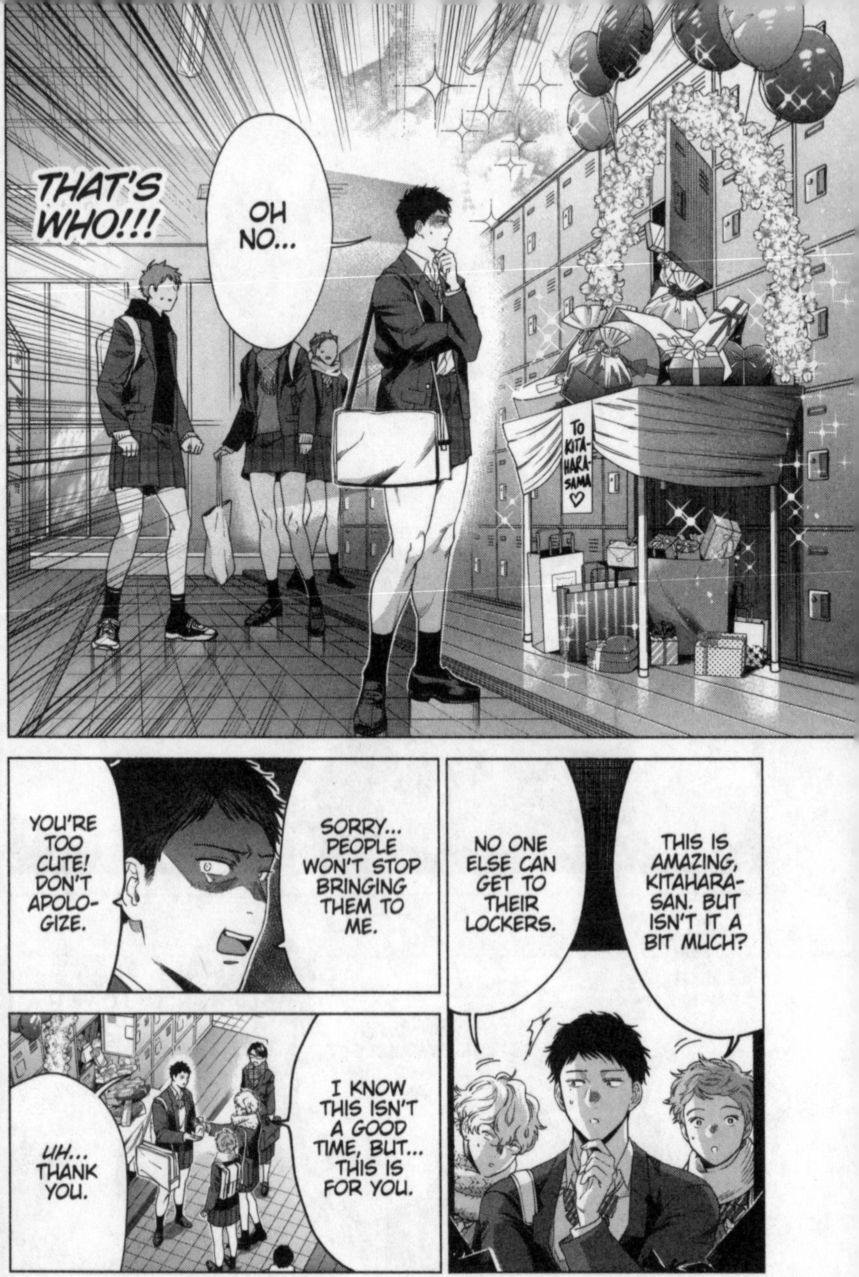
TO KITAHARA-SAMA ♡
OH NO...
THAT'S WHO!!!
THIS IS AMAZING, KITAHARA-SAN. BUT ISN'T IT A BIT MUCH?
NO ONE ELSE CAN GET TO THEIR LOCKERS.
SORRY... PEOPLE WON'T STOP BRINGING THEM TO ME.
YOU'RE TOO CUTE! DON'T APOLOGIZE.
I KNOW THIS ISN'T A GOOD TIME, BUT... THIS IS FOR YOU.
UH... THANK YOU.

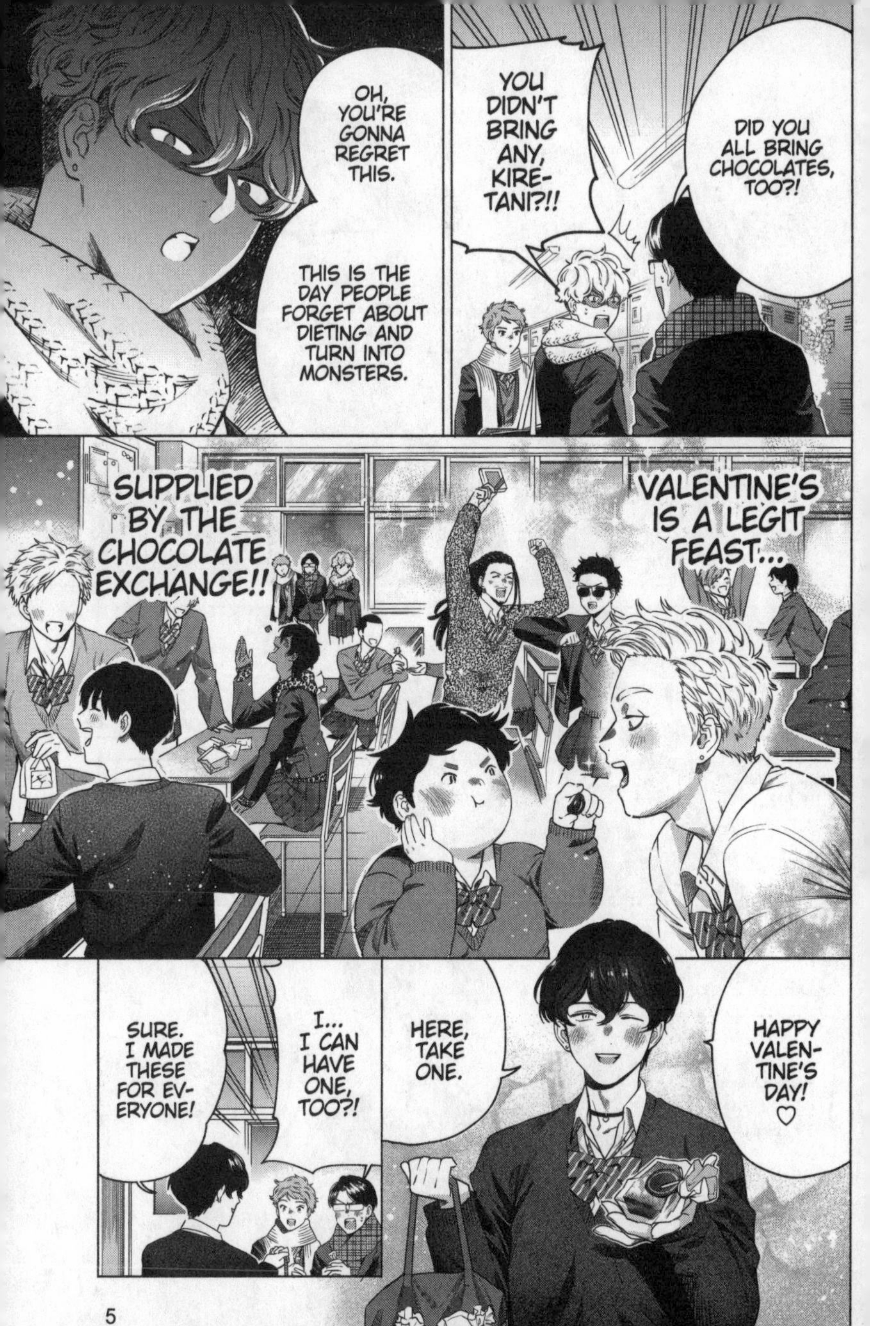
DID YOU ALL BRING CHOCOLATES, TOO?!
YOU DIDN'T BRING ANY, KIRE-TANI?!!
OH, YOU'RE GONNA REGRET THIS.
THIS IS THE DAY PEOPLE FORGET ABOUT DIETING AND TURN INTO MONSTERS.
VALENTINE'S IS A LEGIT FEAST...
SUPPLIED BY THE CHOCOLATE EXCHANGE!!
HAPPY VALEN-TINE'S DAY! ♡
HERE, TAKE ONE.
I... I CAN HAVE ONE, TOO?!
SURE. I MADE THESE FOR EV-ERYONE!

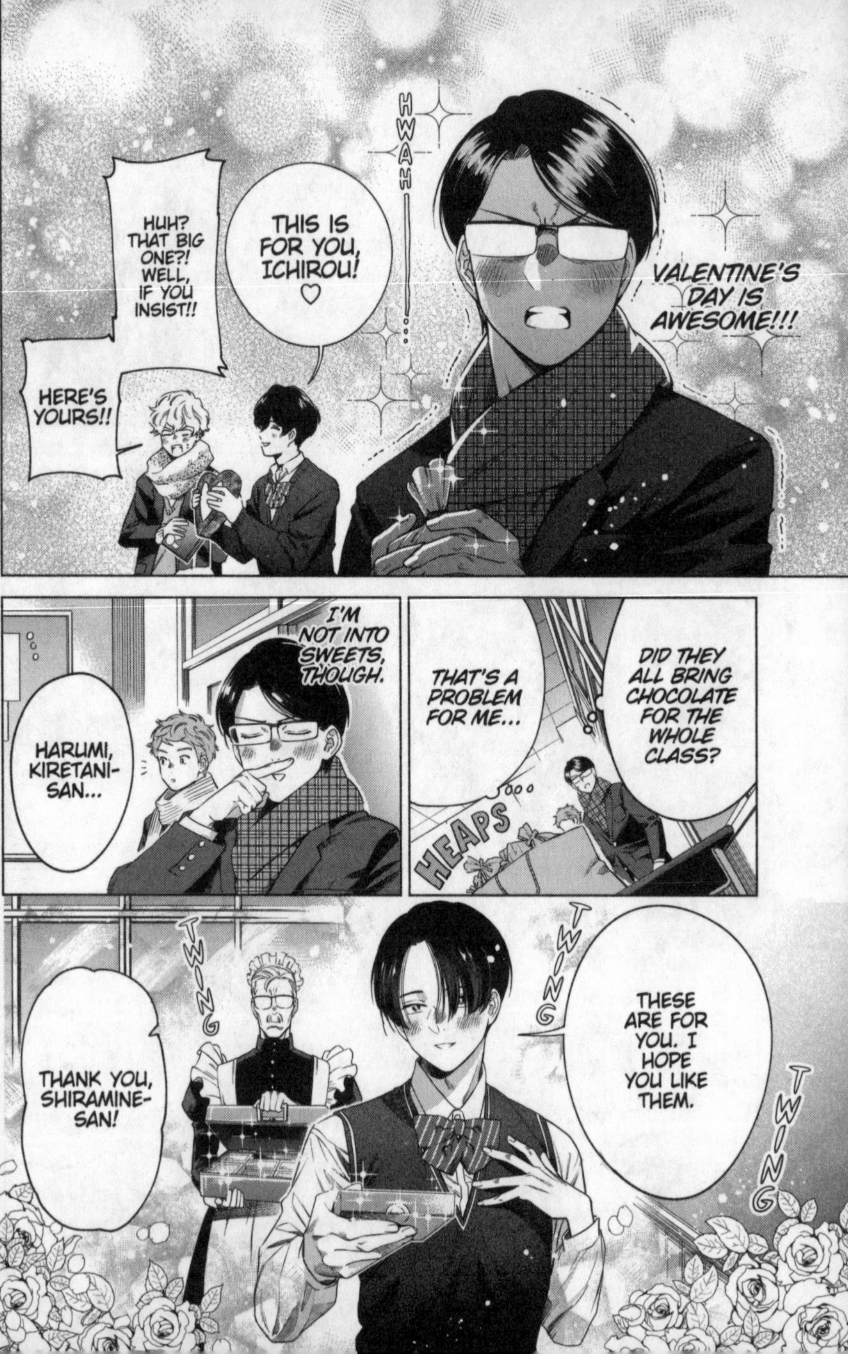
VALENTINE'S DAY IS AWESOME!!!
HWAH...
THIS IS FOR YOU, ICHIROU! ♡
HUH? THAT BIG ONE?! WELL, IF YOU INSIST!!
HERE'S YOURS!!
DID THEY ALL BRING CHOCOLATE FOR THE WHOLE CLASS?
THAT'S A PROBLEM FOR ME...
HEAPS
I'M NOT INTO SWEETS, THOUGH.
HARUMI, KIRETANI-SAN...
TWING
THESE ARE FOR YOU. I HOPE YOU LIKE THEM.
TWING
TWING
THANK YOU, SHIRAMINE-SAN!

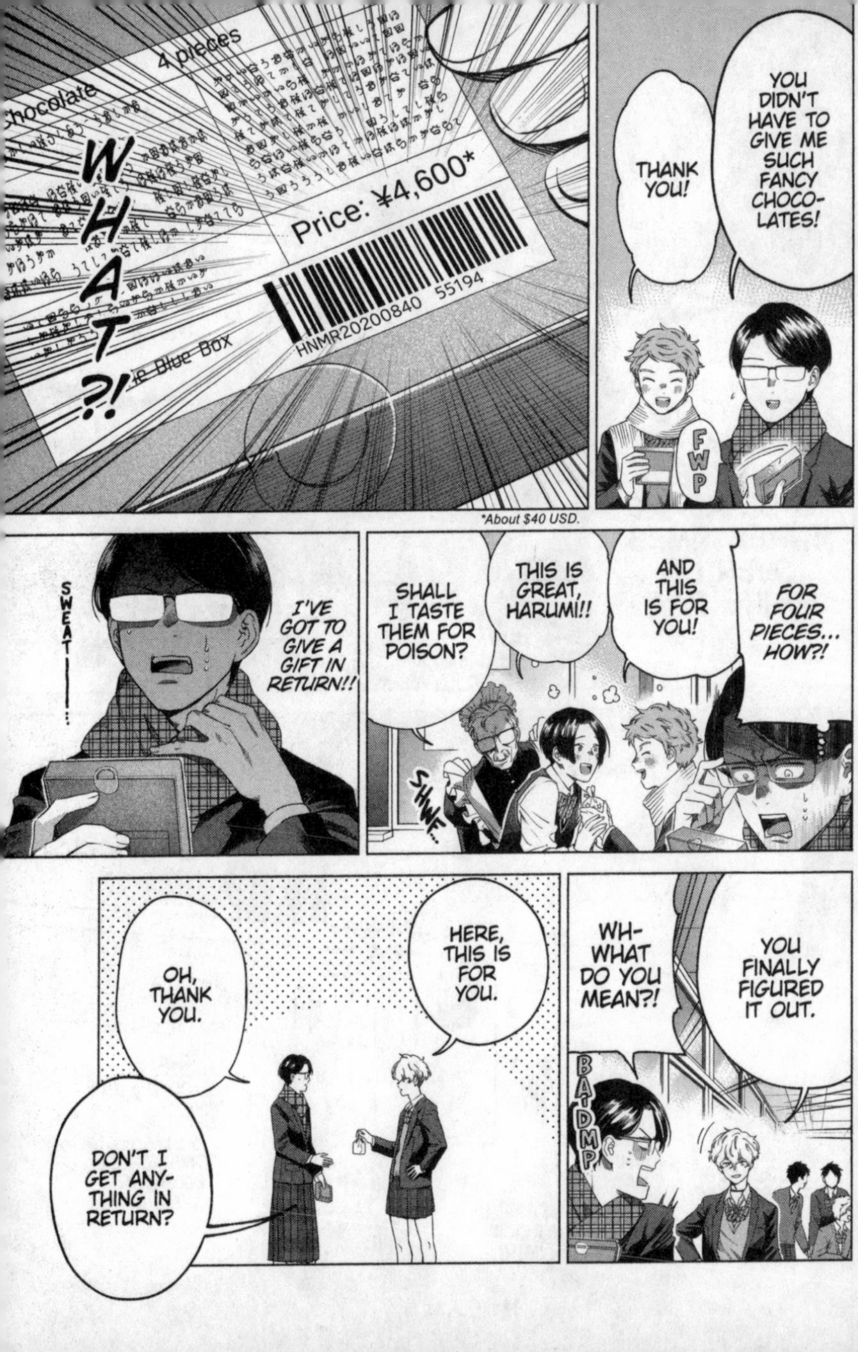

YOU DIDN'T HAVE TO GIVE ME SUCH FANCY CHOCOLATES!
THANK YOU!
FWP
4 pieces
Chocolate
Price: ¥4,600*
HNMR20200840 55194
Blue Box
WHAT?!
FOR FOUR PIECES... HOW?!
AND THIS IS FOR YOU!
THIS IS GREAT, HARUMI!!
SHALL I TASTE THEM FOR POISON?
SHWF...
SWEAT
I'VE GOT TO GIVE A GIFT IN RETURN!!
YOU FINALLY FIGURED IT OUT.
WH-WHAT DO YOU MEAN?!
BADMP
HERE, THIS IS FOR YOU.
OH, THANK YOU.
DON'T I GET ANYTHING IN RETURN?

*About $40 USD.

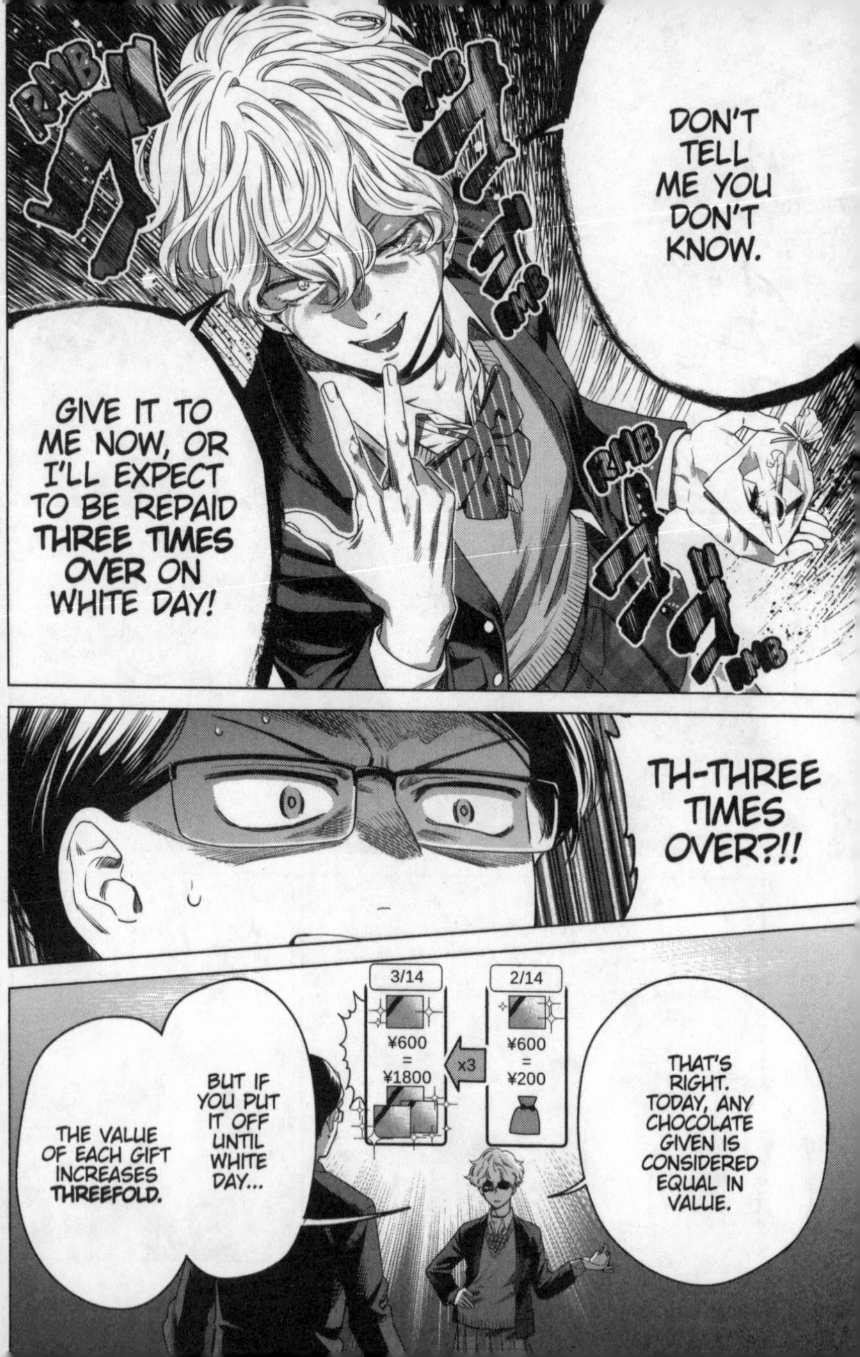
DON'T TELL ME YOU DON'T KNOW.
GIVE IT TO ME NOW, OR I'LL EXPECT TO BE REPAID THREE TIMES OVER ON WHITE DAY!
TH-THREE TIMES OVER?!!
THAT'S RIGHT. TODAY, ANY CHOCOLATE GIVEN IS CONSIDERED EQUAL IN VALUE.
2/14
¥600 = ¥200
x3
3/14
¥600 = ¥1800
BUT IF YOU PUT IT OFF UNTIL WHITE DAY...
THE VALUE OF EACH GIFT INCREASES THREEFOLD.

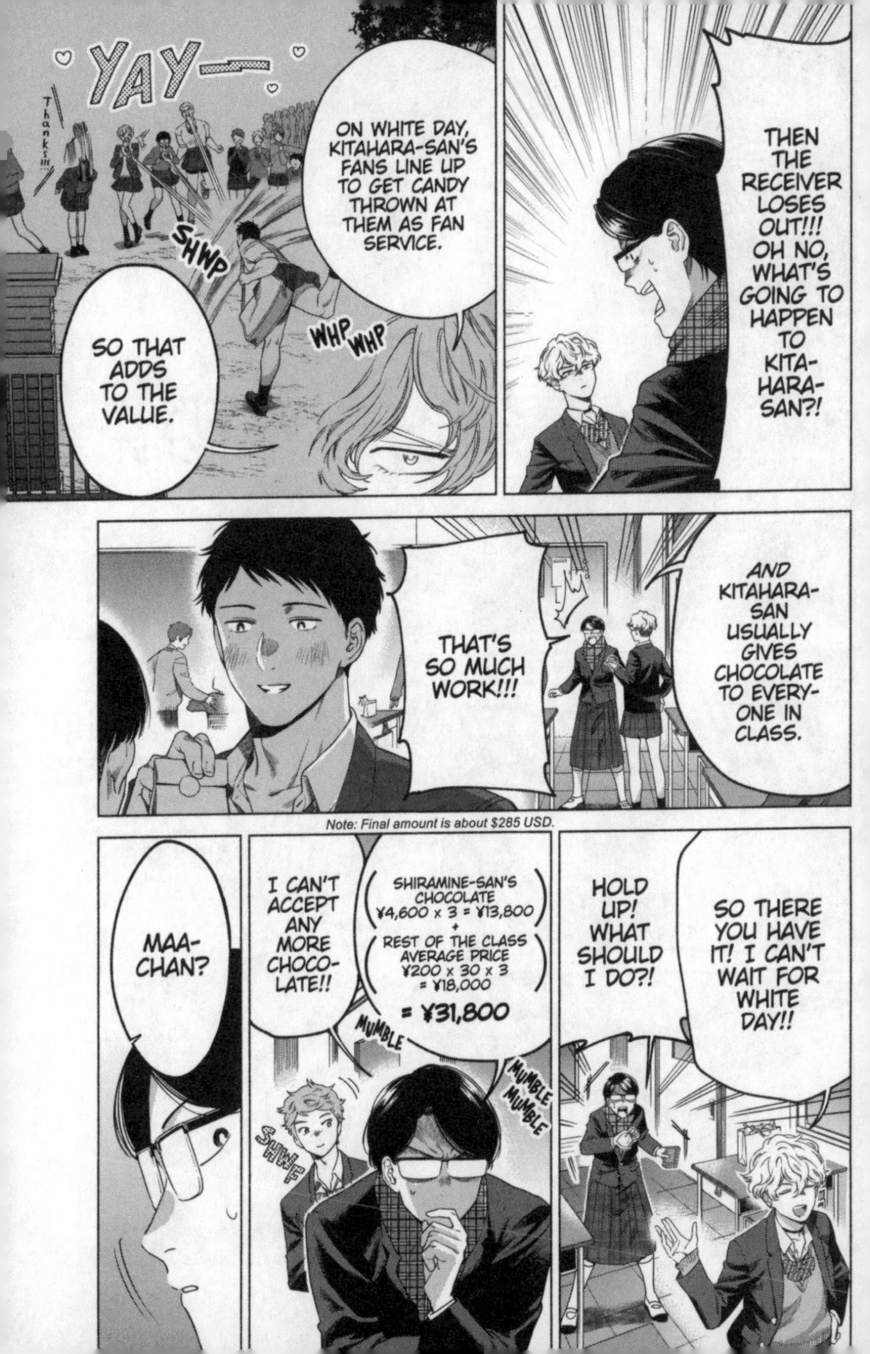
THEN THE RECEIVER LOSES OUT!!! OH NO, WHAT'S GOING TO HAPPEN TO KITA-HARA-SAN?!
YAY—
Thanks!!!
ON WHITE DAY, KITAHARA-SAN'S FANS LINE UP TO GET CANDY THROWN AT THEM AS FAN SERVICE.
SHWP
WHP WHP
SO THAT ADDS TO THE VALUE.
AND KITAHARA-SAN USUALLY GIVES CHOCOLATE TO EVERY-ONE IN CLASS.
THAT'S SO MUCH WORK!!!
Note: Final amount is about $285 USD.
SO THERE YOU HAVE IT! I CAN'T WAIT FOR WHITE DAY!!
HOLD UP! WHAT SHOULD I DO?!
(SHIRAMINE-SAN'S CHOCOLATE ¥4,600 x 3 = ¥13,800) + (REST OF THE CLASS AVERAGE PRICE ¥200 x 30 x 3 = ¥18,000) = ¥31,800
I CAN'T ACCEPT ANY MORE CHOCO-LATE!!
MUMBLE
MUMBLE MUMBLE
SHWF
MAA-CHAN?

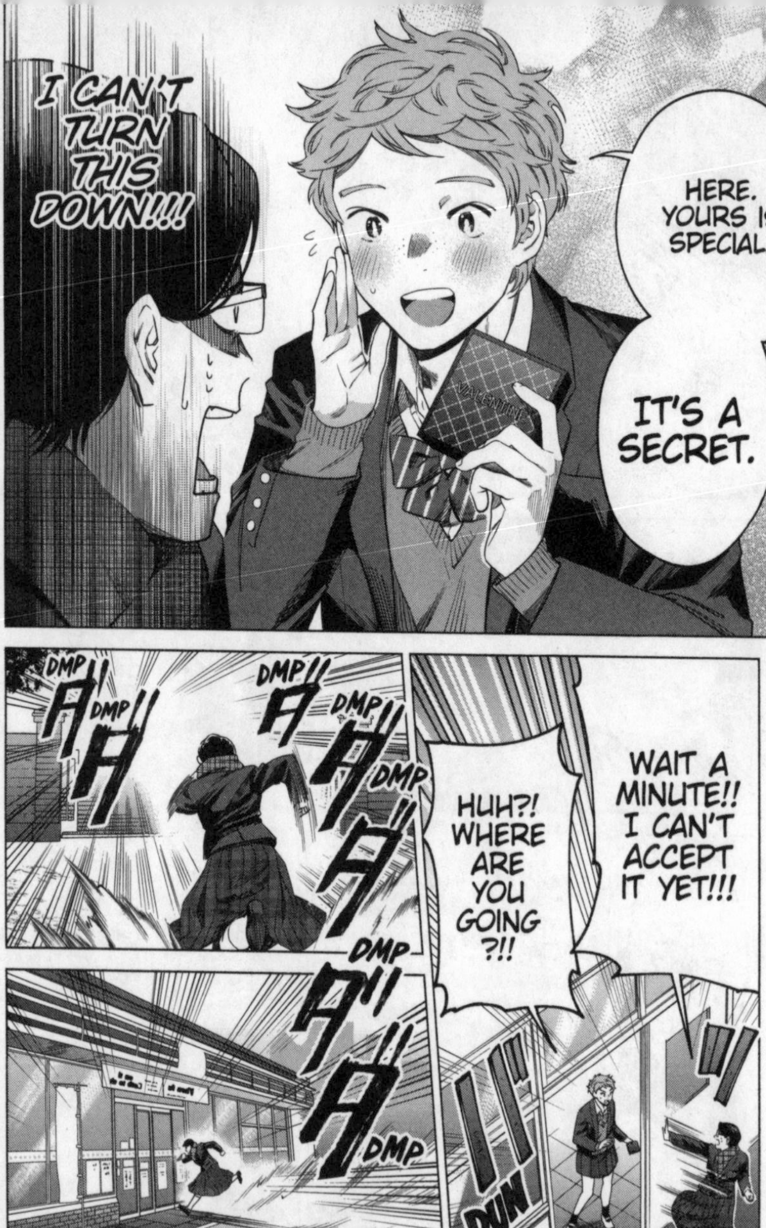
HERE. YOURS IS SPECIAL!
IT'S A SECRET.
VALENTINE
I CAN'T TURN THIS DOWN!!!
WAIT A MINUTE!! I CAN'T ACCEPT IT YET!!!
HUH?! WHERE ARE YOU GOING?!!
DUN
DMP
DMP
DMP
DMP
DMP
DMP
DMP

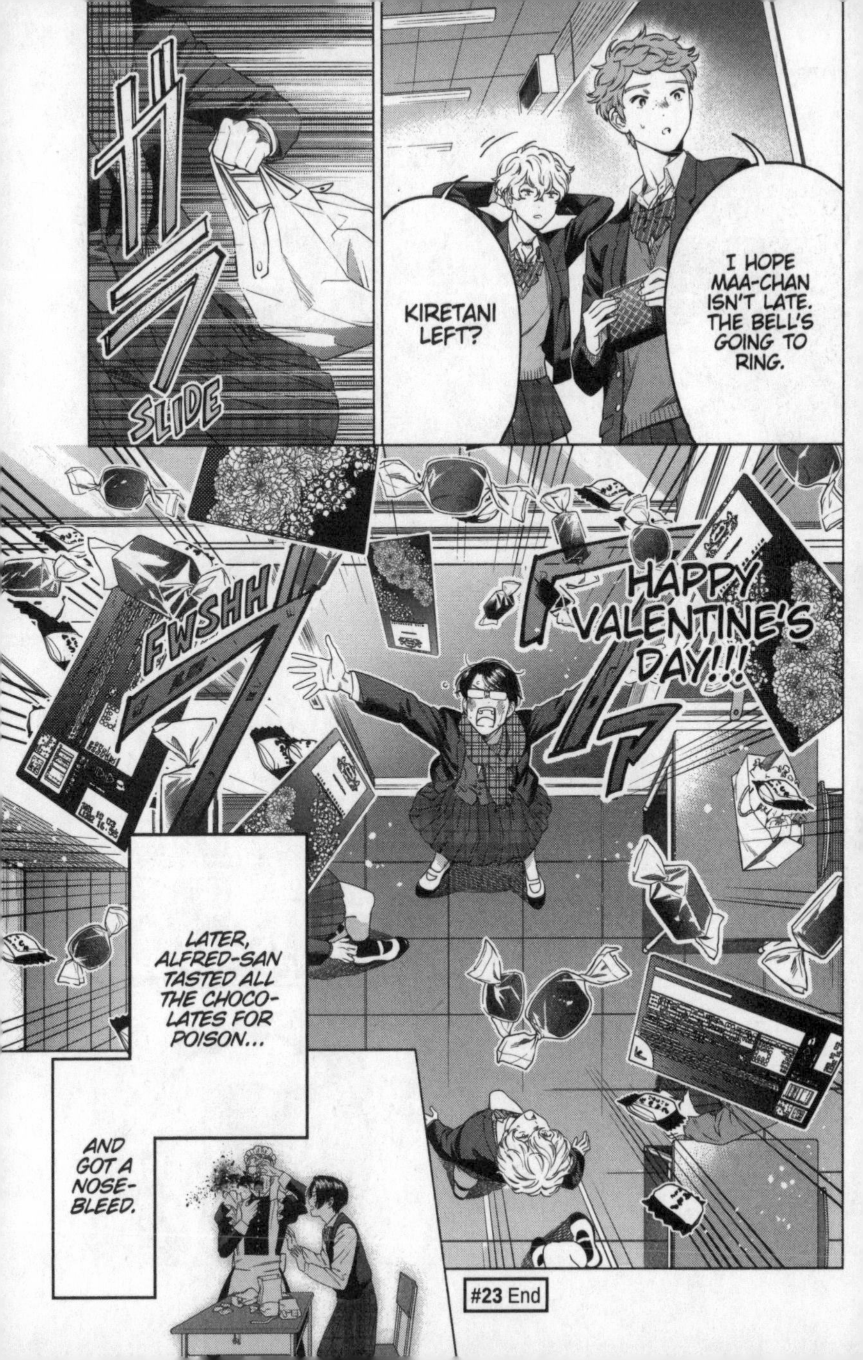
I HOPE MAA-CHAN ISN'T LATE. THE BELL'S GOING TO RING.
KIRETANI LEFT?
SLIDE
HAPPY VALENTINE'S DAY!!!
FWSHH
LATER, ALFRED-SAN TASTED ALL THE CHOCO-LATES FOR POISON...
AND GOT A NOSE-BLEED.
#23 End

THIGH HIGH
Reiwa Hanamaru Academy

HANAMARU PRIVATE HIGH SCHOOL

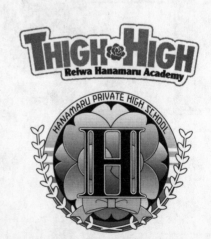

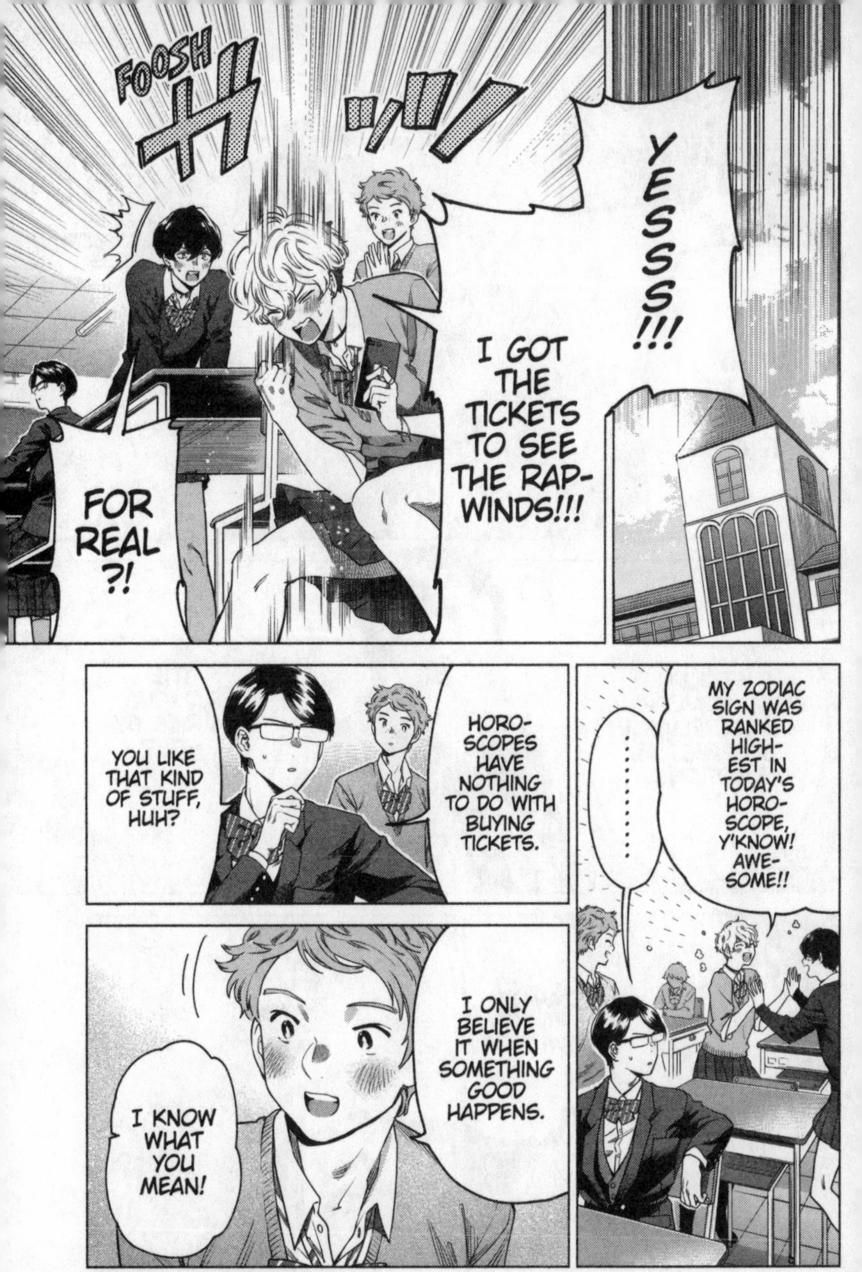
YESSS!!!
I GOT THE TICKETS TO SEE THE RAP-WINDS!!!
FOOSH
FOR REAL?!
MY ZODIAC SIGN WAS RANKED HIGHEST IN TODAY'S HOROSCOPE, Y'KNOW! AWESOME!!
......
HOROSCOPES HAVE NOTHING TO DO WITH BUYING TICKETS.
YOU LIKE THAT KIND OF STUFF, HUH?
I ONLY BELIEVE IT WHEN SOMETHING GOOD HAPPENS.
I KNOW WHAT YOU MEAN!

#24 #itsuptome #tobelieveitornot

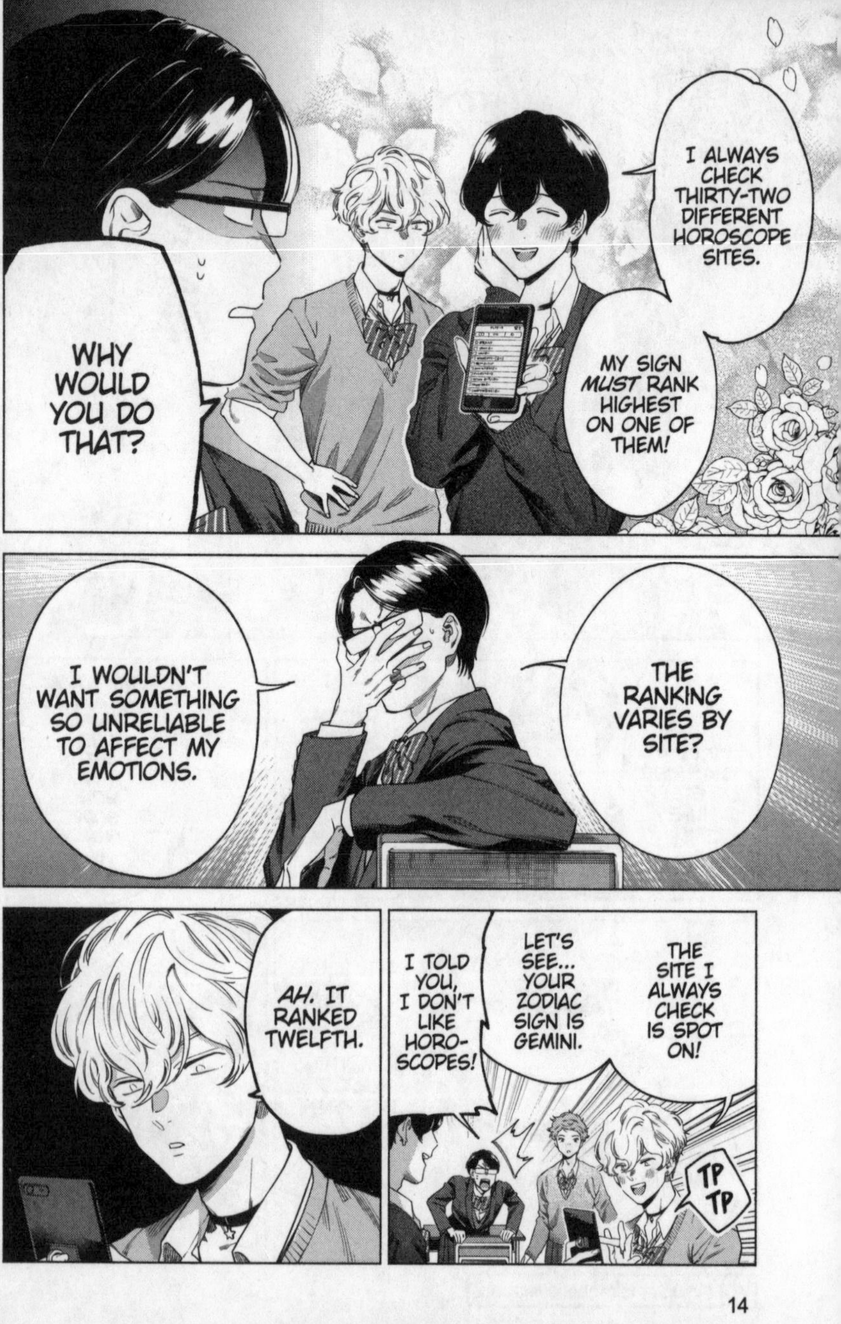
I ALWAYS CHECK THIRTY-TWO DIFFERENT HOROSCOPE SITES.
MY SIGN *MUST* RANK HIGHEST ON ONE OF THEM!
WHY WOULD YOU DO THAT?
THE RANKING VARIES BY SITE?
I WOULDN'T WANT SOMETHING SO UNRELIABLE TO AFFECT MY EMOTIONS.
THE SITE I ALWAYS CHECK IS SPOT ON!
LET'S SEE... YOUR ZODIAC SIGN IS GEMINI.
TP TP
I TOLD YOU, I DON'T LIKE HORO-SCOPES!
AH. IT RANKED TWELFTH.

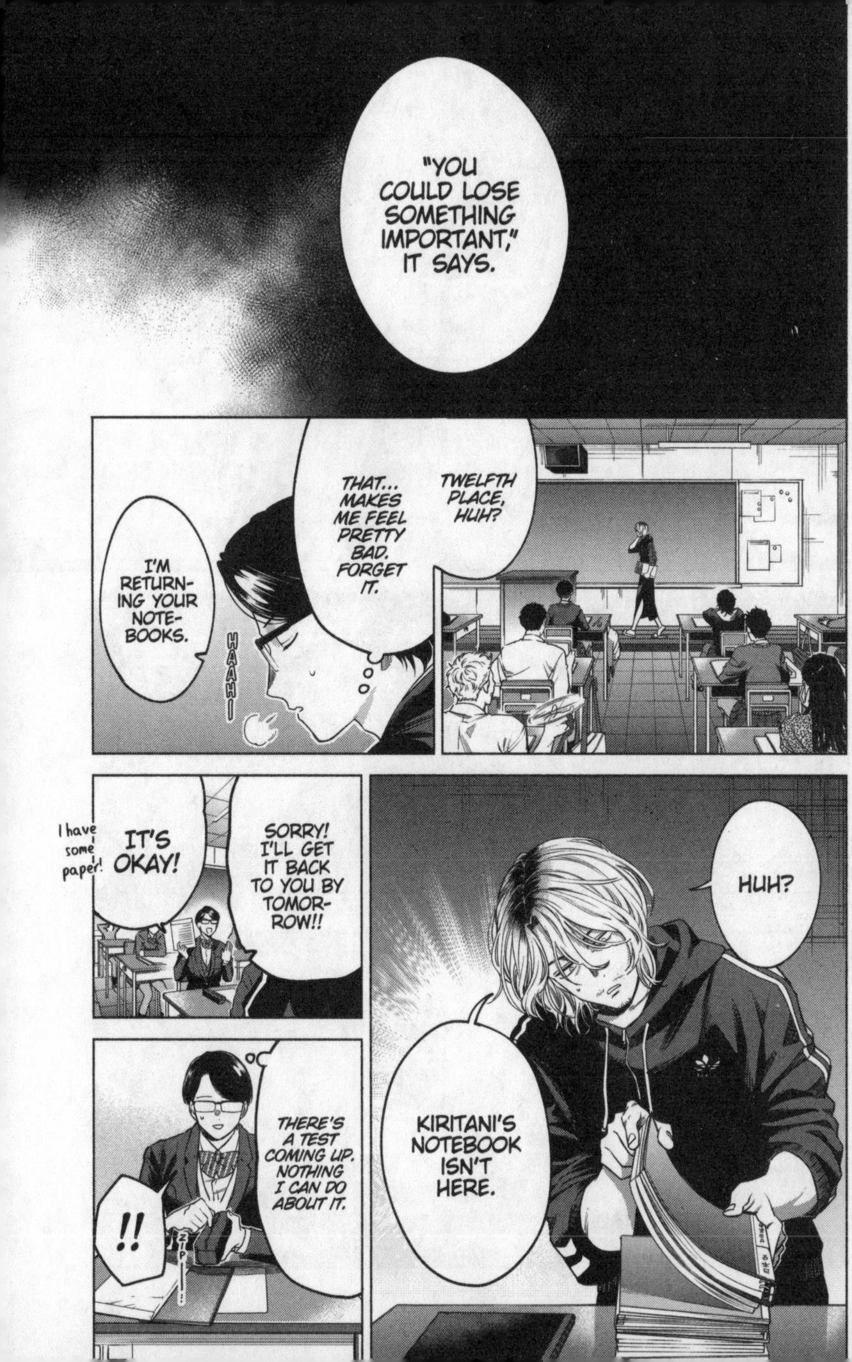
"YOU COULD LOSE SOMETHING IMPORTANT," IT SAYS.
TWELFTH PLACE, HUH?
THAT... MAKES ME FEEL PRETTY BAD. FORGET IT.
I'M RETURNING YOUR NOTEBOOKS.
HAAAH
HUH?
KIRITANI'S NOTEBOOK ISN'T HERE.
SORRY! I'LL GET IT BACK TO YOU BY TOMORROW!!
IT'S OKAY!
I have some paper!
THERE'S A TEST COMING UP. NOTHING I CAN DO ABOUT IT.
!!
ZIP

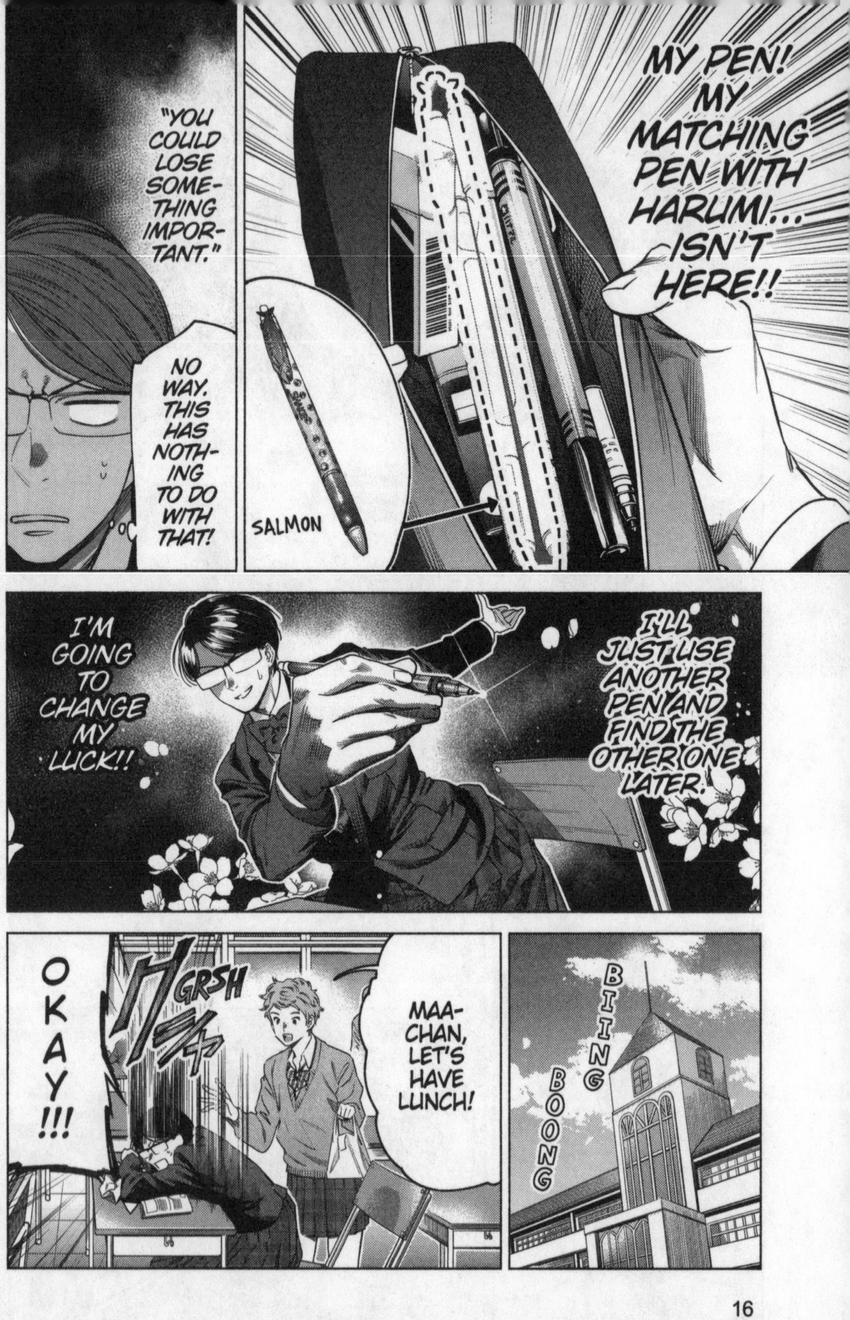
MY PEN! MY MATCHING PEN WITH HARUMI... ISN'T HERE!!
SALMON
"YOU COULD LOSE SOME-THING IMPOR-TANT."
NO WAY. THIS HAS NOTH-ING TO DO WITH THAT!
I'LL JUST USE ANOTHER PEN AND FIND THE OTHER ONE LATER.
I'M GOING TO CHANGE MY LUCK!!
BIING
BOONG
MAA-CHAN, LET'S HAVE LUNCH!
GRSH
OKAY!!!

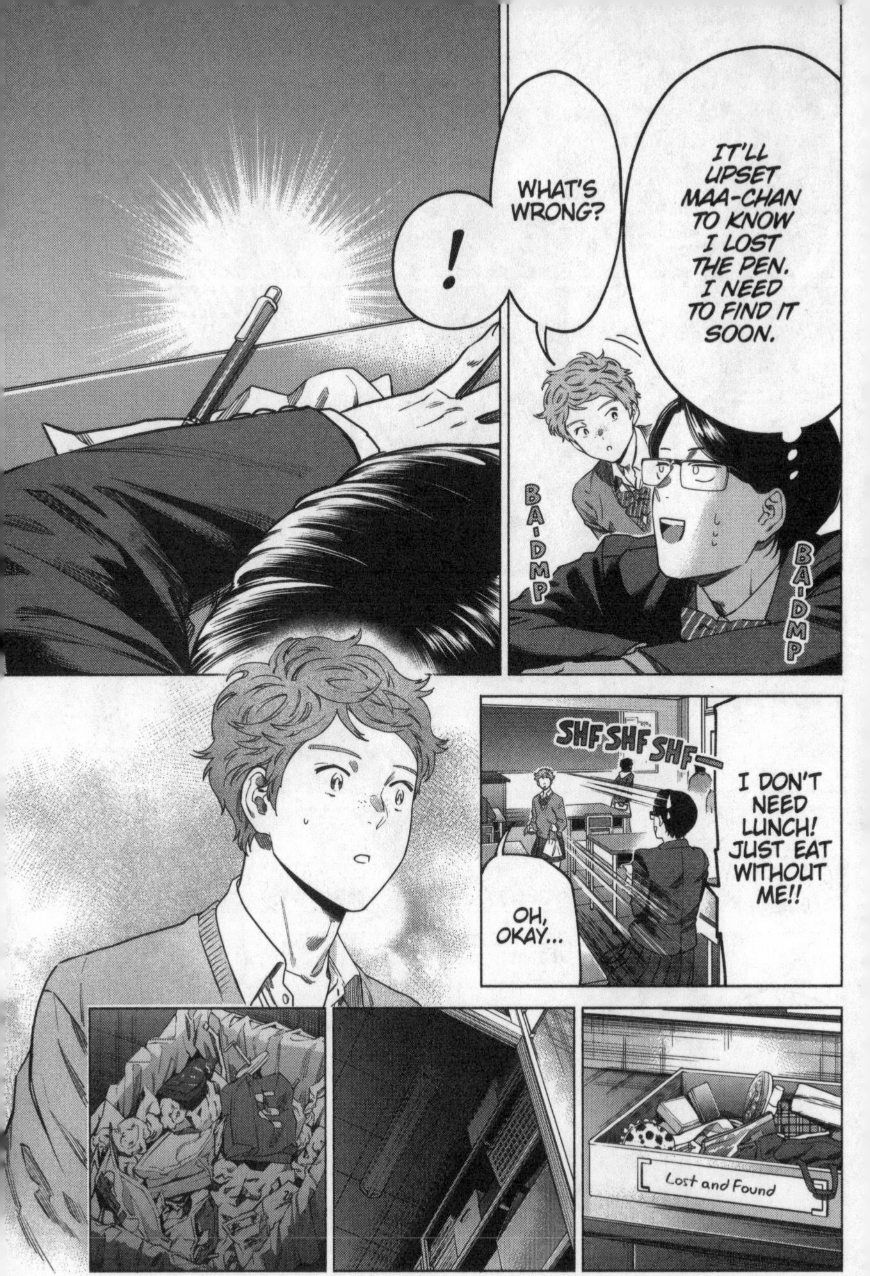

IT'LL UPSET MAA-CHAN TO KNOW I LOST THE PEN. I NEED TO FIND IT SOON.
WHAT'S WRONG?
!
BA-DMP
BA-DMP
SHF SHF SHF
I DON'T NEED LUNCH! JUST EAT WITHOUT ME!!
OH, OKAY...
Lost and Found

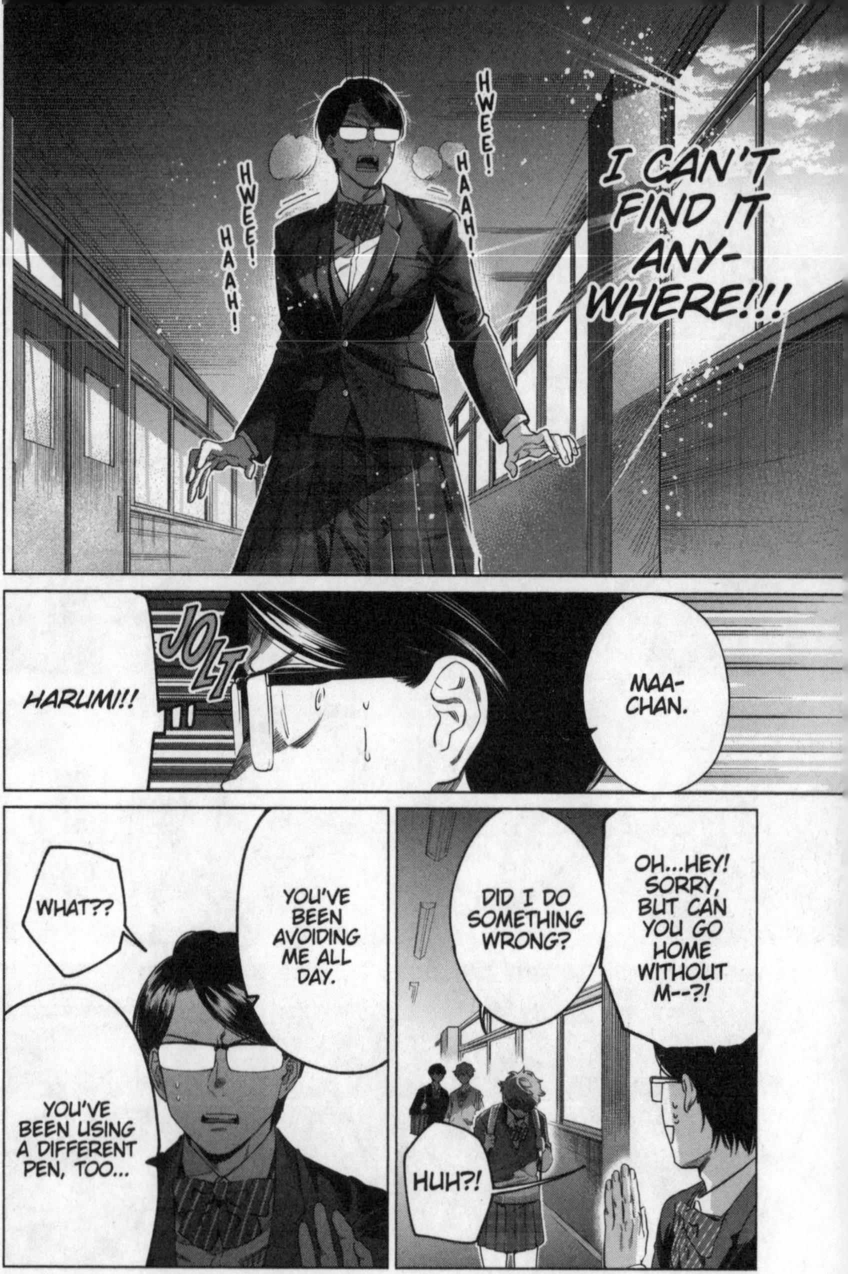
I CAN'T FIND IT ANY-WHERE!!!
HWEE! HAAH!
HWEE! HAAH!
MAA-CHAN.
JOLT
HARUMI!!
OH...HEY! SORRY, BUT CAN YOU GO HOME WITHOUT M--?!
DID I DO SOMETHING WRONG?
HUH?!
YOU'VE BEEN AVOIDING ME ALL DAY.
WHAT??
YOU'VE BEEN USING A DIFFERENT PEN, TOO...

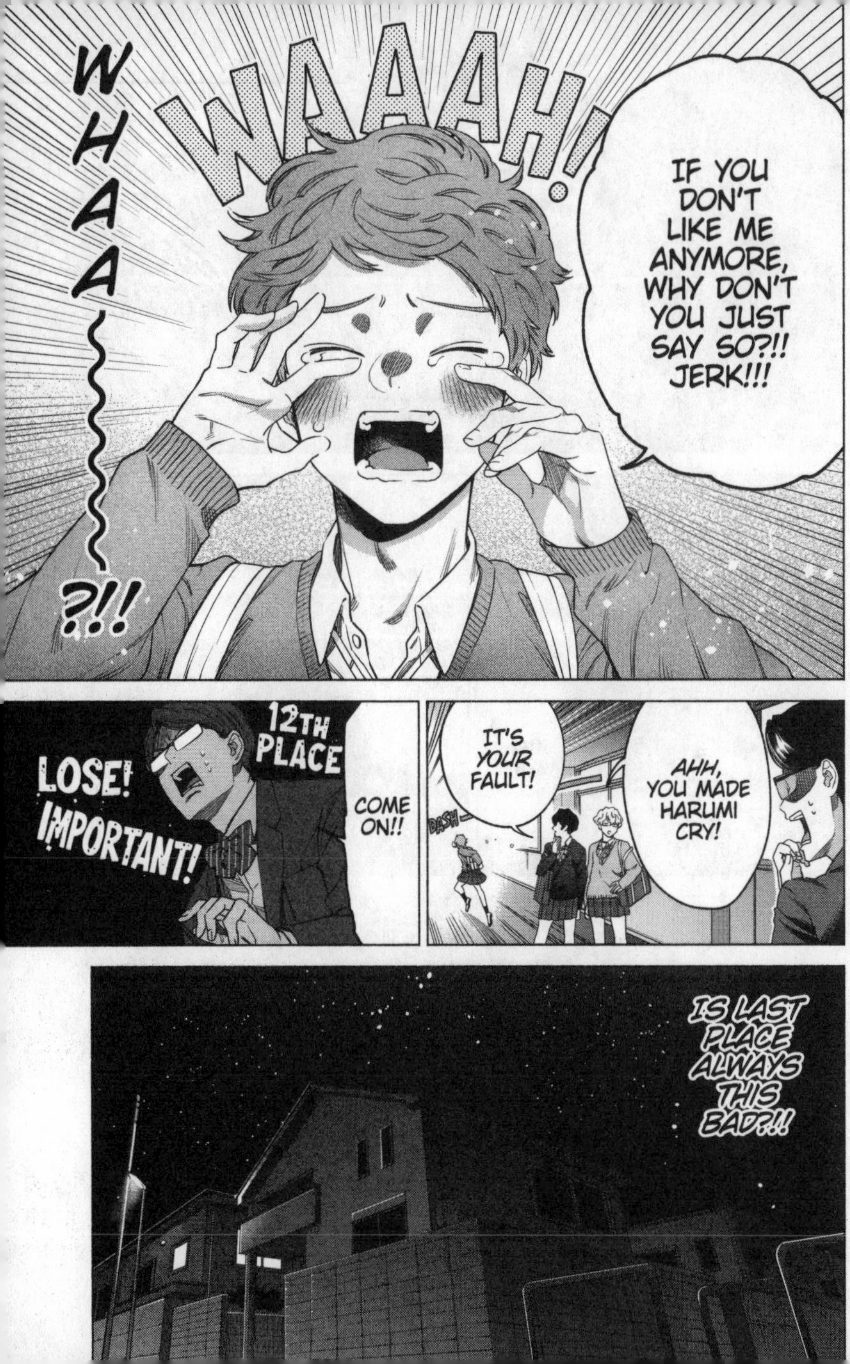
IF YOU DON'T LIKE ME ANYMORE, WHY DON'T YOU JUST SAY SO?!! JERK!!!
WAAAH!
WHAAA~?!!
AHH, YOU MADE HARUMI CRY!
IT'S YOUR FAULT!
DASH
COME ON!!
12TH PLACE
LOSE! IMPORTANT!
IS LAST PLACE ALWAYS THIS BAD?!!

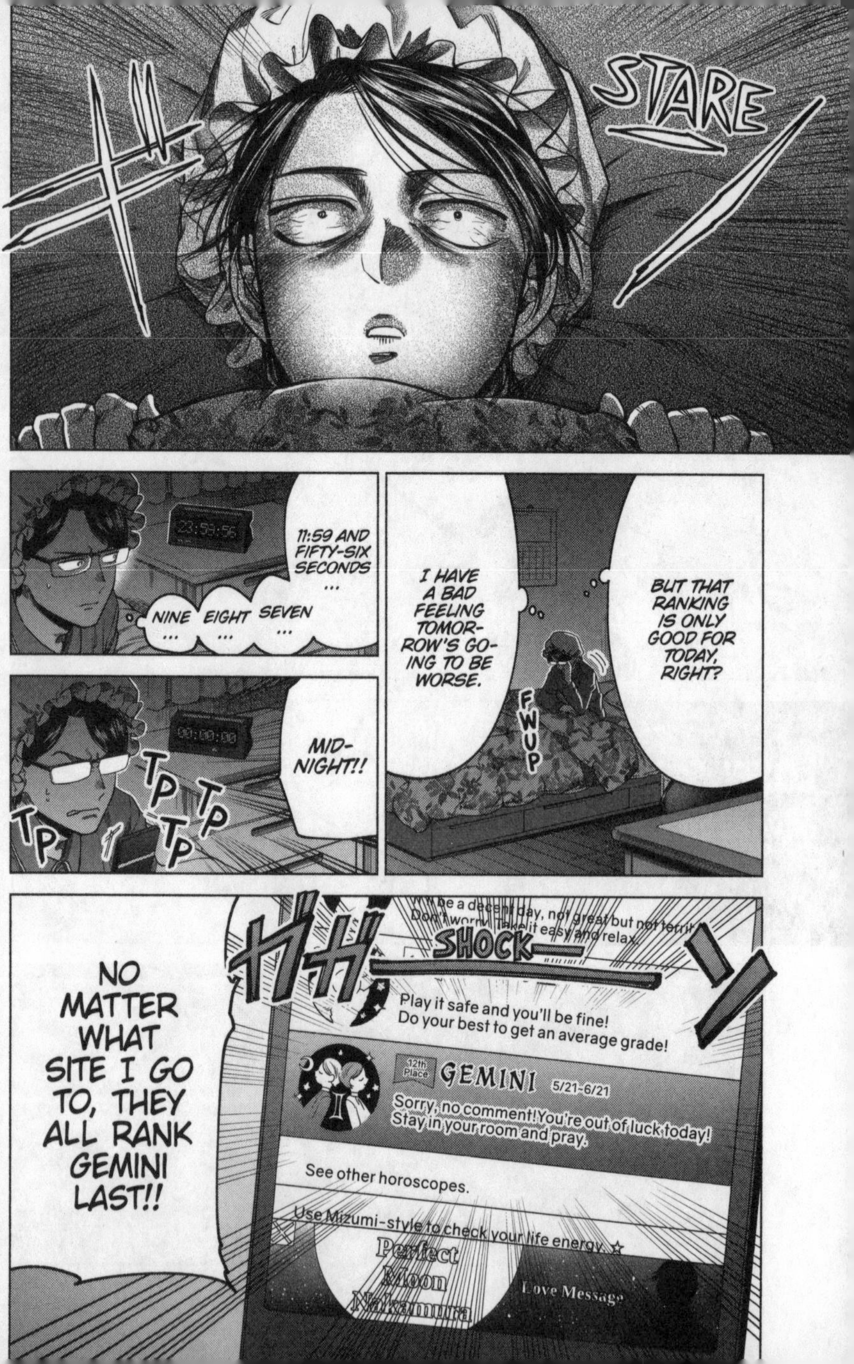
STARE
BUT THAT RANKING IS ONLY GOOD FOR TODAY, RIGHT?
I HAVE A BAD FEELING TOMORROW'S GOING TO BE WORSE.
FWUP
23:59:56
11:59 AND FIFTY-SIX SECONDS ...
NINE ... EIGHT ... SEVEN ...
00:00:00
MIDNIGHT!!
TP TP TP TP TP
ガガ
SHOCK—
Play it safe and you'll be fine!
Do your best to get an average grade!
12th Place
GEMINI 5/21-6/21
Sorry, no comment! You're out of luck today!
Stay in your room and pray.
See other horoscopes.
Use Mizumi-style to check your life energy.☆
Perfect Moon Nakamura
Love Message
NO MATTER WHAT SITE I GO TO, THEY ALL RANK GEMINI LAST!!

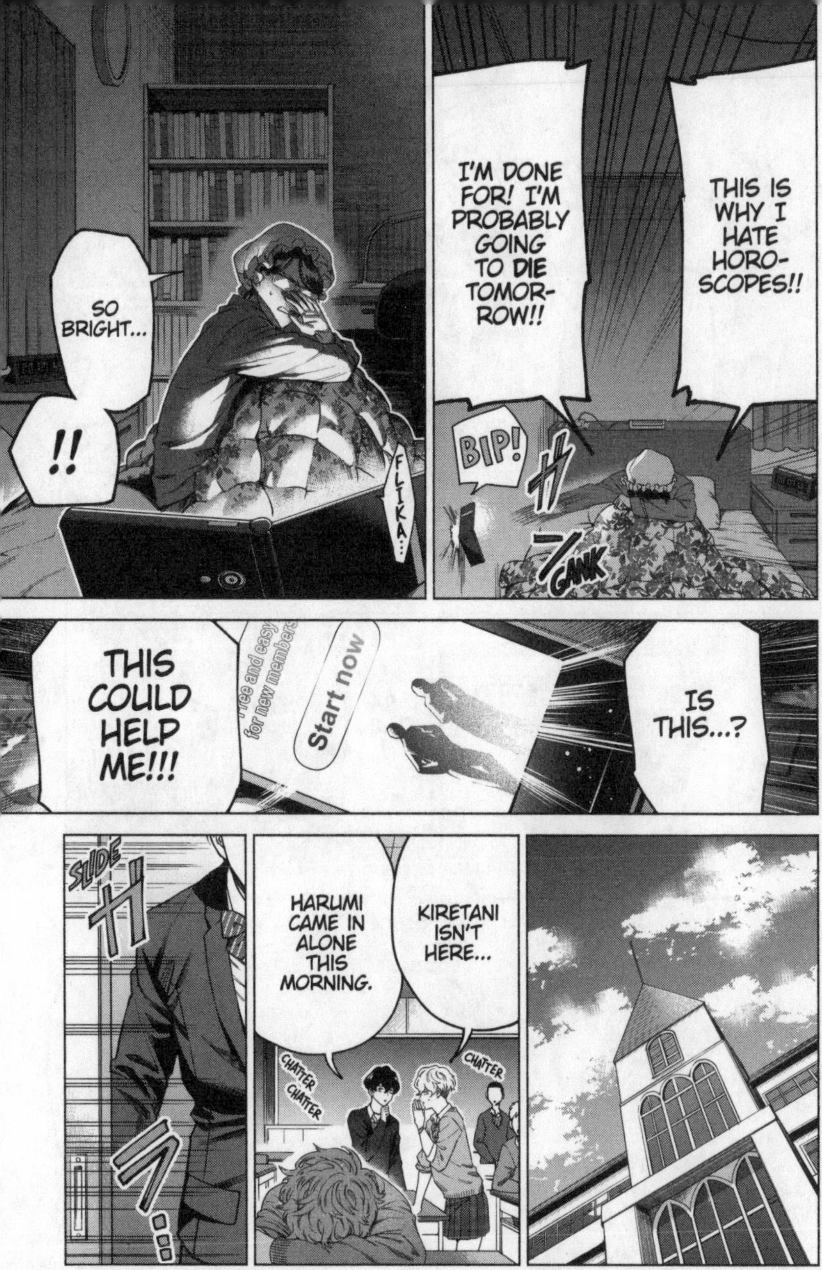
THIS IS WHY I HATE HORO-SCOPES!!
I'M DONE FOR! I'M PROBABLY GOING TO DIE TOMOR-ROW!!
BIP!
GANK
SO BRIGHT...
!!
FLIKA...
IS THIS...?
Start now
ree and easy
for new members
THIS COULD HELP ME!!!
KIRETANI ISN'T HERE...
HARUMI CAME IN ALONE THIS MORNING.
CHATTER
CHATTER
CHATTER
SLIDE
...

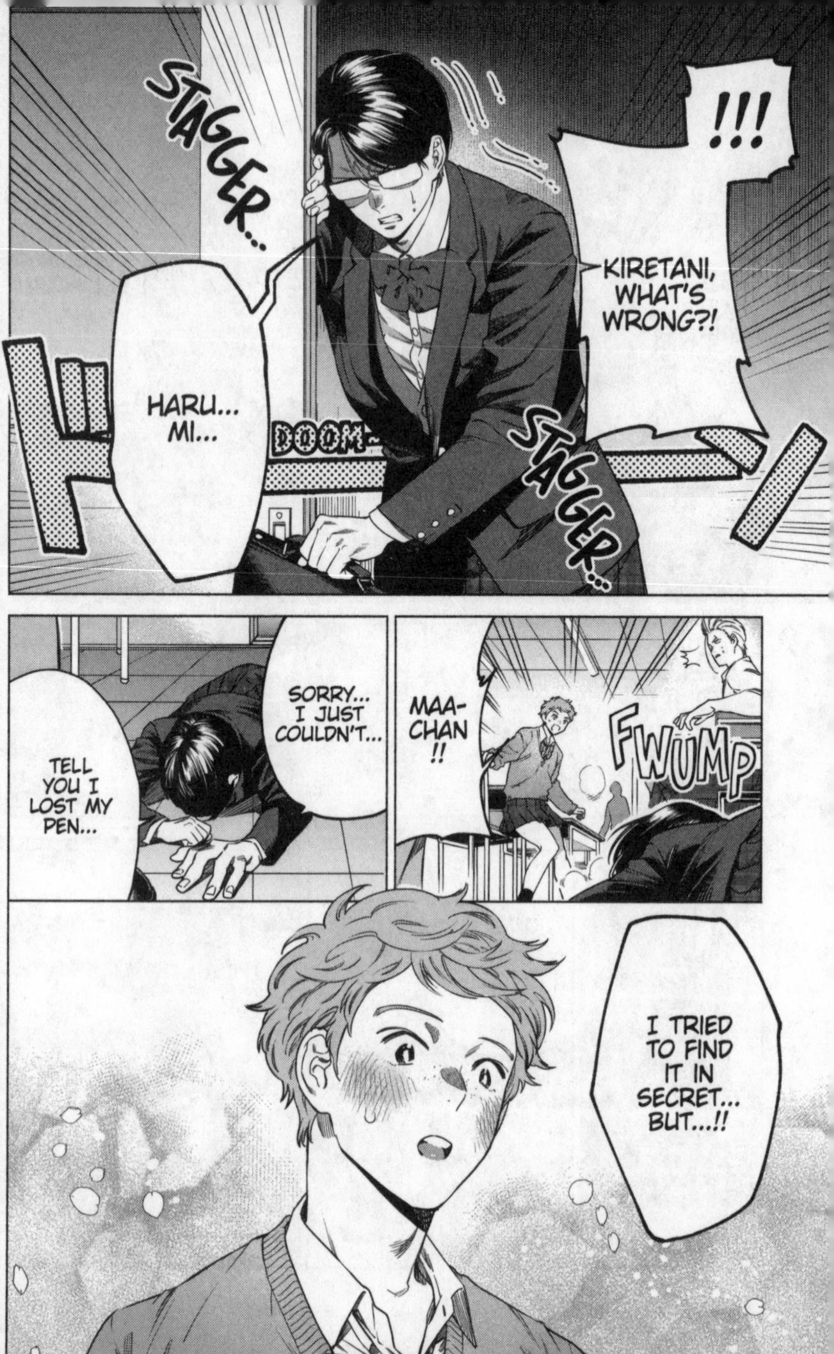
!!!
KIRETANI, WHAT'S WRONG?!
STAGGER...
STAGGER...
HARU... MI...
DOOM
FWUMP
MAA-CHAN !!
SORRY... I JUST COULDN'T...
TELL YOU I LOST MY PEN...
I TRIED TO FIND IT IN SECRET... BUT...!!

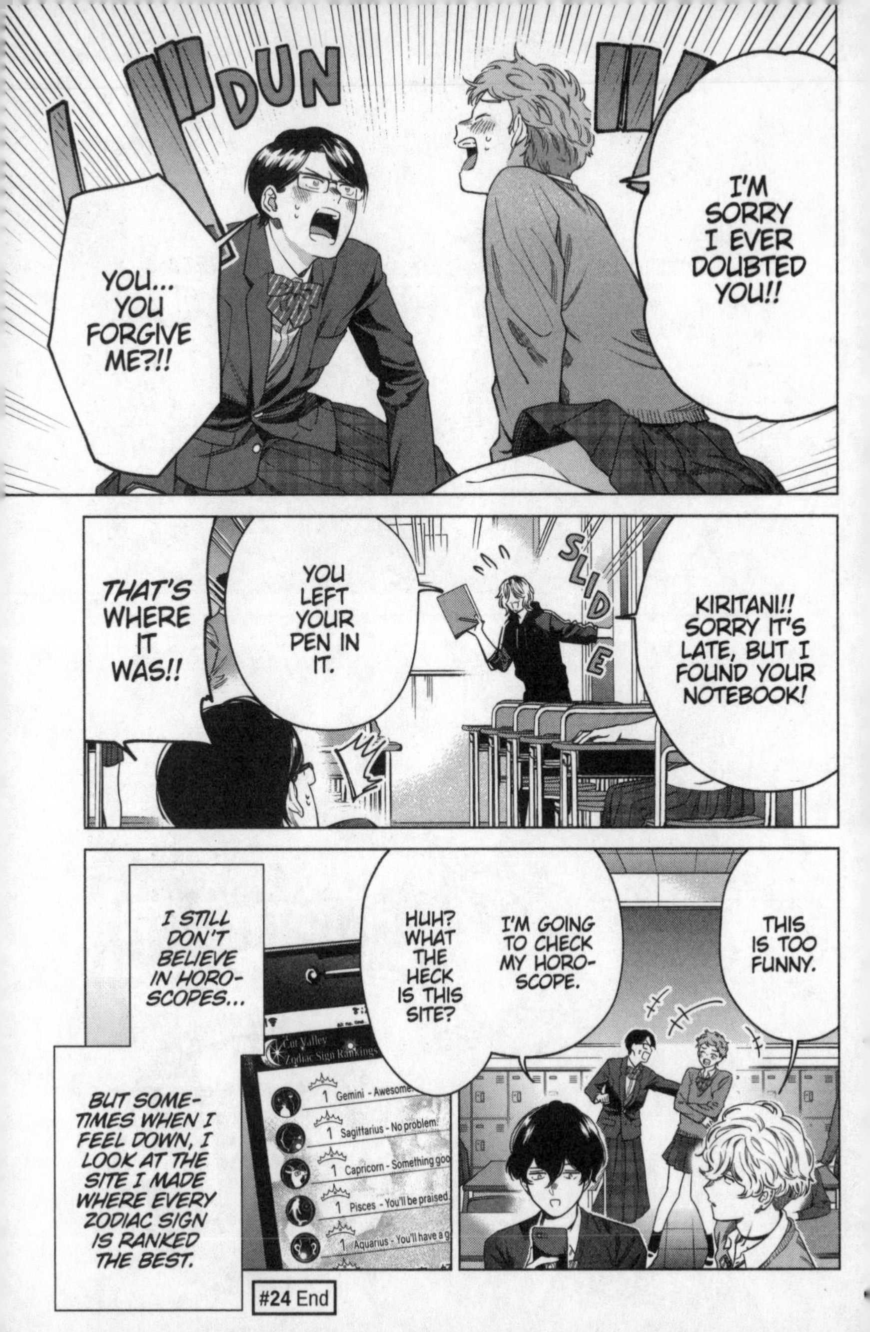
DUN
I'M SORRY I EVER DOUBTED YOU!!
YOU... YOU FORGIVE ME?!!
KIRITANI!! SORRY IT'S LATE, BUT I FOUND YOUR NOTEBOOK!
SLIDE
YOU LEFT YOUR PEN IN IT.
THAT'S WHERE IT WAS!!
THIS IS TOO FUNNY.
I'M GOING TO CHECK MY HOROSCOPE.
HUH? WHAT THE HECK IS THIS SITE?
I STILL DON'T BELIEVE IN HOROSCOPES...
Cut Valley Zodiac Sign Rankings
1 Gemini - Awesome
1 Sagittarius - No problem.
1 Capricorn - Something goo
1 Pisces - You'll be praised.
1 Aquarius - You'll have a g
BUT SOMETIMES WHEN I FEEL DOWN, I LOOK AT THE SITE I MADE WHERE EVERY ZODIAC SIGN IS RANKED THE BEST.

#24 End

THIGH HIGH
Reiwa Hanamaru Academy

HANAMARU PRIVATE HIGH SCHOOL

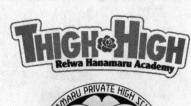

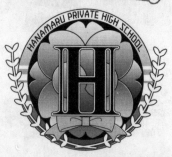

#25 #mighty #Mushasan

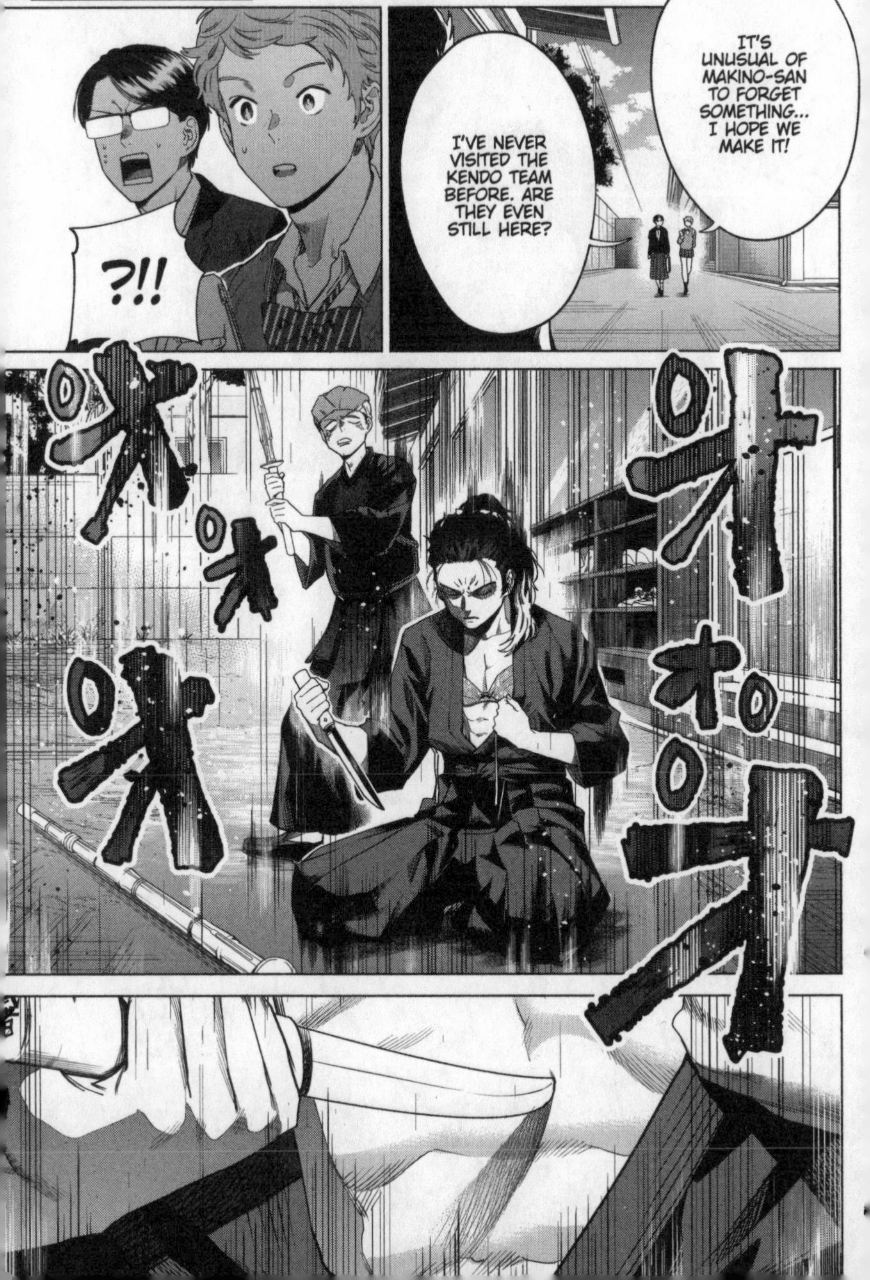

IT'S UNUSUAL OF MAKINO-SAN TO FORGET SOMETHING... I HOPE WE MAKE IT!
I'VE NEVER VISITED THE KENDO TEAM BEFORE. ARE THEY EVEN STILL HERE?
?!!

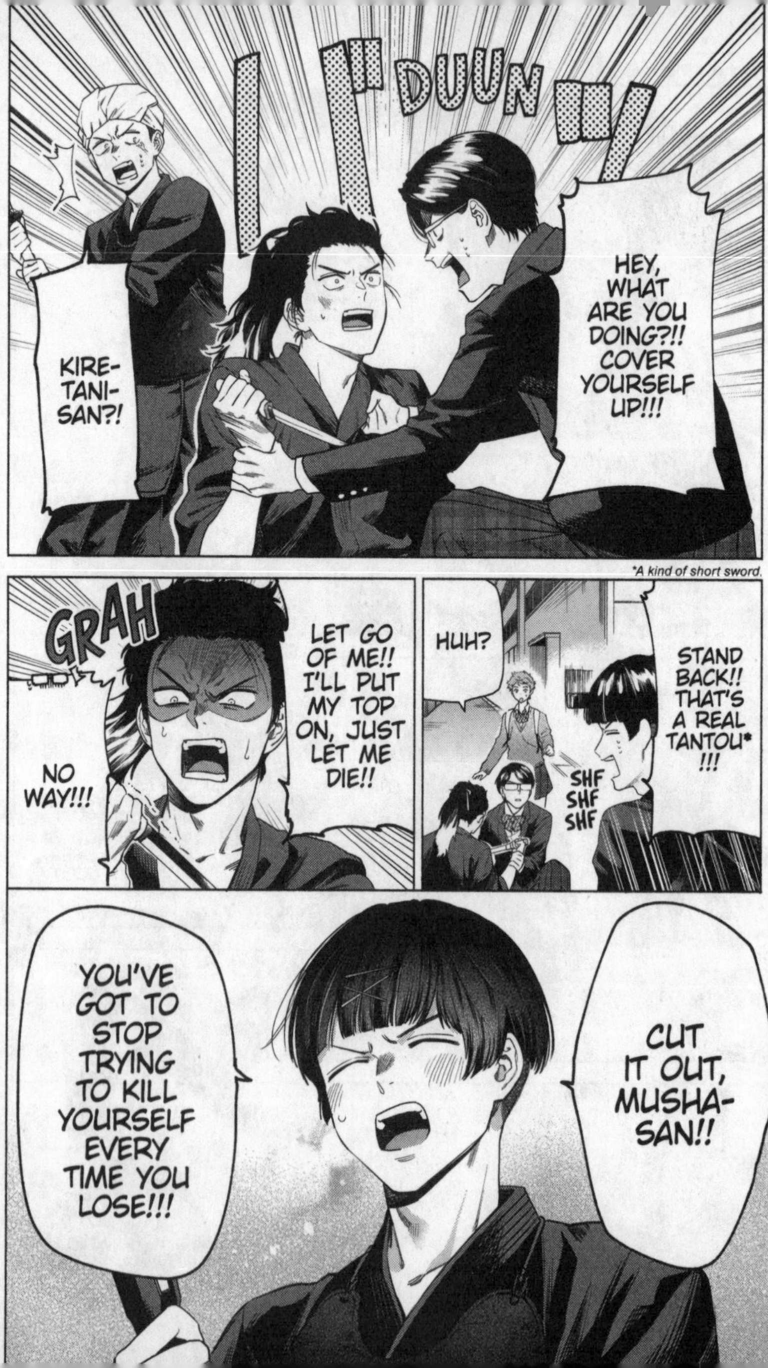
DUUN
HEY, WHAT ARE YOU DOING?!! COVER YOURSELF UP!!!
KIRE-TANI-SAN?!
STAND BACK!! THAT'S A REAL TANTOU* !!!
SHF SHF SHF
HUH?
LET GO OF ME!! I'LL PUT MY TOP ON, JUST LET ME DIE!!
GRAH
NO WAY!!!
CUT IT OUT, MUSHA-SAN!!
YOU'VE GOT TO STOP TRYING TO KILL YOURSELF EVERY TIME YOU LOSE!!!
*A kind of short sword.

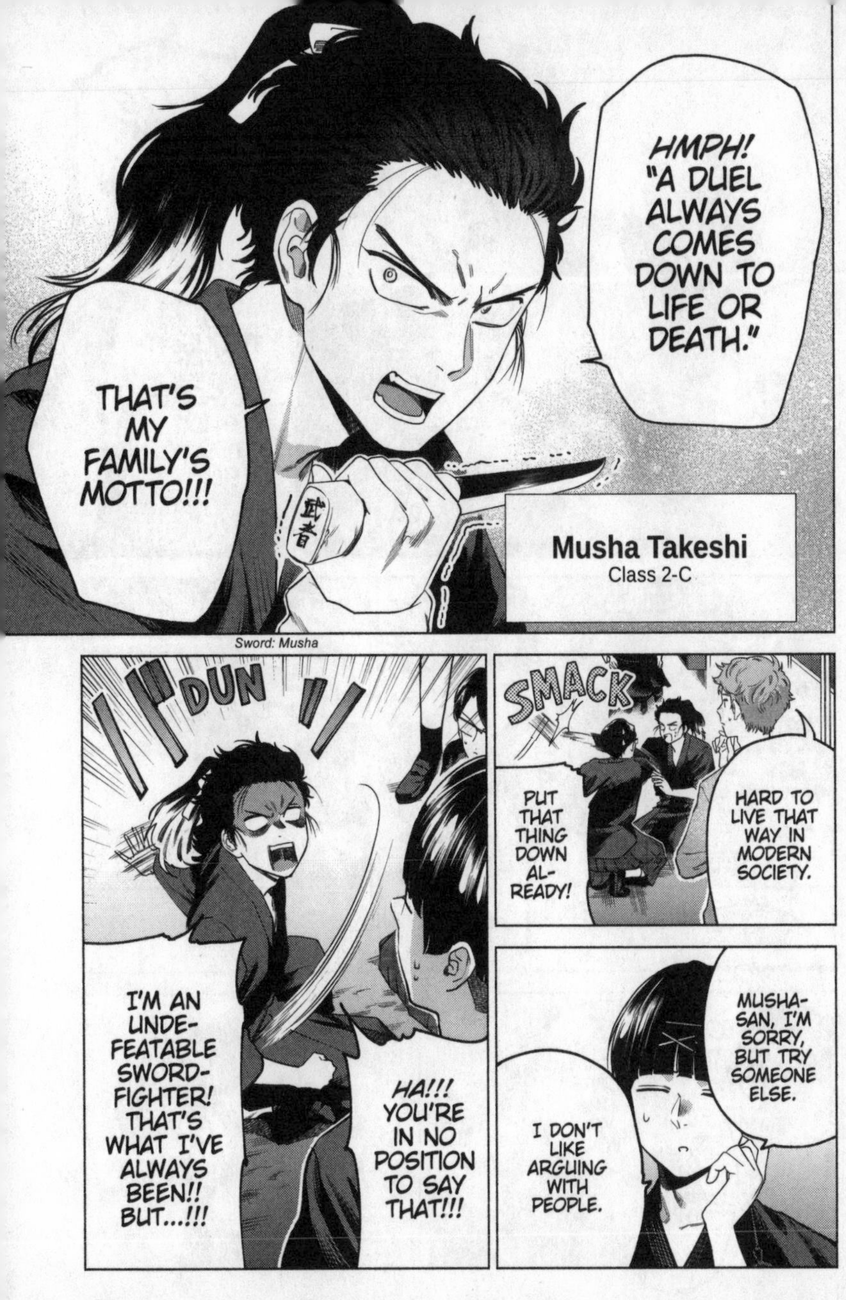
HMPH! "A DUEL ALWAYS COMES DOWN TO LIFE OR DEATH."
THAT'S MY FAMILY'S MOTTO!!!
武者
Musha Takeshi
Class 2-C
SMACK
HARD TO LIVE THAT WAY IN MODERN SOCIETY.
PUT THAT THING DOWN AL-READY!
MUSHA-SAN, I'M SORRY, BUT TRY SOMEONE ELSE.
I DON'T LIKE ARGUING WITH PEOPLE.
DUN
HA!!! YOU'RE IN NO POSITION TO SAY THAT!!!
I'M AN UNDE-FEATABLE SWORD-FIGHTER! THAT'S WHAT I'VE ALWAYS BEEN!! BUT...!!!

Sword: Musha

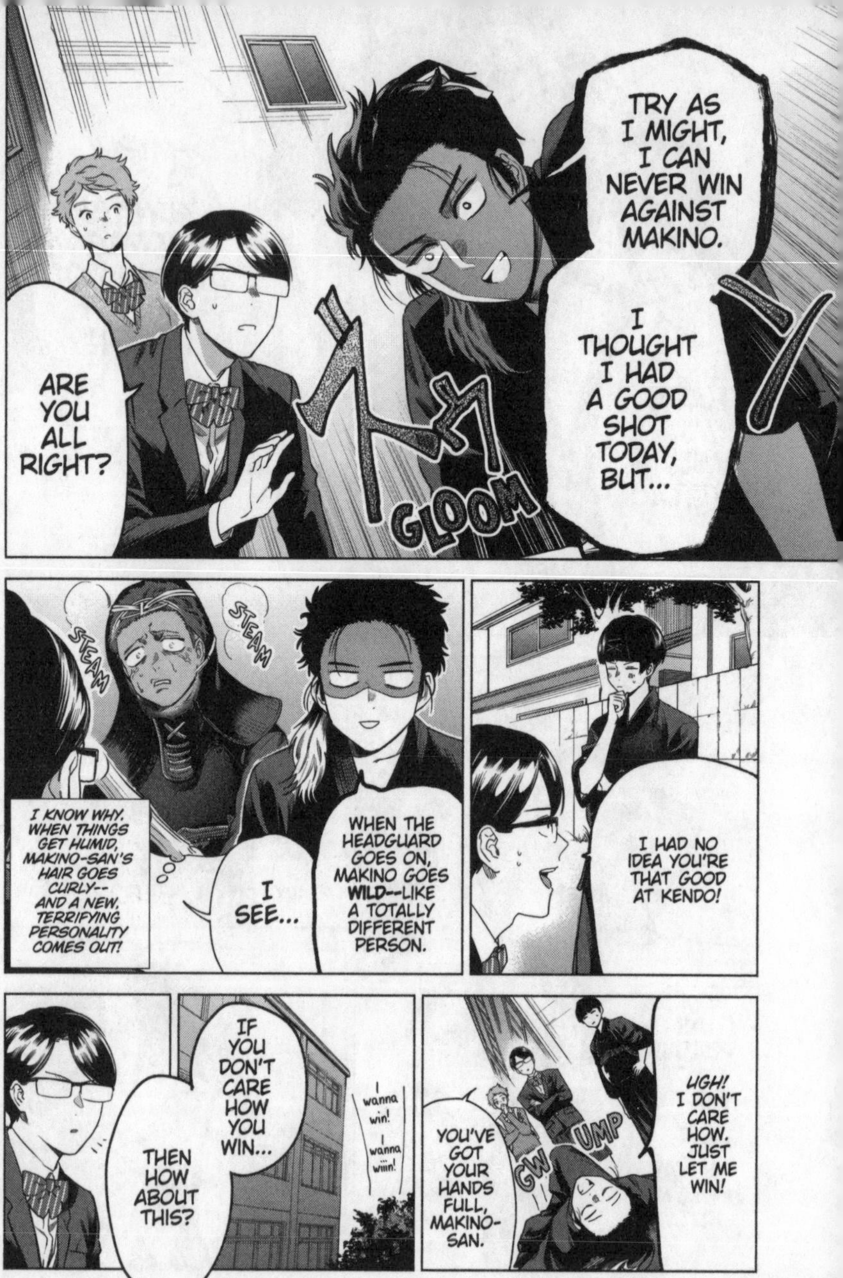
TRY AS I MIGHT, I CAN NEVER WIN AGAINST MAKINO.
I THOUGHT I HAD A GOOD SHOT TODAY, BUT...
GLOOM
ARE YOU ALL RIGHT?
I HAD NO IDEA YOU'RE THAT GOOD AT KENDO!
STEAM
STEAM
WHEN THE HEADGUARD GOES ON, MAKINO GOES WILD--LIKE A TOTALLY DIFFERENT PERSON.
I SEE...
I KNOW WHY. WHEN THINGS GET HUMID, MAKINO-SAN'S HAIR GOES CURLY-- AND A NEW, TERRIFYING PERSONALITY COMES OUT!
UGH! I DON'T CARE HOW. JUST LET ME WIN!
GWUMP
YOU'VE GOT YOUR HANDS FULL, MAKINO-SAN.
I wanna win! I wanna ... wiiin!
IF YOU DON'T CARE HOW YOU WIN...
THEN HOW ABOUT THIS?

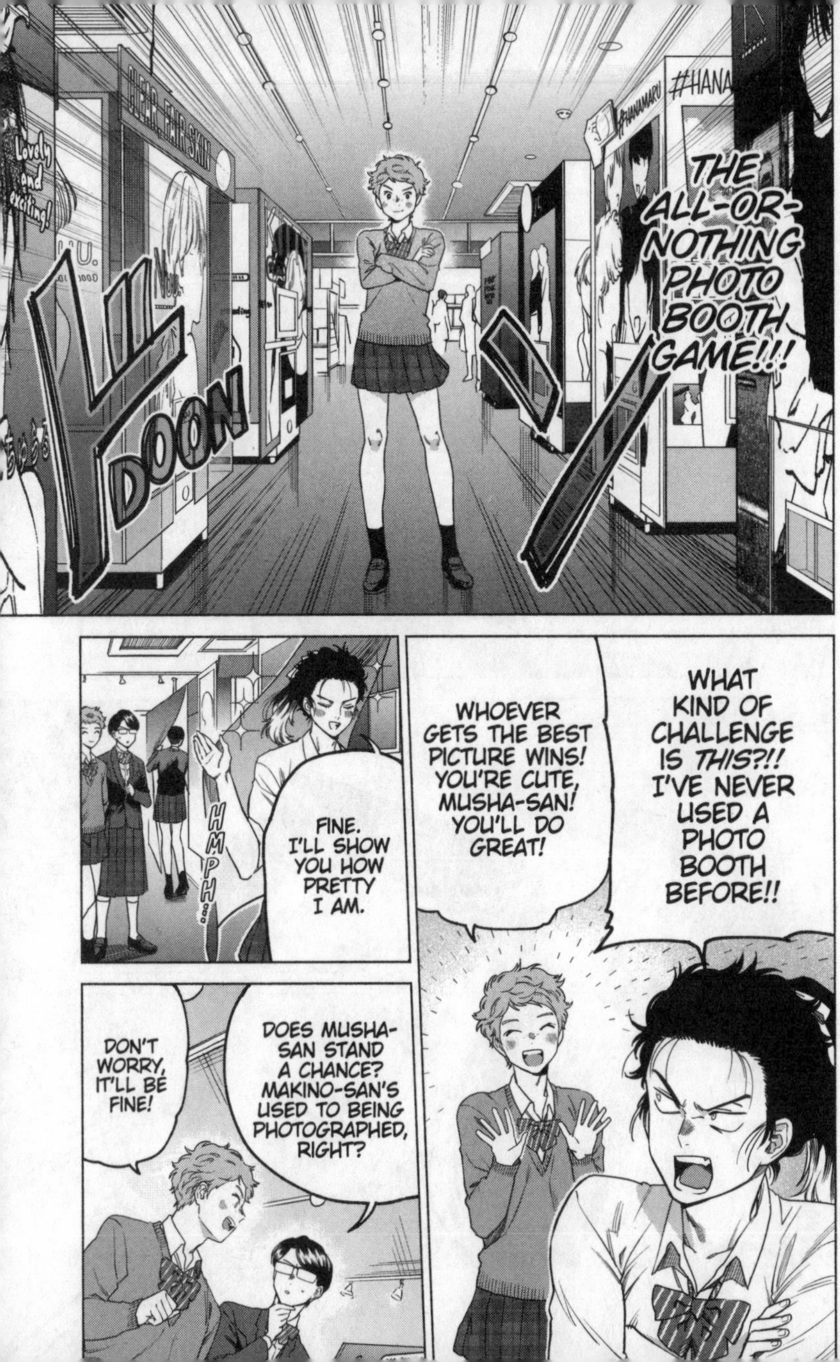
#HANAMARU
THE ALL-OR-NOTHING PHOTO BOOTH GAME!!!
DOON
Lovely and exciting!
WHAT KIND OF CHALLENGE IS *THIS*?!! I'VE NEVER USED A PHOTO BOOTH BEFORE!!
WHOEVER GETS THE BEST PICTURE WINS! YOU'RE CUTE, MUSHA-SAN! YOU'LL DO GREAT!
FINE. I'LL SHOW YOU HOW PRETTY I AM.
HMPH...
DOES MUSHA-SAN STAND A CHANCE? MAKINO-SAN'S USED TO BEING PHOTOGRAPHED, RIGHT?
DON'T WORRY, IT'LL BE FINE!

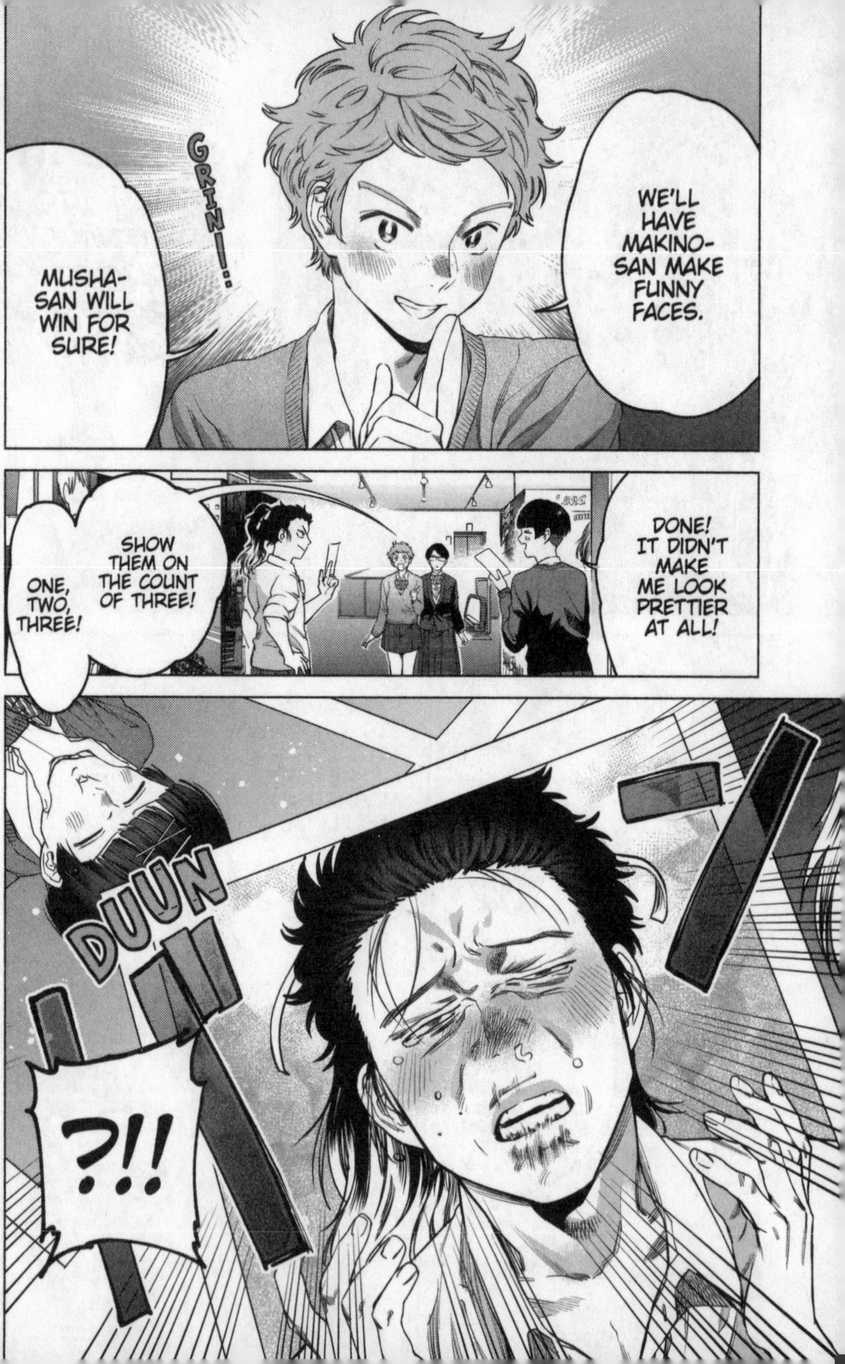
WE'LL HAVE MAKINO-SAN MAKE FUNNY FACES.
GRIN!!
MUSHA-SAN WILL WIN FOR SURE!
DONE! IT DIDN'T MAKE ME LOOK PRETTIER AT ALL!
SHOW THEM ON THE COUNT OF THREE!
ONE, TWO, THREE!
DUUN
?!!

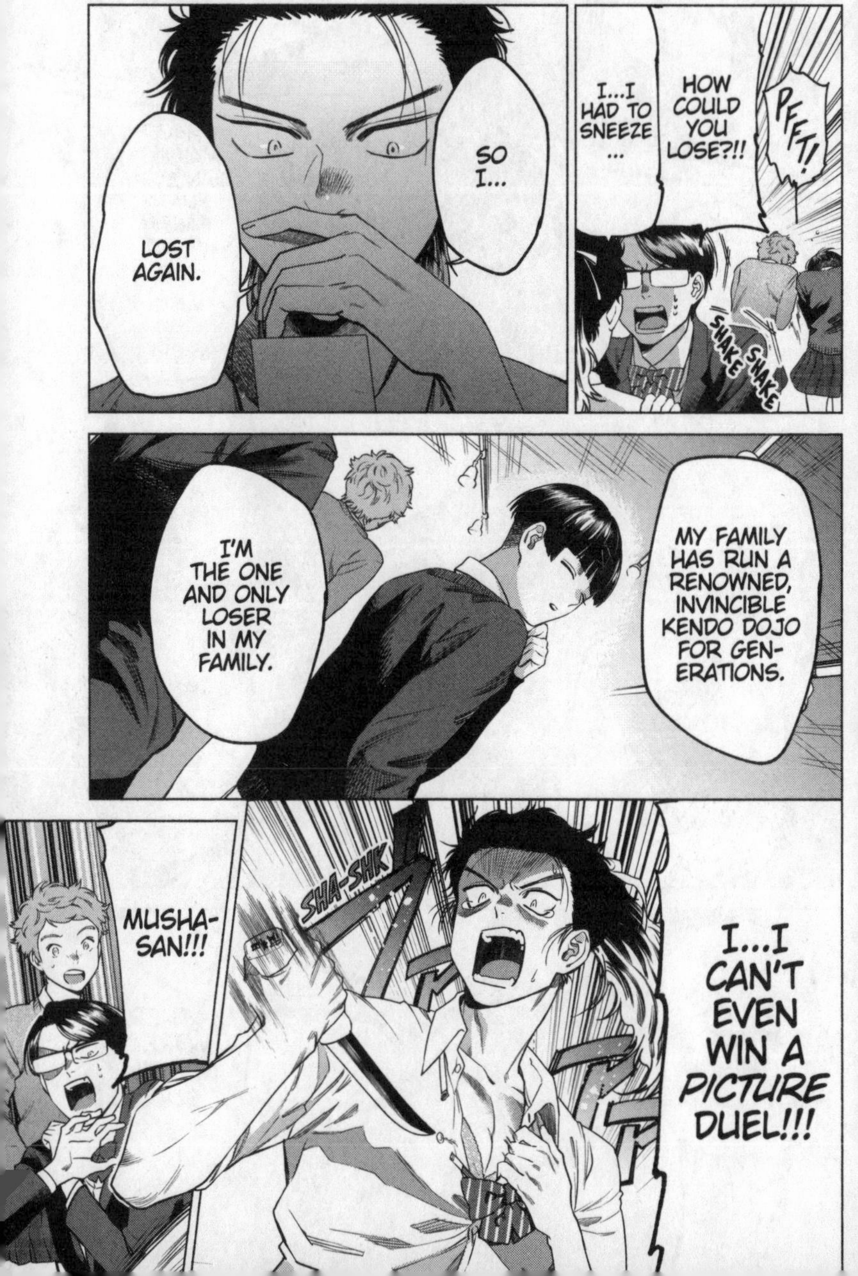
PFFT!!
HOW COULD YOU LOSE?!!
I...I HAD TO SNEEZE ...
SHAKE SHAKE
SO I...
LOST AGAIN.
MY FAMILY HAS RUN A RENOWNED, INVINCIBLE KENDO DOJO FOR GEN-ERATIONS.
I'M THE ONE AND ONLY LOSER IN MY FAMILY.
I...I CAN'T EVEN WIN A PICTURE DUEL!!!
SHA-SHK
MUSHA-SAN!!!

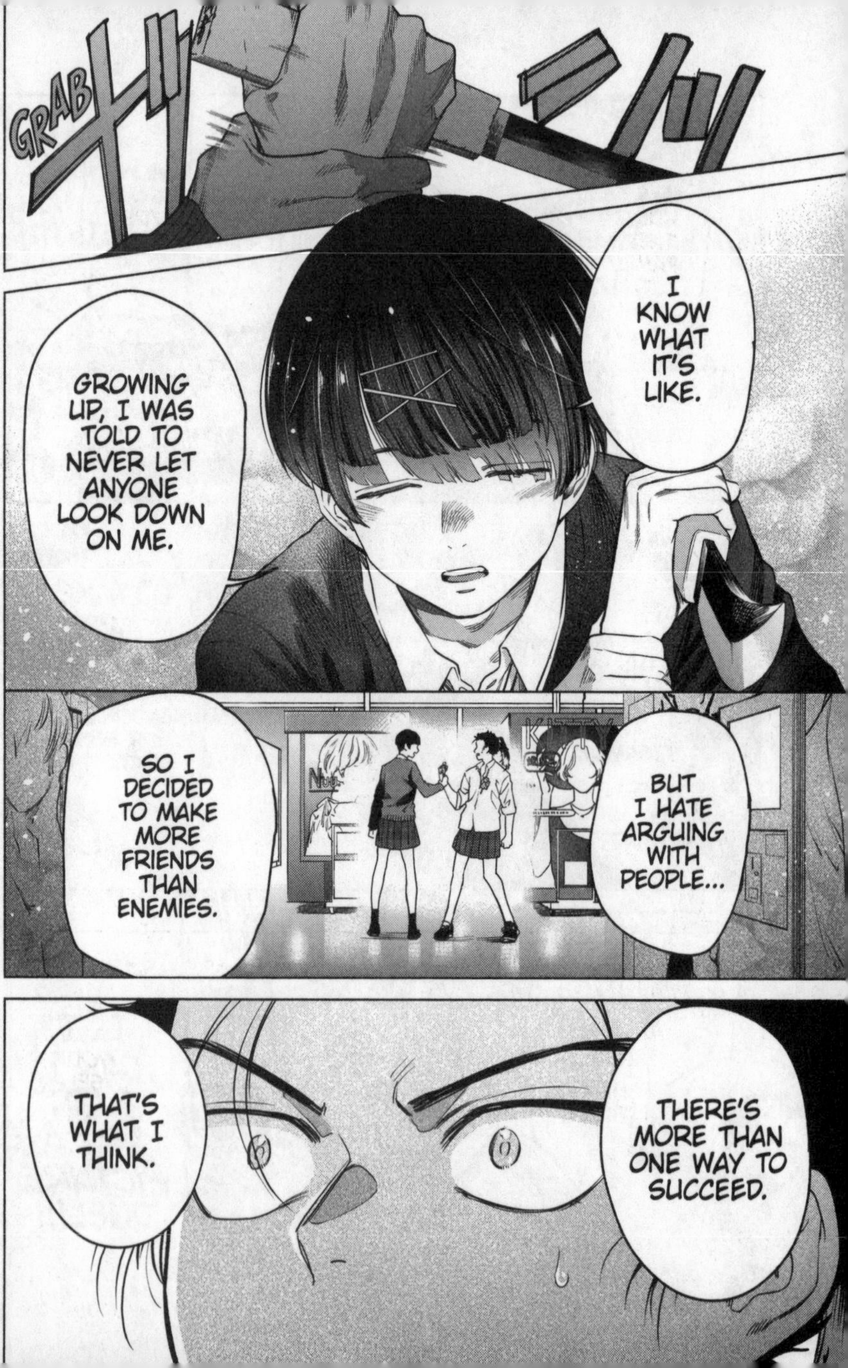
GRAB
I KNOW WHAT IT'S LIKE.
GROWING UP, I WAS TOLD TO NEVER LET ANYONE LOOK DOWN ON ME.
BUT I HATE ARGUING WITH PEOPLE...
SO I DECIDED TO MAKE MORE FRIENDS THAN ENEMIES.
THERE'S MORE THAN ONE WAY TO SUCCEED.
THAT'S WHAT I THINK.

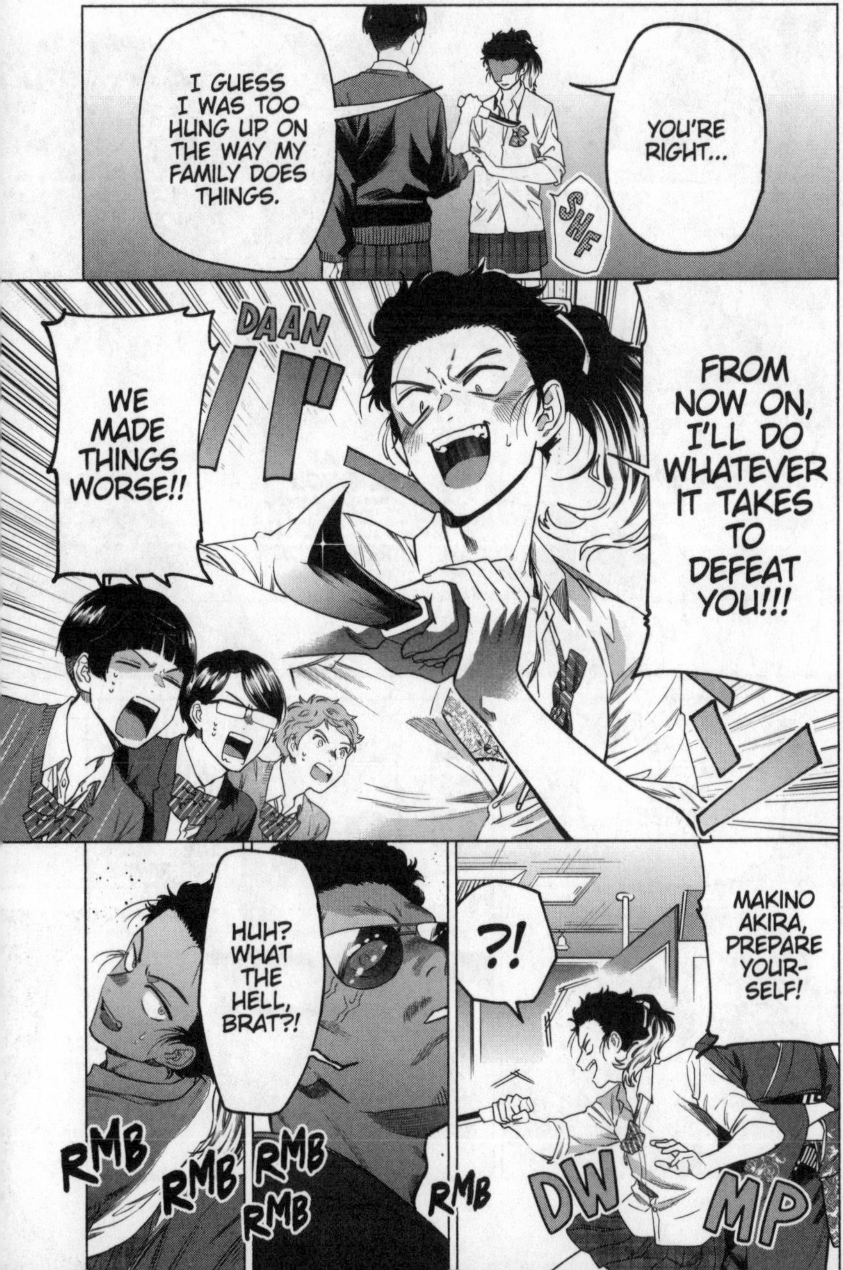
YOU'RE RIGHT...
SHF
I GUESS I WAS TOO HUNG UP ON THE WAY MY FAMILY DOES THINGS.
FROM NOW ON, I'LL DO WHATEVER IT TAKES TO DEFEAT YOU!!!
DAAN
WE MADE THINGS WORSE!!
MAKINO AKIRA, PREPARE YOUR-SELF!
?!
DWMP
RMB
HUH? WHAT THE HELL, BRAT?!
RMB RMB RMB RMB

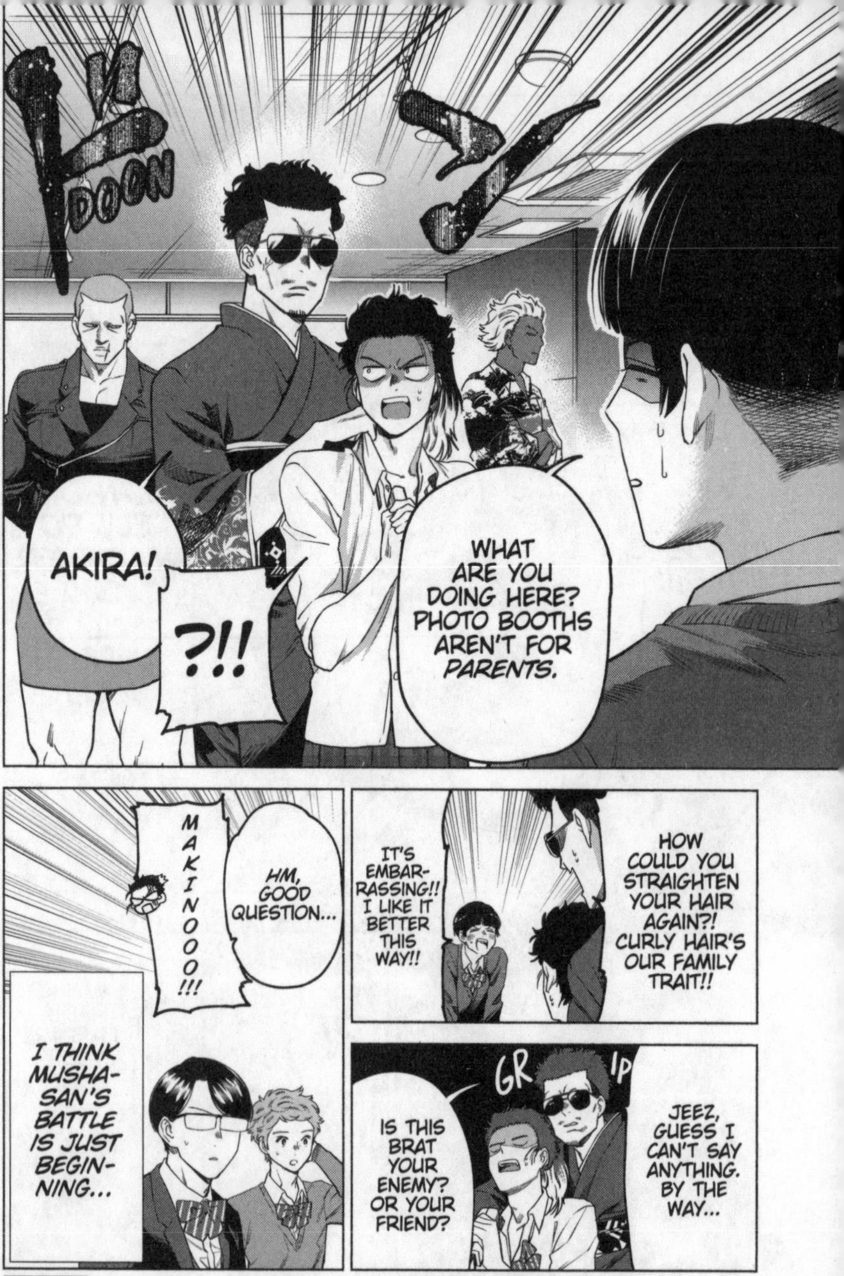
DOON
WHAT ARE YOU DOING HERE? PHOTO BOOTHS AREN'T FOR PARENTS.
?!!
AKIRA!
HOW COULD YOU STRAIGHTEN YOUR HAIR AGAIN?! CURLY HAIR'S OUR FAMILY TRAIT!!
IT'S EMBARRASSING!! I LIKE IT BETTER THIS WAY!!
JEEZ, GUESS I CAN'T SAY ANYTHING. BY THE WAY...
GRIP
IS THIS BRAT YOUR ENEMY? OR YOUR FRIEND?
HM, GOOD QUESTION...
MAKINOOOO!!!
I THINK MUSHA-SAN'S BATTLE IS JUST BEGINNING...

#25 End

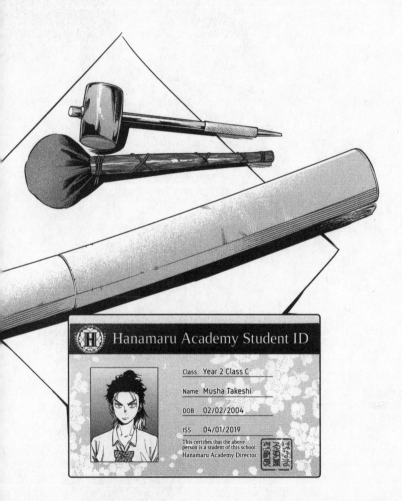

Hanamaru Academy Student ID

Class   Year 2 Class C

Name   Musha Takeshi

DOB   02/02/2004

ISS   04/01/2019

This certifies that the above
person is a student of this school.
Hanamaru Academy Director

THIGH HIGH
Reiwa Hanamaru Academy

HANAMARU PRIVATE HIGH SCHOOL

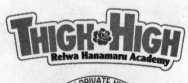

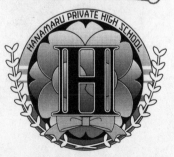

#26 #classrep #goesbad #inApril

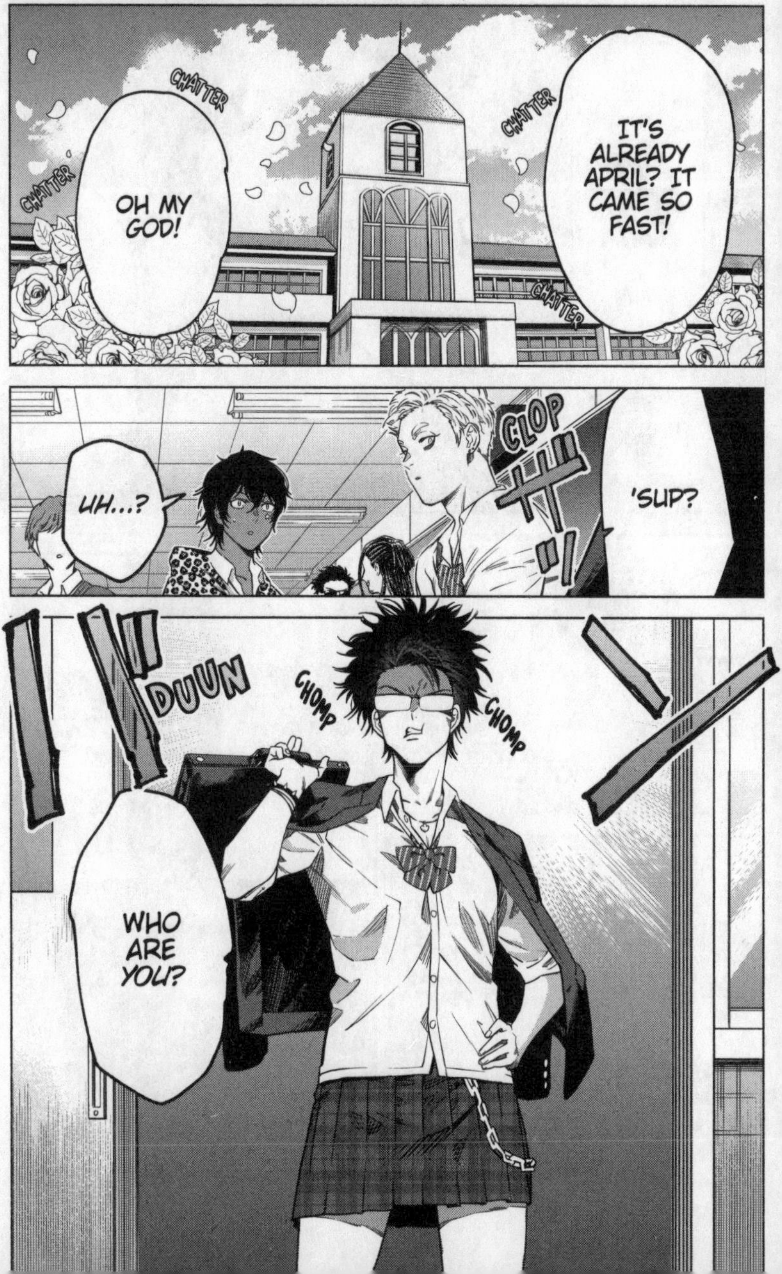
CHATTER
IT'S ALREADY APRIL? IT CAME SO FAST!
CHATTER
CHATTER
OH MY GOD!
CHATTER
'SUP?
CLOP
UH...?
CHOMP
CHOMP
DUUN
WHO ARE YOU?

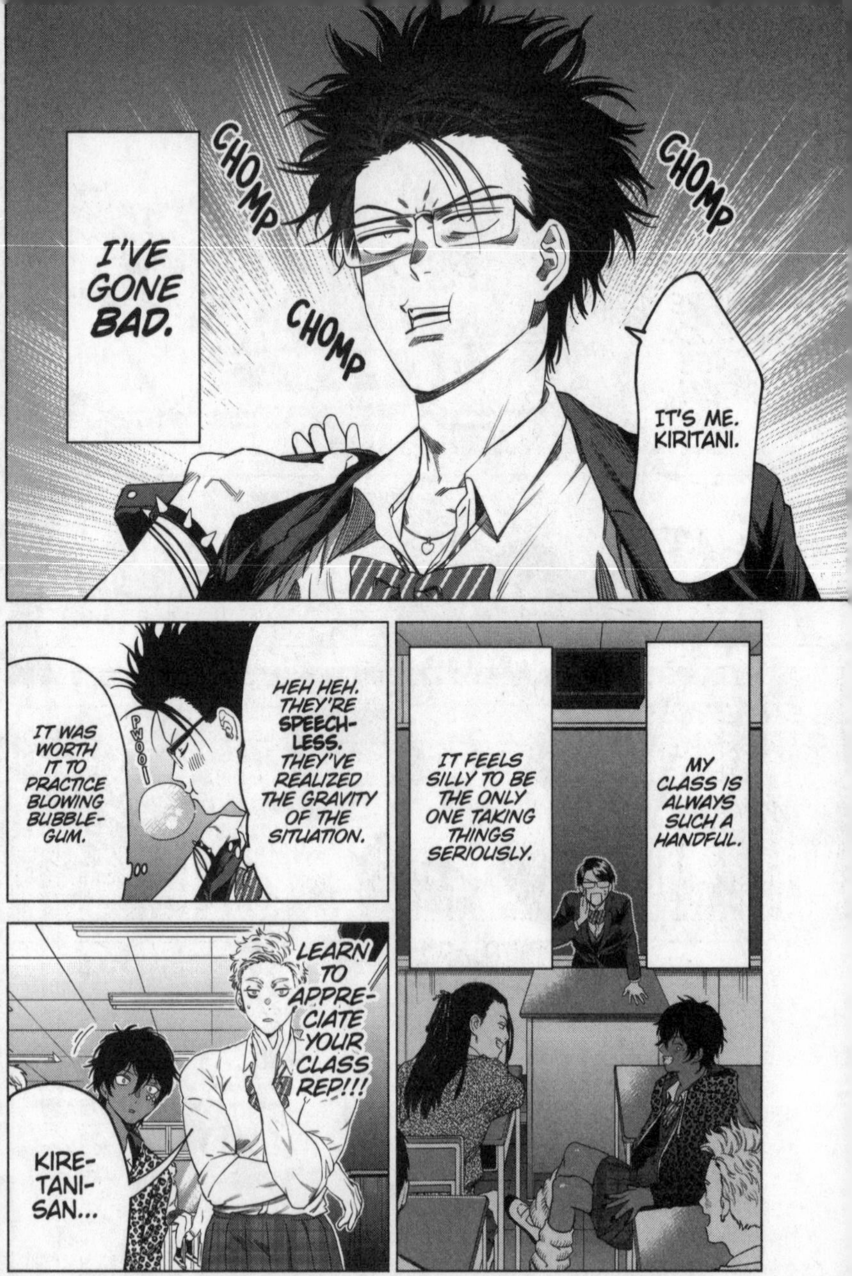
CHOMP
CHOMP
I'VE GONE BAD.
CHOMP
IT'S ME. KIRITANI.
MY CLASS IS ALWAYS SUCH A HANDFUL.
IT FEELS SILLY TO BE THE ONLY ONE TAKING THINGS SERIOUSLY.
HEH HEH. THEY'RE SPEECH-LESS. THEY'VE REALIZED THE GRAVITY OF THE SITUATION.
PWOO!
IT WAS WORTH IT TO PRACTICE BLOWING BUBBLE-GUM.
LEARN TO APPRE-CIATE YOUR CLASS REP!!!
KIRE-TANI-SAN...

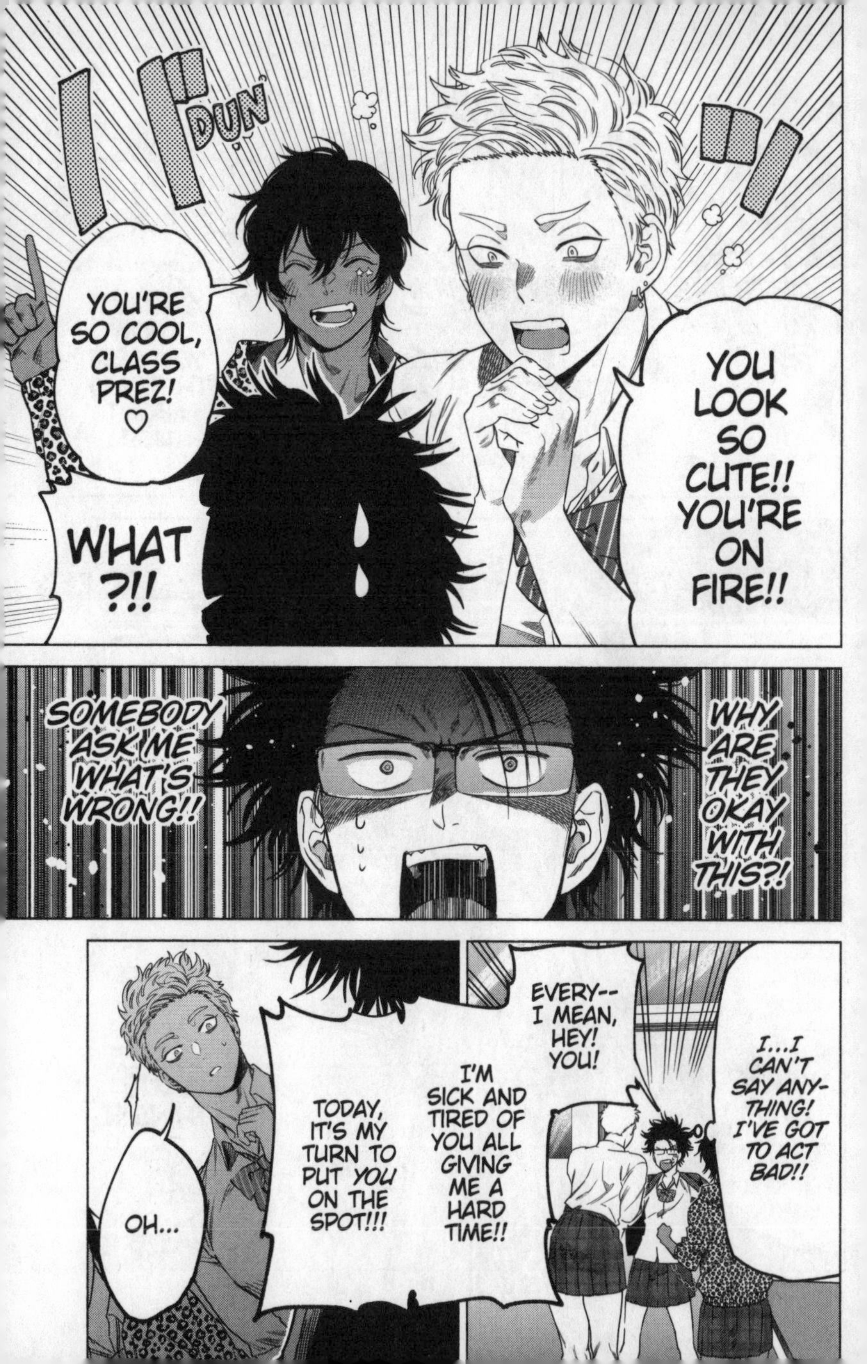
YOU LOOK SO CUTE!! YOU'RE ON FIRE!!
DUN
YOU'RE SO COOL, CLASS PREZ! ♡
WHAT?!!
WHY ARE THEY OKAY WITH THIS?!
SOMEBODY ASK ME WHAT'S WRONG!!
I...I CAN'T SAY ANY-THING! I'VE GOT TO ACT BAD!!
EVERY-- I MEAN, HEY! YOU!
I'M SICK AND TIRED OF YOU ALL GIVING ME A HARD TIME!!
TODAY, IT'S MY TURN TO PUT *YOU* ON THE SPOT!!!
OH...

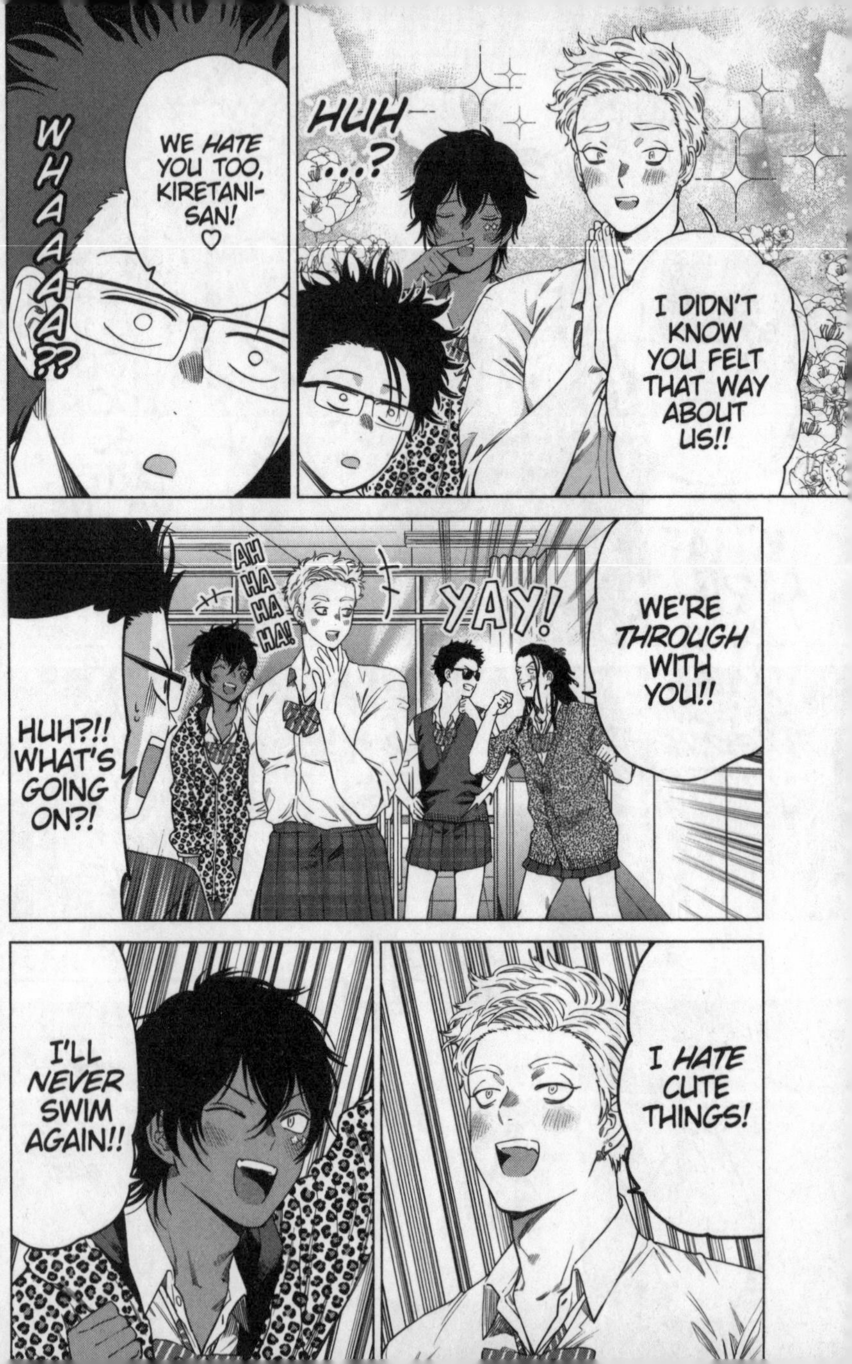
I DIDN'T KNOW YOU FELT THAT WAY ABOUT US!!
HUH...?
WE HATE YOU TOO, KIRETANI-SAN! ♡
WHAAAAAA??
WE'RE THROUGH WITH YOU!!
YAY!
AH HA HA HA HA!
HUH?!! WHAT'S GOING ON?!
I HATE CUTE THINGS!
I'LL NEVER SWIM AGAIN!!

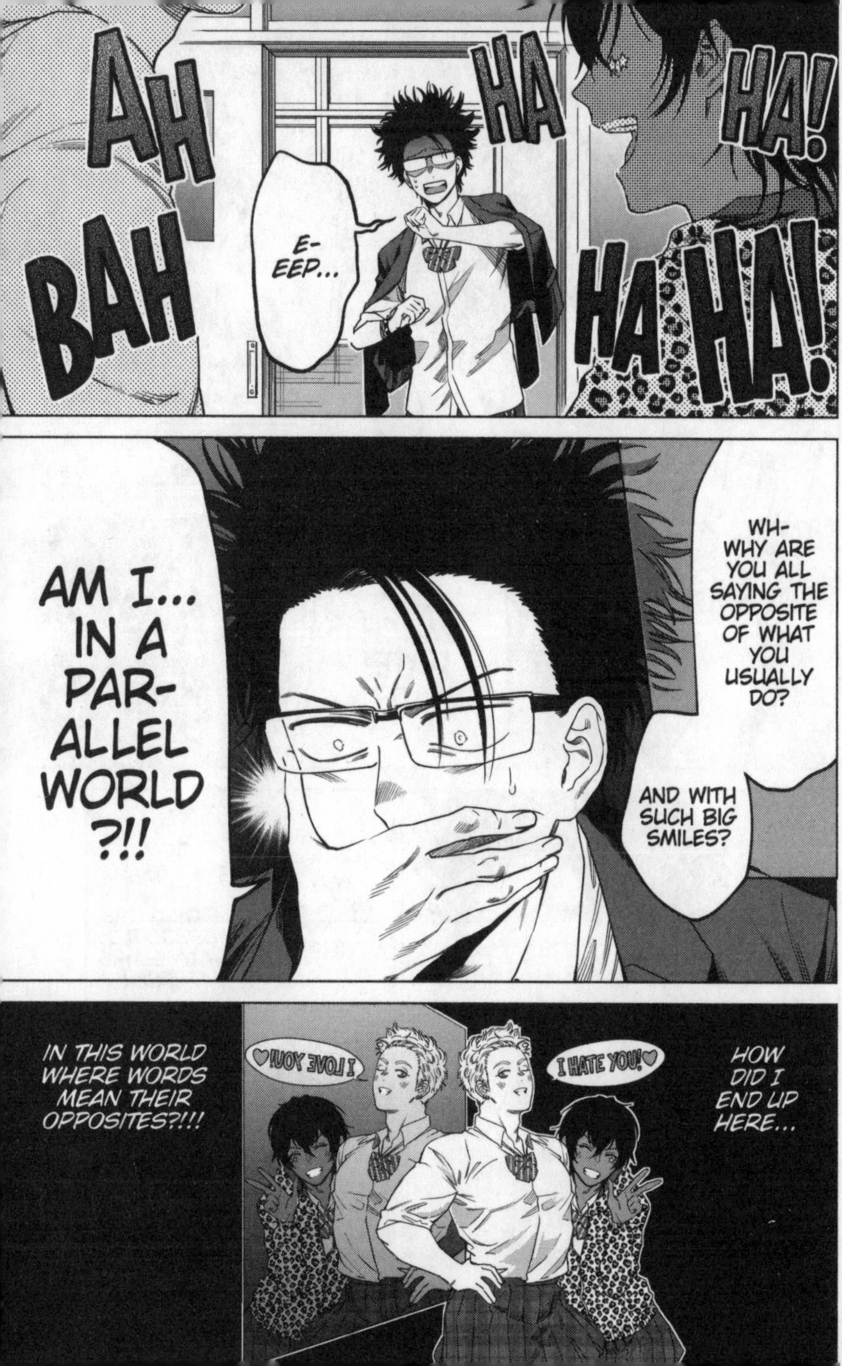
HA HA!
HA HA HA!
E-EEP...
AH BAH
WH- WHY ARE YOU ALL SAYING THE OPPOSITE OF WHAT YOU USUALLY DO?
AND WITH SUCH BIG SMILES?
AM I... IN A PAR-ALLEL WORLD ?!!
HOW DID I END UP HERE...
I HATE YOU!♥
I LOVE YOU!♥
IN THIS WORLD WHERE WORDS MEAN THEIR OPPOSITES?!!!

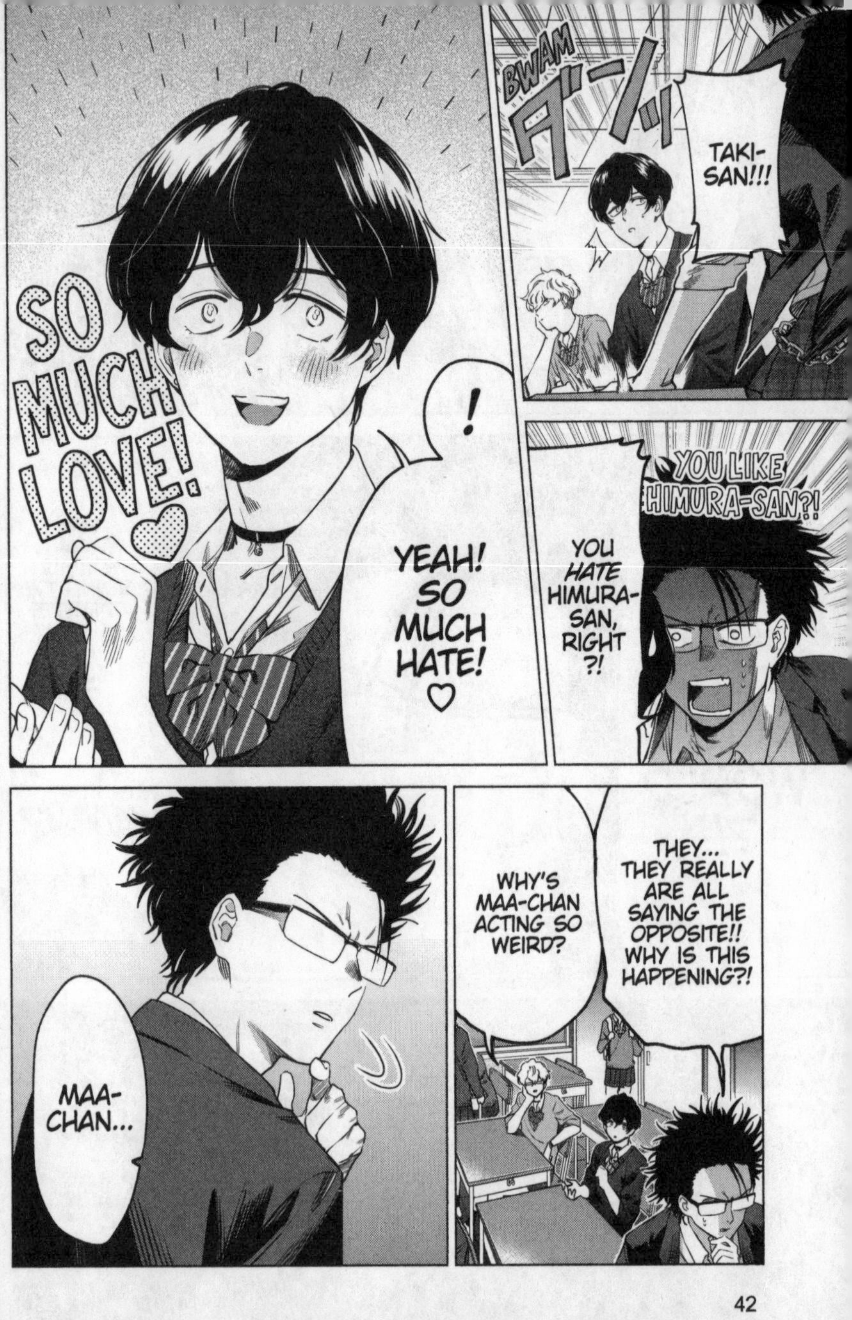
BWAM
TAKI-SAN!!!
YOU LIKE HIMURA-SAN?!
YOU HATE HIMURA-SAN, RIGHT?!
!
YEAH! SO MUCH HATE! ♡
SO MUCH LOVE! ♡
THEY... THEY REALLY ARE ALL SAYING THE OPPOSITE!! WHY IS THIS HAPPENING?!
WHY'S MAA-CHAN ACTING SO WEIRD?
MAA-CHAN...

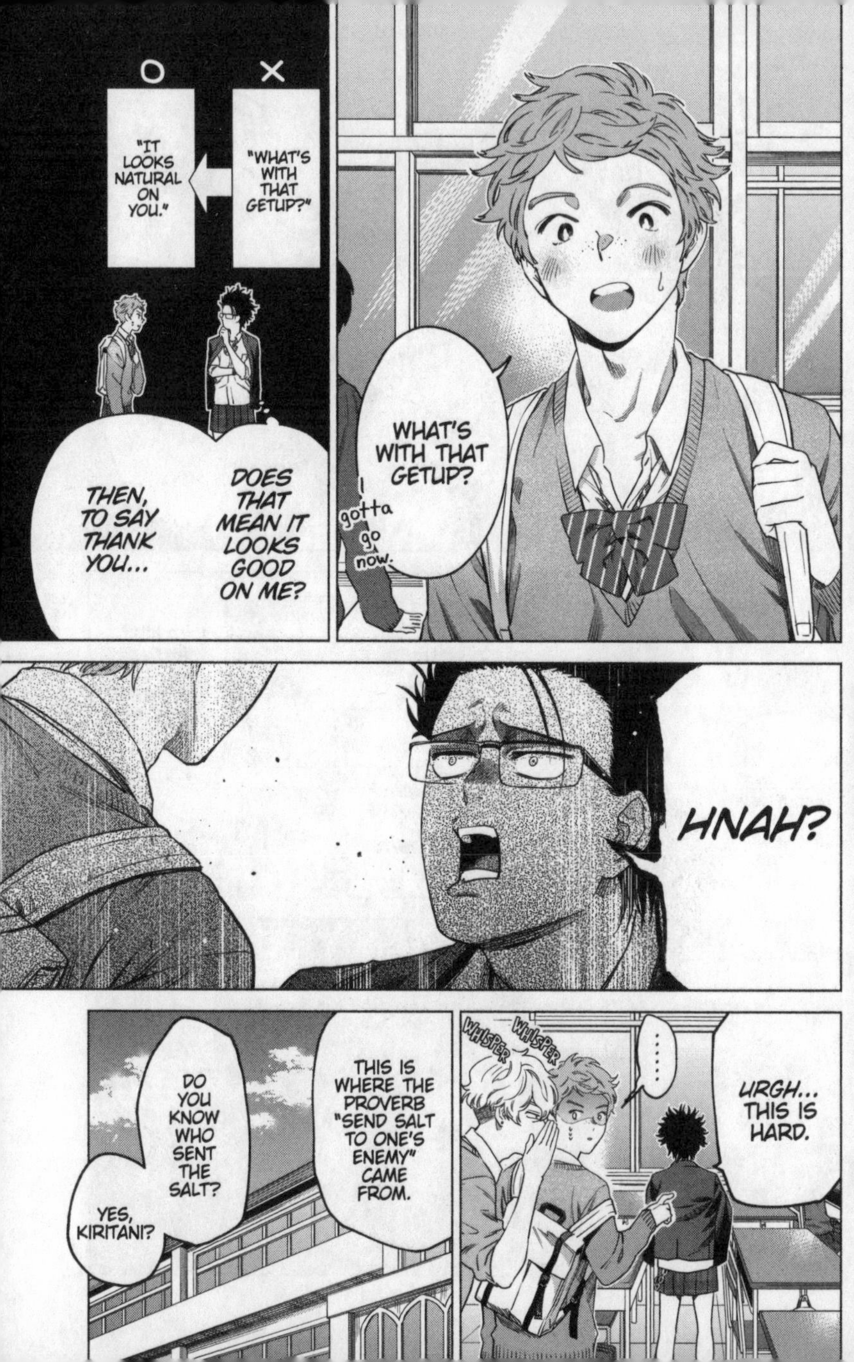
WHAT'S WITH THAT GETUP?
I gotta go now.
×
"WHAT'S WITH THAT GETUP?"
O
"IT LOOKS NATURAL ON YOU."
DOES THAT MEAN IT LOOKS GOOD ON ME?
THEN, TO SAY THANK YOU...
HNAH?
URGH... THIS IS HARD.
......
WHISPER
WHISPER
THIS IS WHERE THE PROVERB "SEND SALT TO ONE'S ENEMY" CAME FROM.
DO YOU KNOW WHO SENT THE SALT?
YES, KIRITANI?

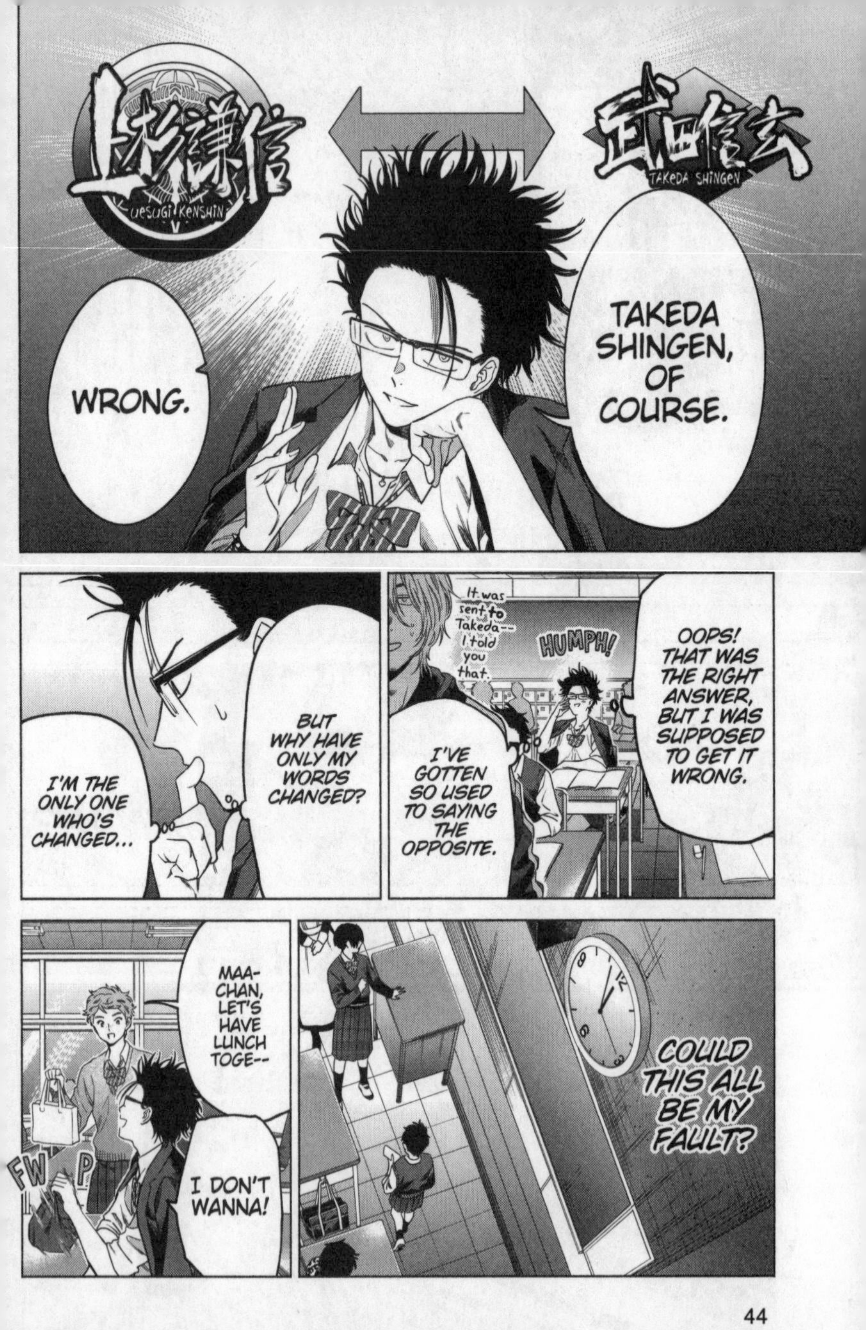
武田信玄
TAKEDA SHINGEN
上杉謙信
UESUGI KENSHIN
TAKEDA SHINGEN, OF COURSE.
WRONG.
OOPS! THAT WAS THE RIGHT ANSWER, BUT I WAS SUPPOSED TO GET IT WRONG.
HUMPH!
It was sent to Takeda-- I told you that.
I'VE GOTTEN SO USED TO SAYING THE OPPOSITE.
BUT WHY HAVE ONLY MY WORDS CHANGED?
I'M THE ONLY ONE WHO'S CHANGED...
COULD THIS ALL BE MY FAULT?
MAA-CHAN, LET'S HAVE LUNCH TOGE--
FWP
I DON'T WANNA!

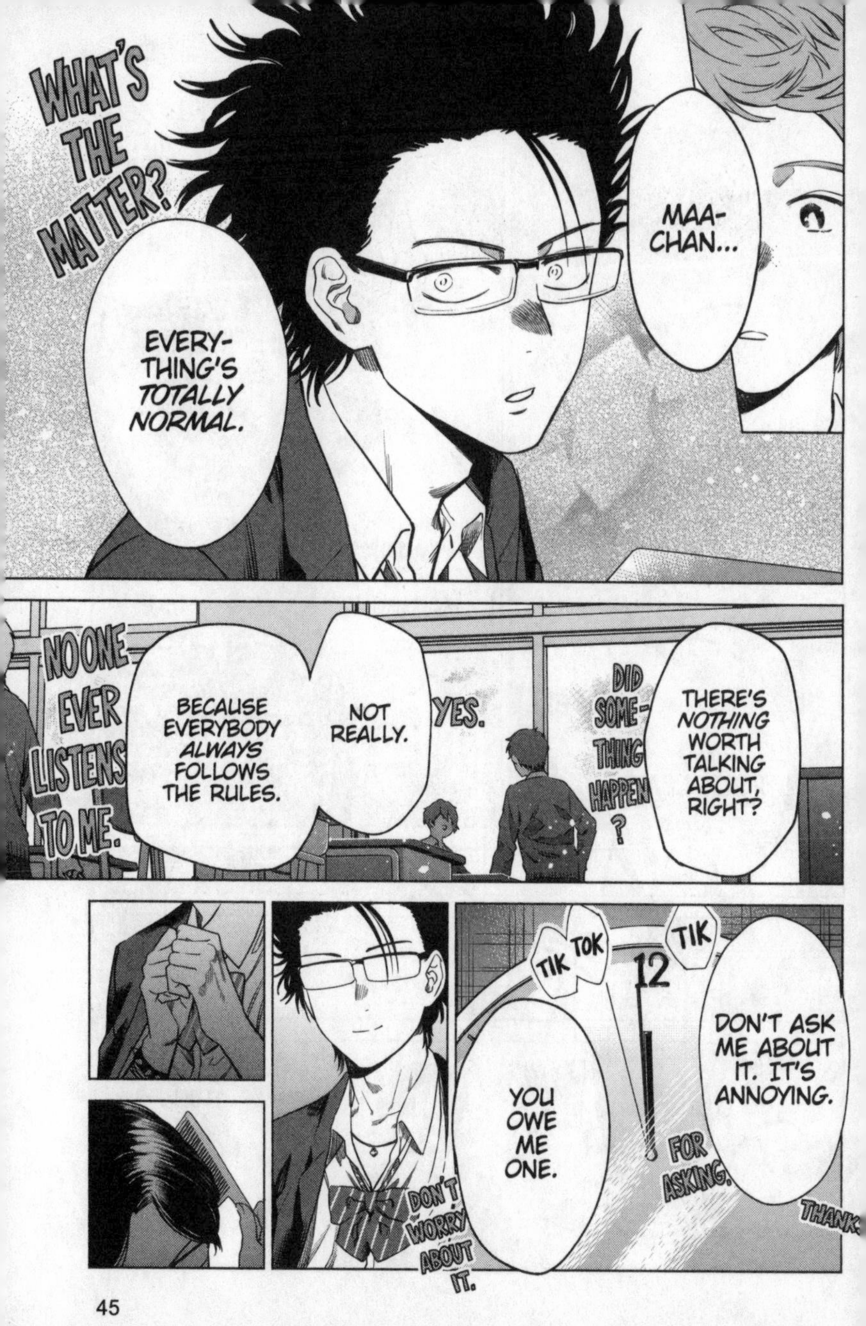
MAA-CHAN...
WHAT'S THE MATTER?
EVERY-THING'S *TOTALLY NORMAL.*
THERE'S *NOTHING* WORTH TALKING ABOUT, RIGHT?
DID SOME-THING HAPPEN?
YES.
NOT REALLY.
BECAUSE EVERYBODY *ALWAYS* FOLLOWS THE RULES.
NO ONE EVER LISTENS TO ME.
TIK
TOK
TIK
12
DON'T ASK ME ABOUT IT. IT'S ANNOYING.
THANK
FOR ASKING.
YOU OWE ME ONE.
DON'T WORRY ABOUT IT.

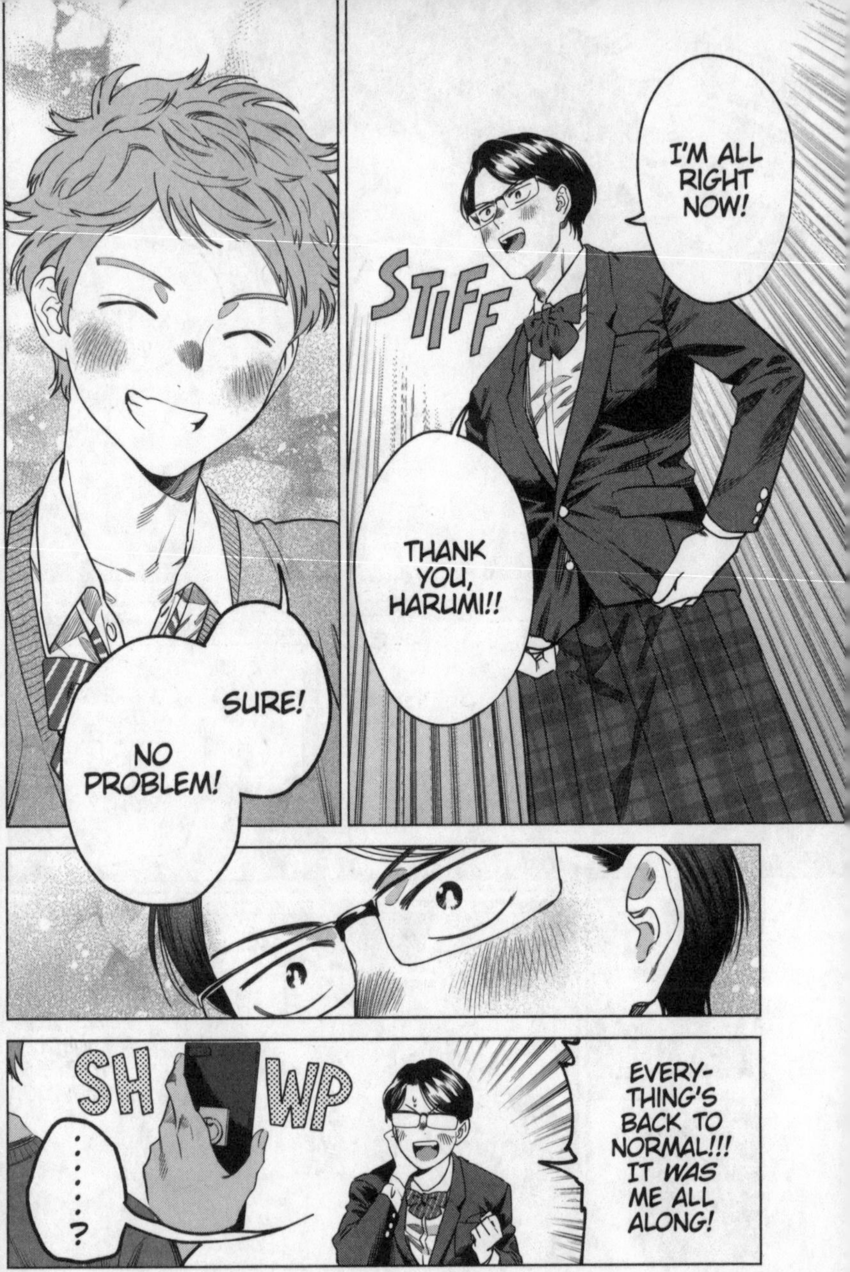
I'M ALL RIGHT NOW!
STIFF
THANK YOU, HARUMI!!
SURE!
NO PROBLEM!
EVERY-THING'S BACK TO NORMAL!!! IT *WAS* ME ALL ALONG!
SHWP
......?

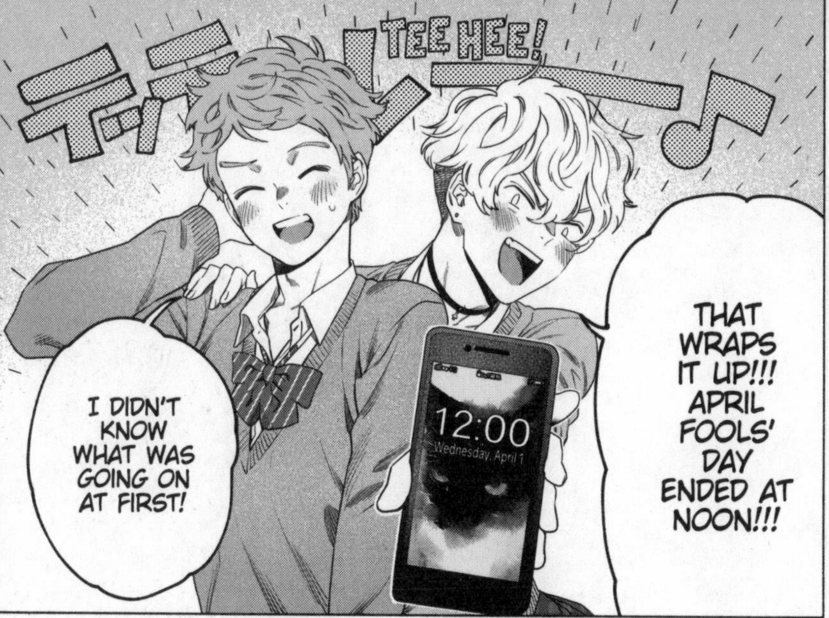
TEE HEE!
テッテレー♪
THAT WRAPS IT UP!!! APRIL FOOLS' DAY ENDED AT NOON!!!
12:00
Wednesday, April 1
I DIDN'T KNOW WHAT WAS GOING ON AT FIRST!

※ In some areas, April Fools' Day pranks must end by 12:00 PM.

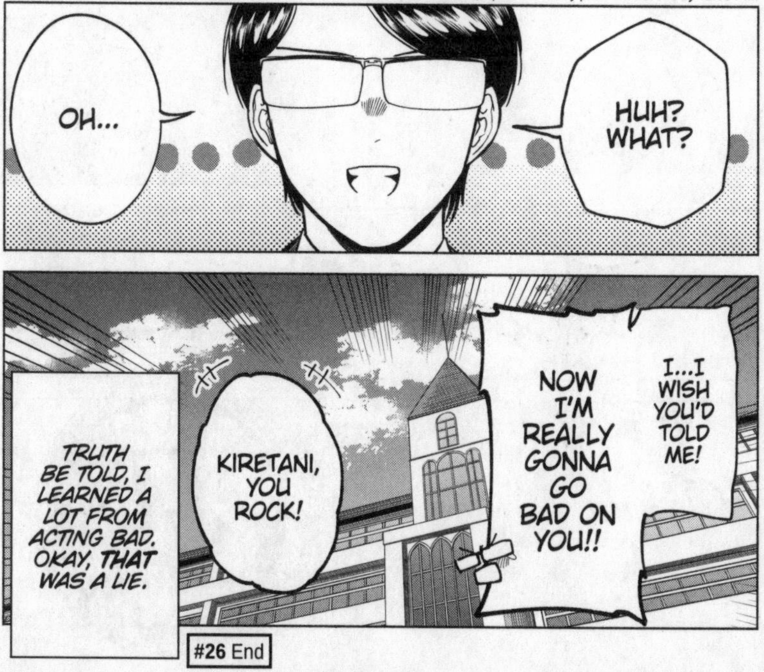
HUH? WHAT?
OH...
I...I WISH YOU'D TOLD ME!
NOW I'M REALLY GONNA GO BAD ON YOU!!
KIRETANI, YOU ROCK!
TRUTH BE TOLD, I LEARNED A LOT FROM ACTING BAD. OKAY, THAT WAS A LIE.

#26 End

THIGH HIGH
Reiwa Hanamaru Academy

HANAMARU PRIVATE HIGH SCHOOL

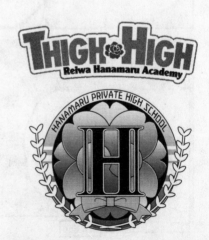

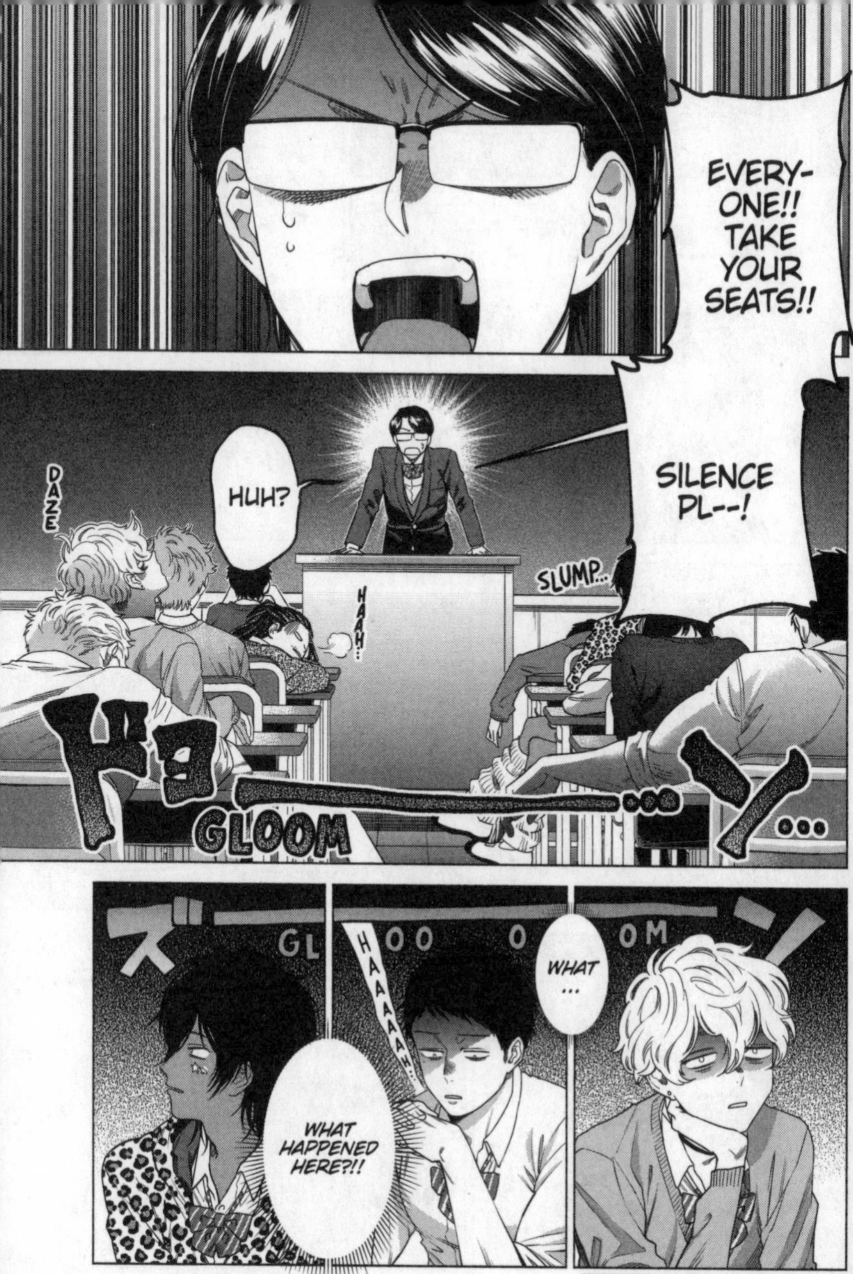
EVERY-ONE!! TAKE YOUR SEATS!!
SILENCE PL--!
SLUMP...
HAAAH...
HUH?
DAZE
ドヨーーー...ン...
GLOOM
WHAT ...
HAAAAAAH...
ズーーン
GL OO O OM
WHAT HAPPENED HERE?!!

#27 #goforitClassA #closecall

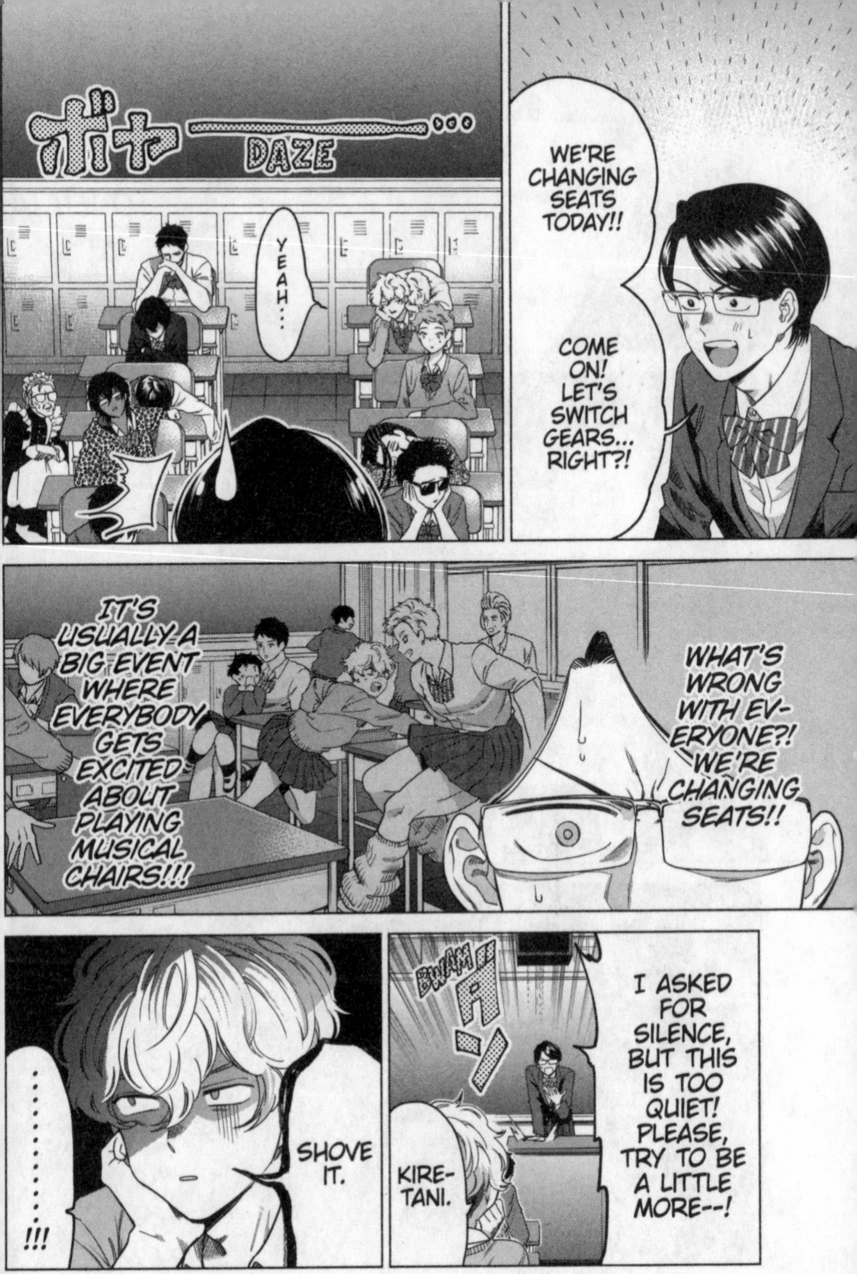
WE'RE CHANGING SEATS TODAY!!
COME ON! LET'S SWITCH GEARS... RIGHT?!
ボケー———…
DAZE
YEAH...
WHAT'S WRONG WITH EV-ERYONE?! WE'RE CHANGING SEATS!!
IT'S USUALLY A BIG EVENT WHERE EVERYBODY GETS EXCITED ABOUT PLAYING MUSICAL CHAIRS!!!
BWAM
I ASKED FOR SILENCE, BUT THIS IS TOO QUIET! PLEASE, TRY TO BE A LITTLE MORE--!
KIRE-TANI.
SHOVE IT.
.........!!!

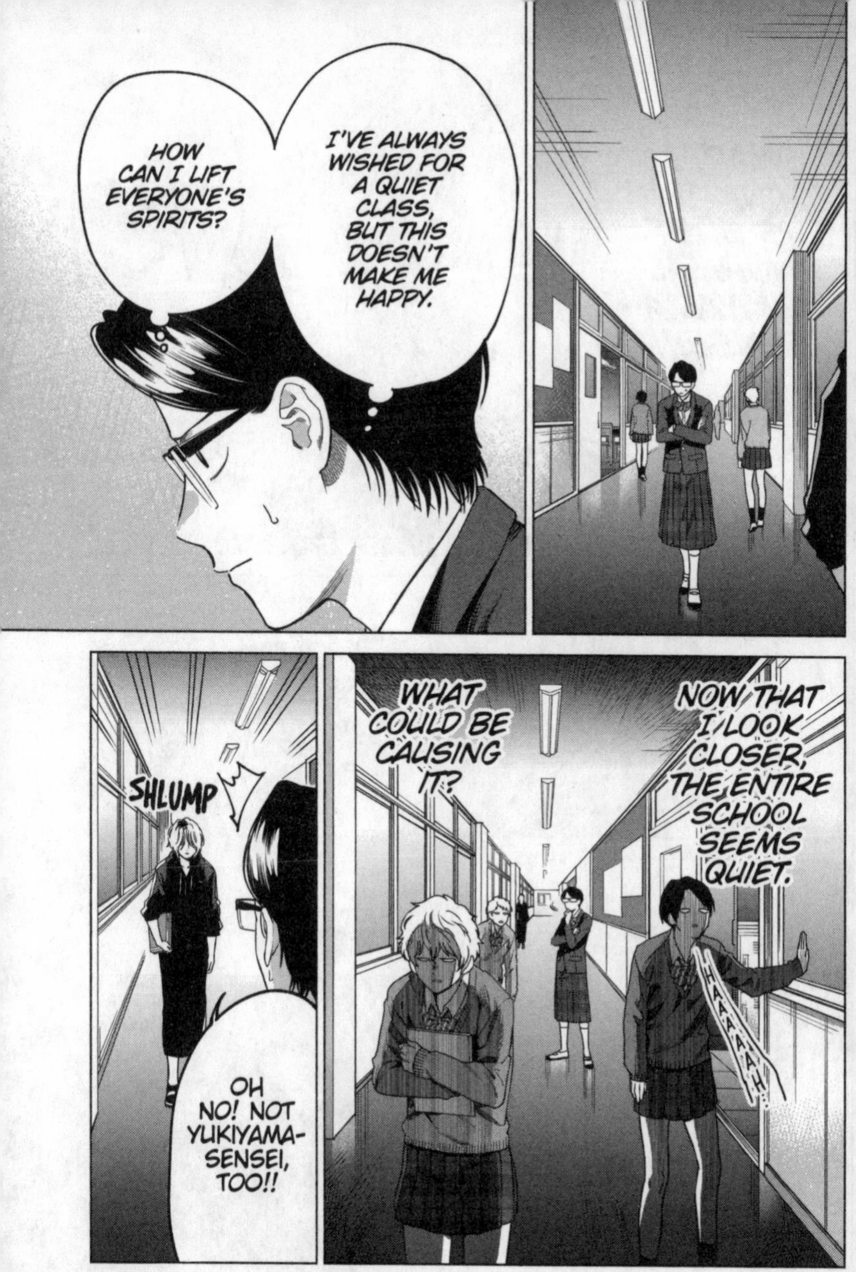
I'VE ALWAYS WISHED FOR A QUIET CLASS, BUT THIS DOESN'T MAKE ME HAPPY.
HOW CAN I LIFT EVERYONE'S SPIRITS?
NOW THAT I LOOK CLOSER, THE ENTIRE SCHOOL SEEMS QUIET.
WHAT COULD BE CAUSING IT?
HAAAAAAH
SHLUMP
OH NO! NOT YUKIYAMA-SENSEI, TOO!!

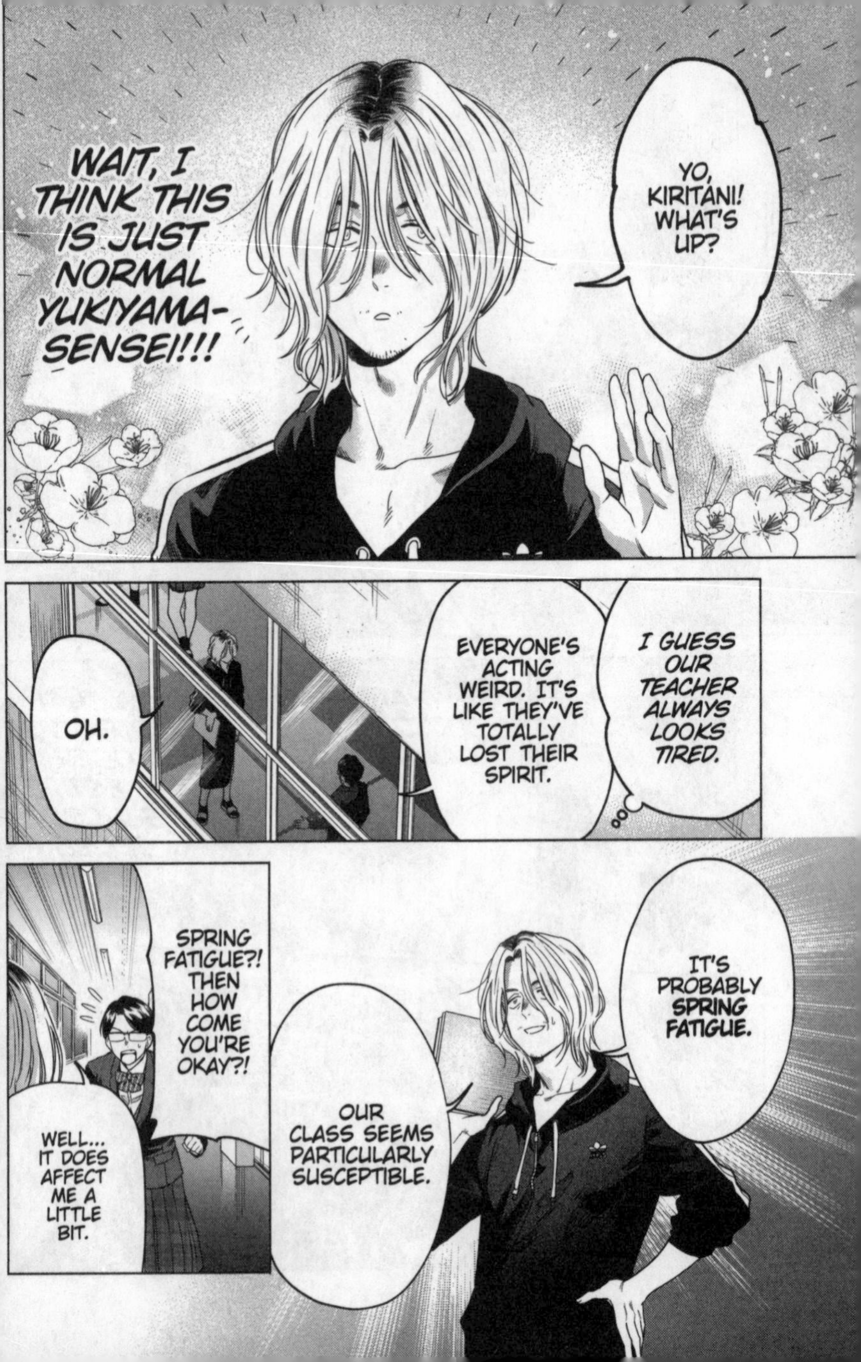
YO, KIRITANI! WHAT'S UP?
WAIT, I THINK THIS IS JUST NORMAL YUKIYAMA-SENSEI!!!
I GUESS OUR TEACHER ALWAYS LOOKS TIRED.
EVERYONE'S ACTING WEIRD. IT'S LIKE THEY'VE TOTALLY LOST THEIR SPIRIT.
OH.
IT'S PROBABLY SPRING FATIGUE.
OUR CLASS SEEMS PARTICULARLY SUSCEPTIBLE.
SPRING FATIGUE?! THEN HOW COME YOU'RE OKAY?!
WELL... IT DOES AFFECT ME A LITTLE BIT.

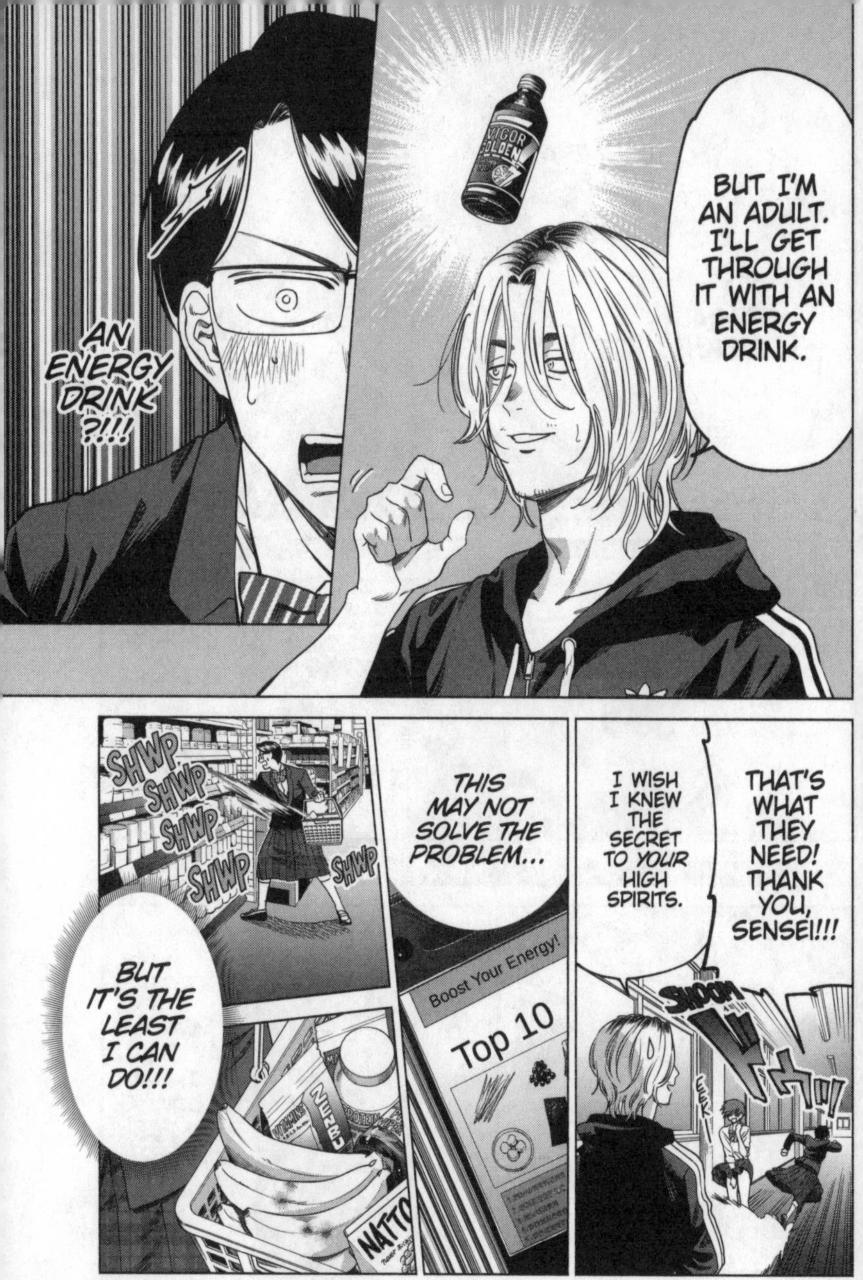
BUT I'M AN ADULT. I'LL GET THROUGH IT WITH AN ENERGY DRINK.
VIGOR GOLDEN
AN ENERGY DRINK ?!!!
THAT'S WHAT THEY NEED! THANK YOU, SENSEI!!!
I WISH I KNEW THE SECRET TO *YOUR* HIGH SPIRITS.
SHOOM
EEK
THIS MAY NOT SOLVE THE PROBLEM...
Boost Your Energy!
Top 10
SHWP
SHWP
SHWP
SHWP
SHWP
BUT IT'S THE LEAST I CAN DO!!!
VITAMINS
ZENBU
PROTEIN
NATTO

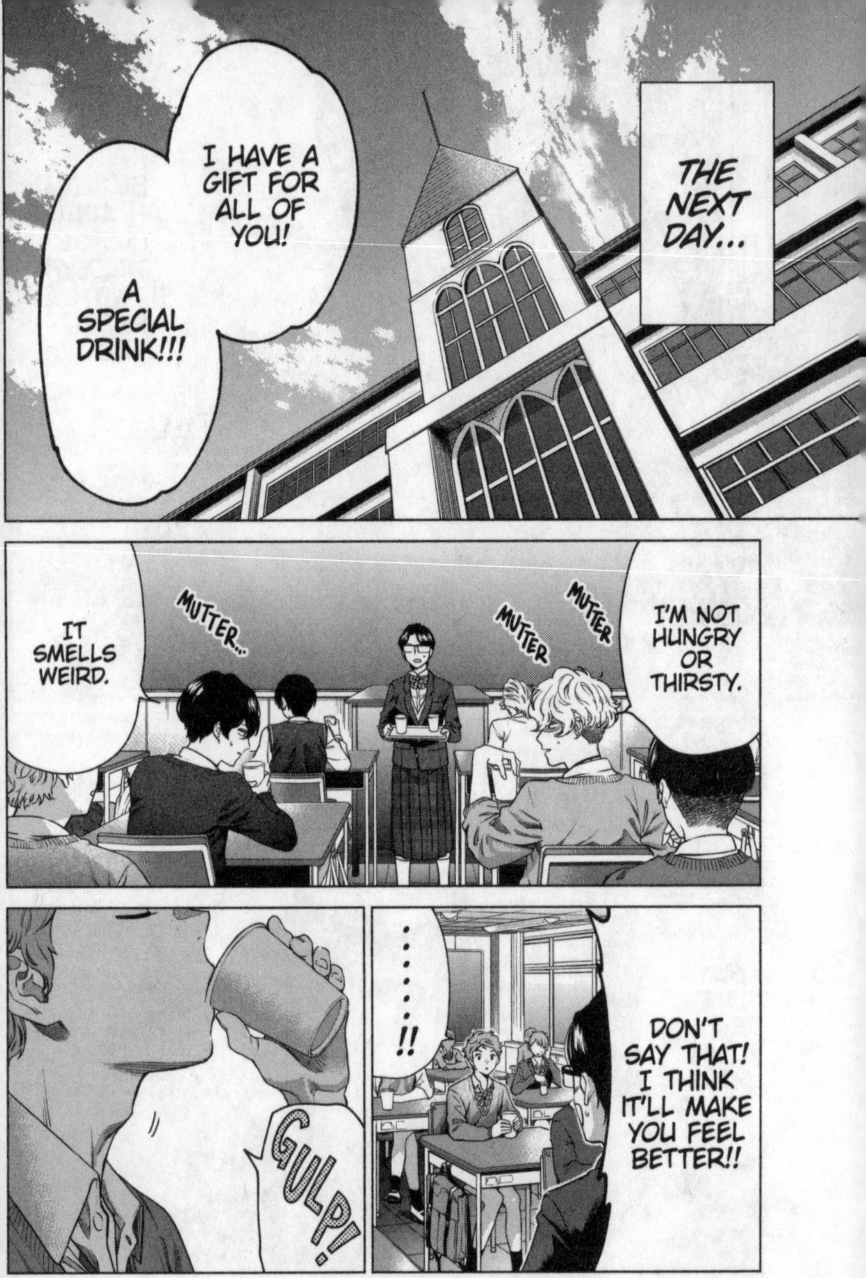
THE NEXT DAY...
I HAVE A GIFT FOR ALL OF YOU!
A SPECIAL DRINK!!!
I'M NOT HUNGRY OR THIRSTY.
MUTTER
MUTTER
MUTTER...
IT SMELLS WEIRD.
DON'T SAY THAT! I THINK IT'LL MAKE YOU FEEL BETTER!!
......!!
GULP!!

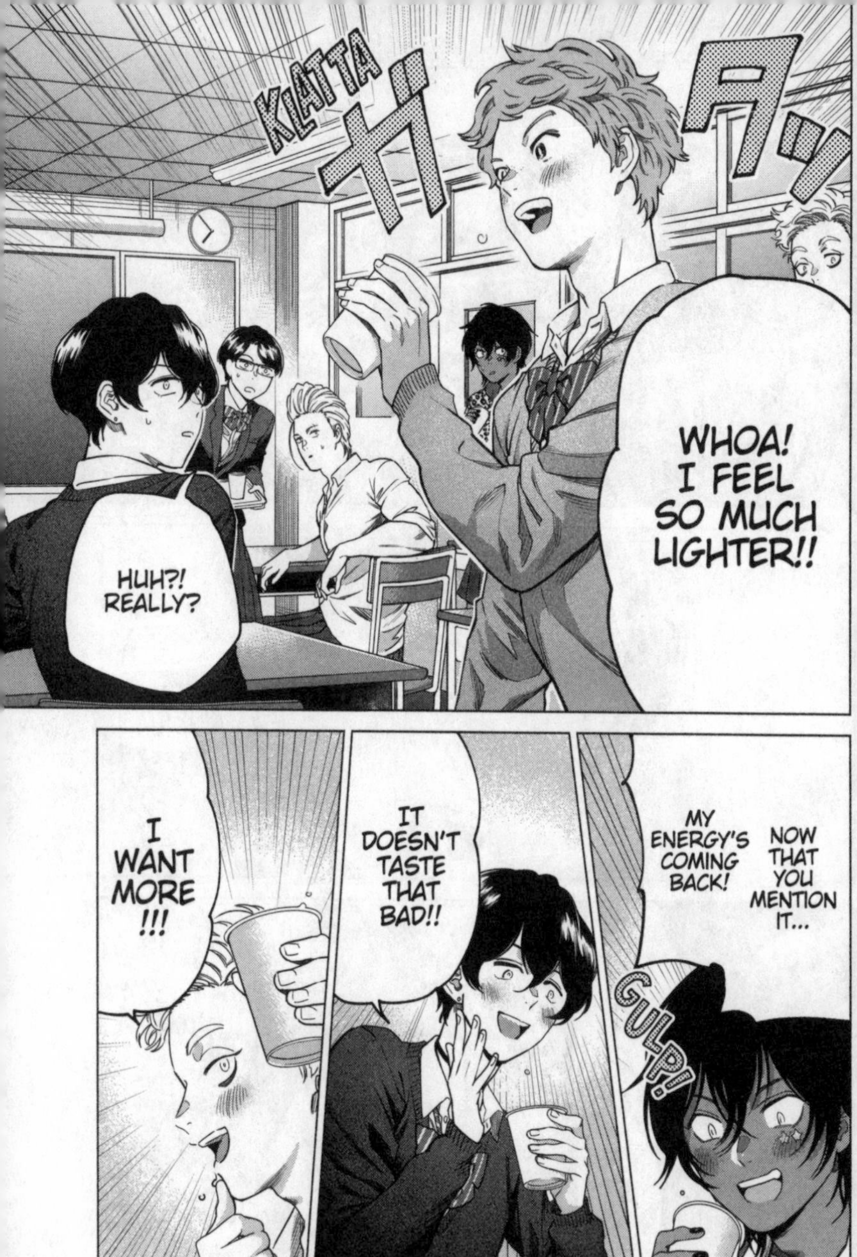
KLATTA
WHOA! I FEEL SO MUCH LIGHTER!!
HUH?! REALLY?
NOW THAT YOU MENTION IT...
MY ENERGY'S COMING BACK!
GULP!
IT DOESN'T TASTE THAT BAD!!
I WANT MORE!!!

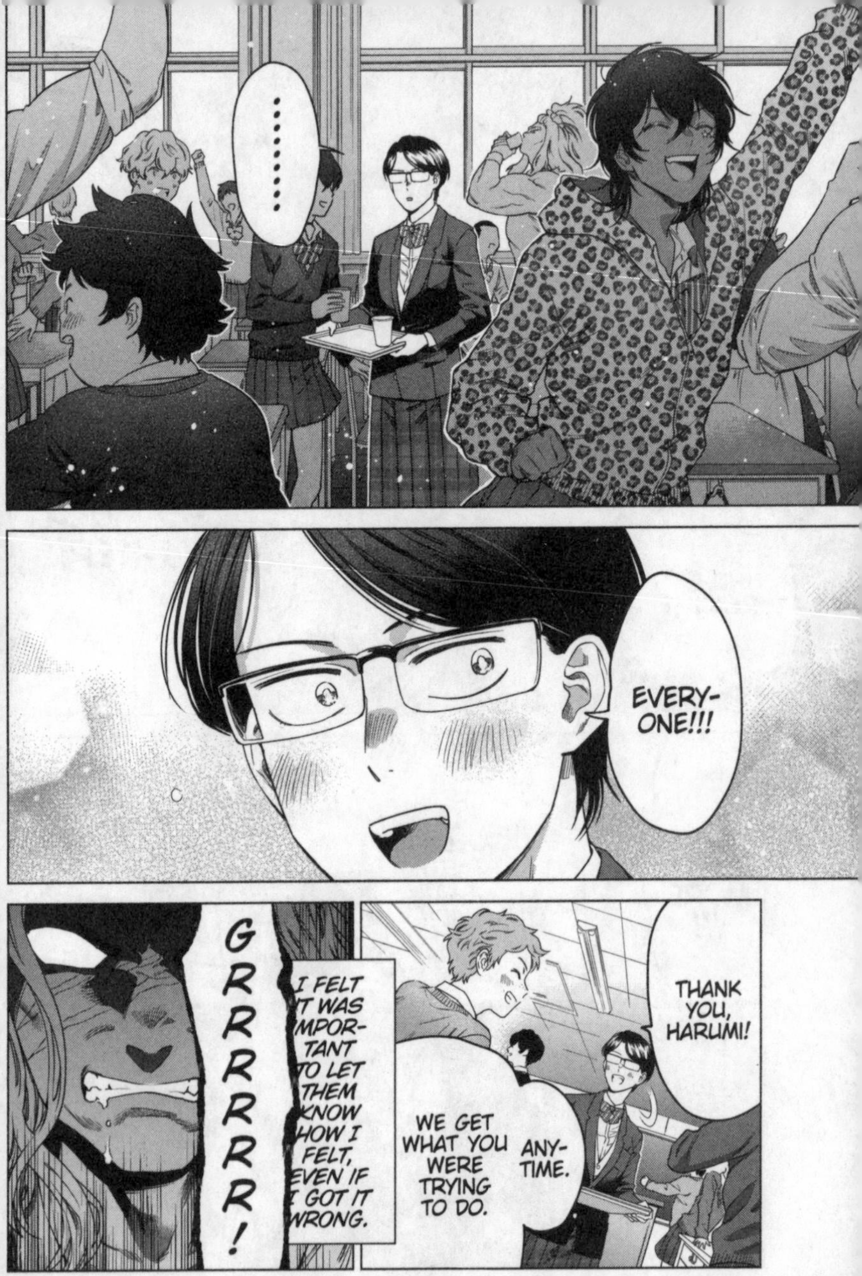
......
EVERY-ONE!!!
THANK YOU, HARUMI!
ANY-TIME.
WE GET WHAT YOU WERE TRYING TO DO.
I FELT IT WAS IMPOR-TANT TO LET THEM KNOW HOW I FELT, EVEN IF I GOT IT WRONG.
GRRRRRR!

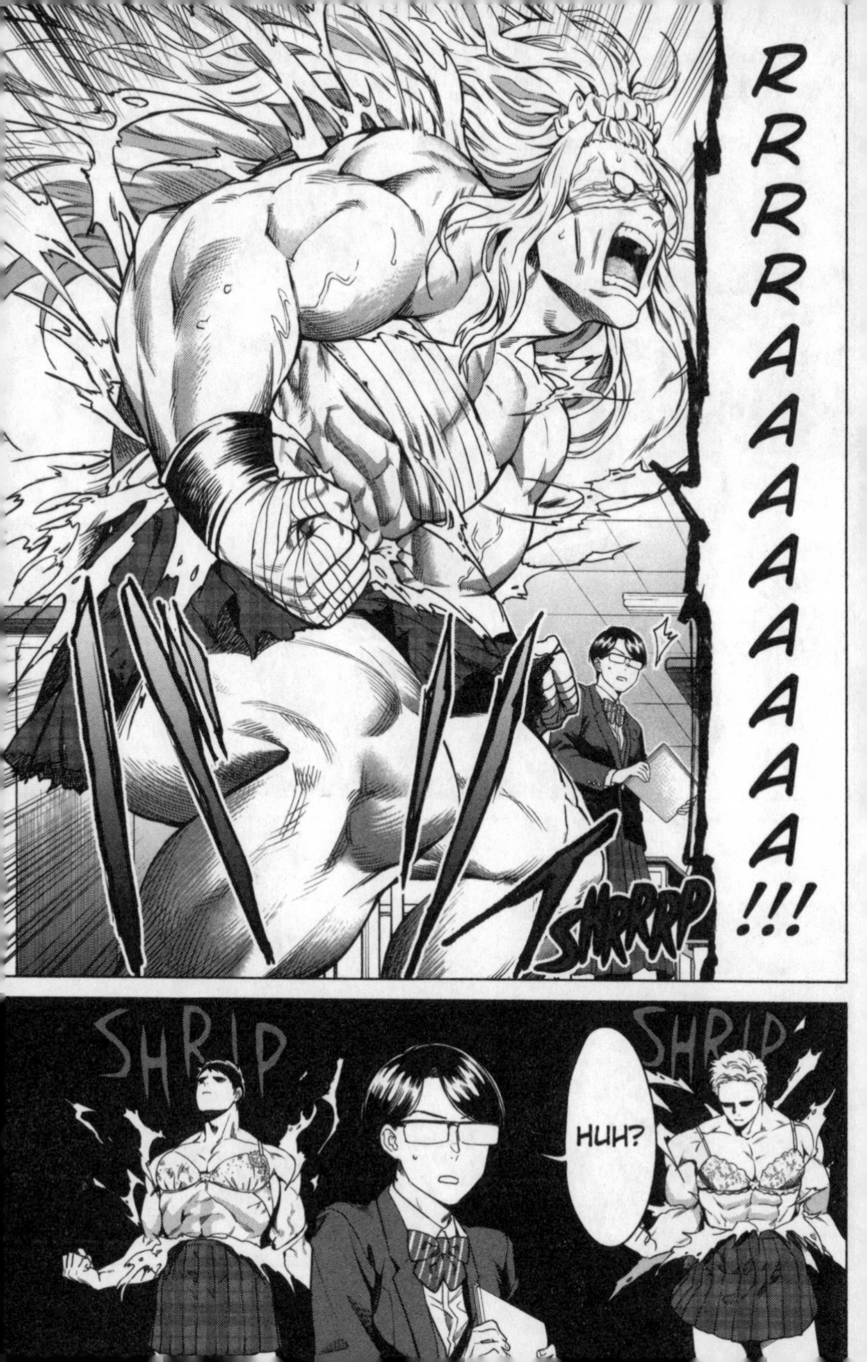
RRRRAAAAAAAA!!!
SHRRRP
SHRIP
HUH?
SHRIP

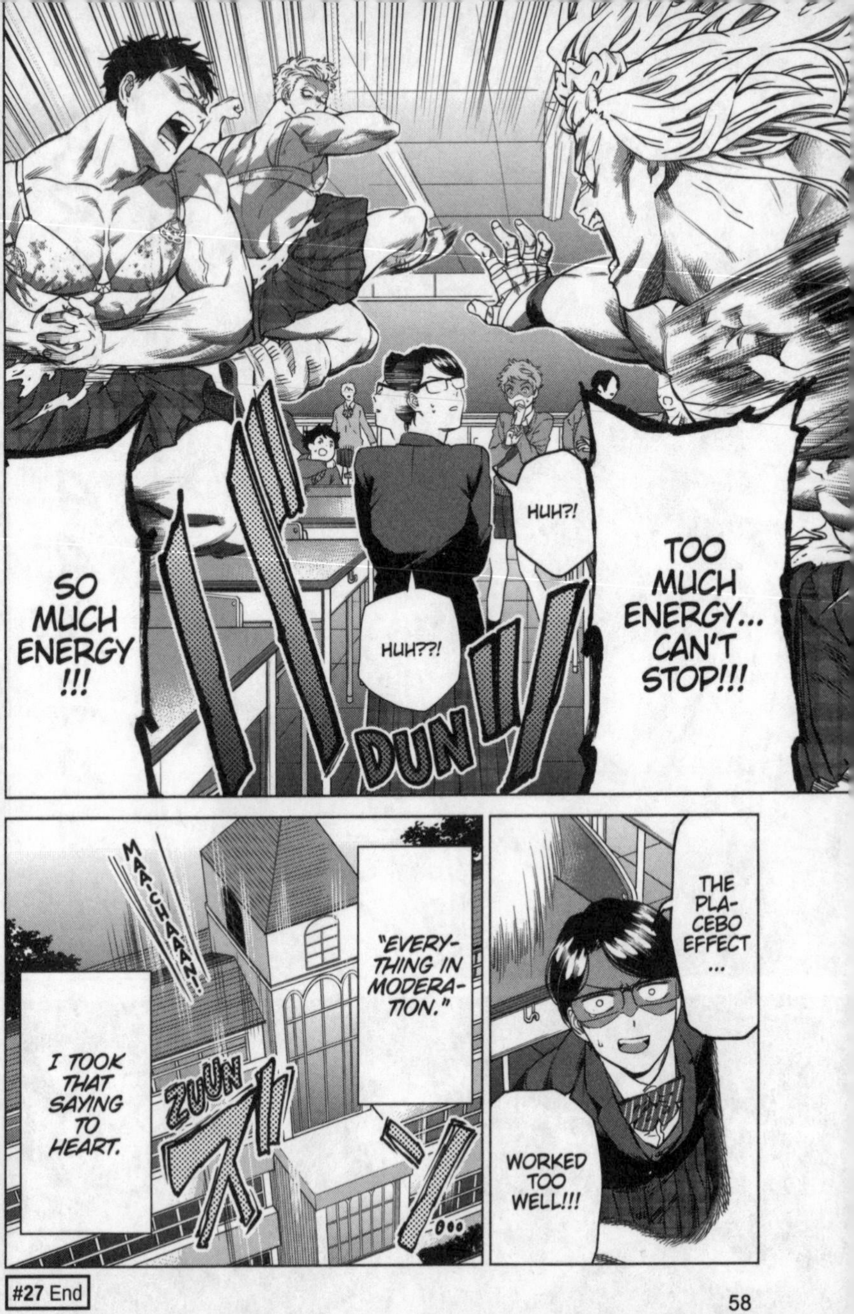
TOO MUCH ENERGY... CAN'T STOP!!!
HUH?!
HUH??!
DUN
SO MUCH ENERGY!!!
THE PLACEBO EFFECT...
WORKED TOO WELL!!!
"EVERYTHING IN MODERATION."
MAA-CHAAAN!
I TOOK THAT SAYING TO HEART.
ZUUN

#27 End

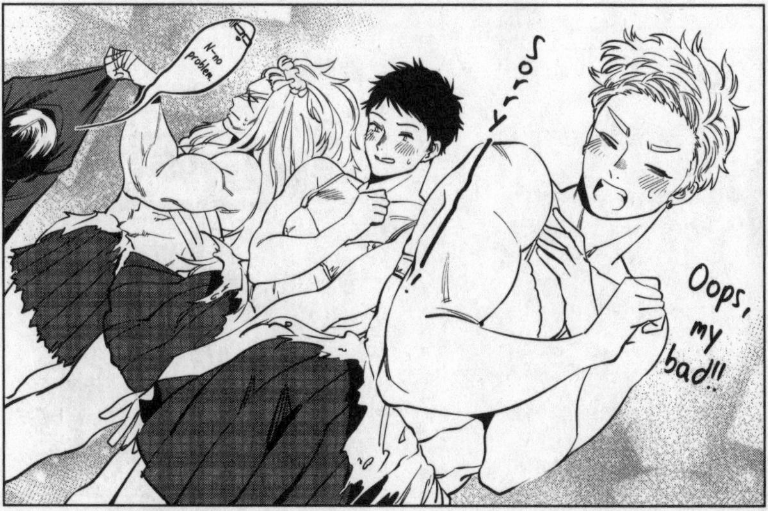
Oops, my bad!!
Sorry
N-no problem.

THIGH HIGH
Reiwa Hanamaru Academy

HANAMARU PRIVATE HIGH SCHOOL

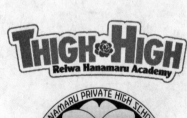

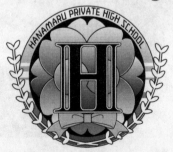

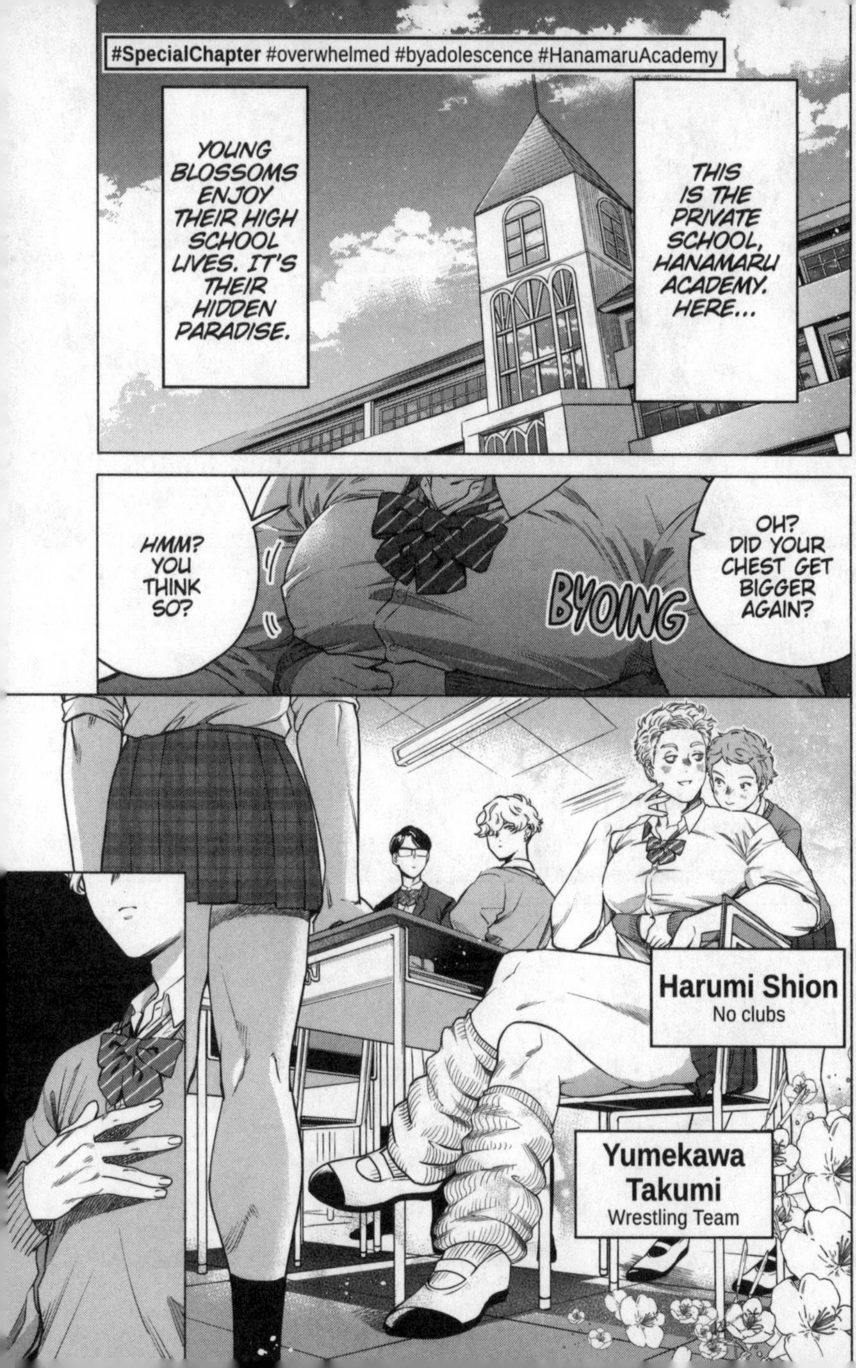
#SpecialChapter #overwhelmed #byadolescence #HanamaruAcademy
THIS IS THE PRIVATE SCHOOL, HANAMARU ACADEMY. HERE...
YOUNG BLOSSOMS ENJOY THEIR HIGH SCHOOL LIVES. IT'S THEIR HIDDEN PARADISE.
OH? DID YOUR CHEST GET BIGGER AGAIN?
BYOING
HMM? YOU THINK SO?
Harumi Shion
No clubs
Yumekawa Takumi
Wrestling Team

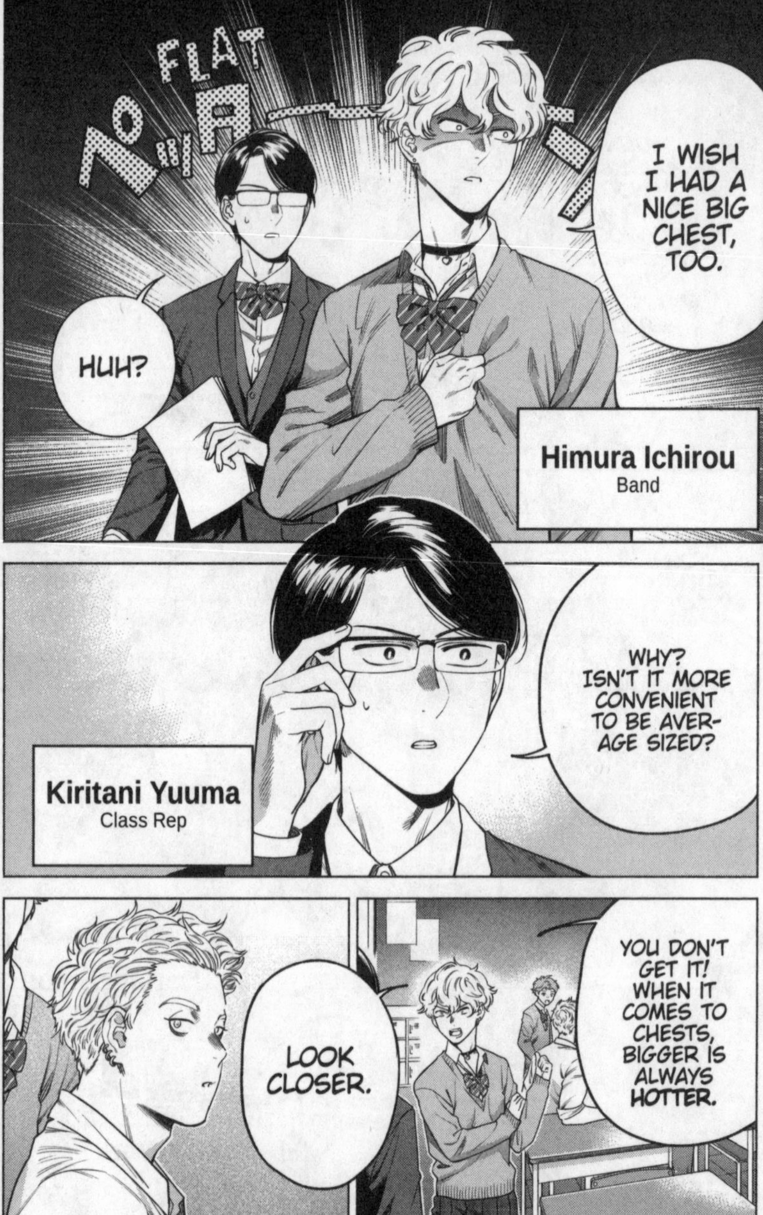
FLAT
I WISH I HAD A NICE BIG CHEST, TOO.
HUH?
Himura Ichirou
Band
WHY? ISN'T IT MORE CONVENIENT TO BE AVER-AGE SIZED?
Kiritani Yuuma
Class Rep
YOU DON'T GET IT! WHEN IT COMES TO CHESTS, BIGGER IS ALWAYS HOTTER.
LOOK CLOSER.

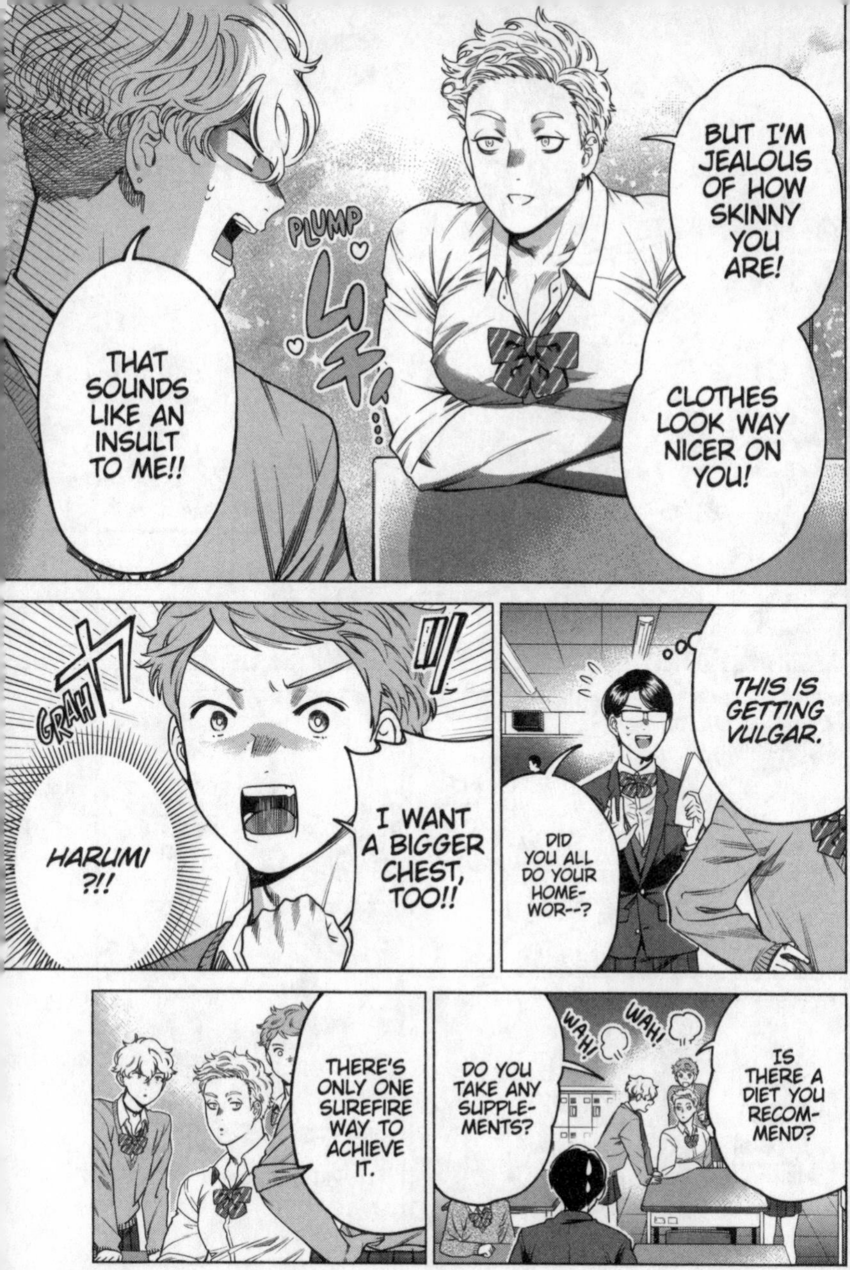
BUT I'M JEALOUS OF HOW SKINNY YOU ARE!
CLOTHES LOOK WAY NICER ON YOU!
PLUMP
ムチ…
THAT SOUNDS LIKE AN INSULT TO ME!!
THIS IS GETTING VULGAR.
DID YOU ALL DO YOUR HOME-WOR--?
I WANT A BIGGER CHEST, TOO!!
GRAH
HARUMI ?!!
IS THERE A DIET YOU RECOMMEND?
WAH!
WAH!
DO YOU TAKE ANY SUPPLEMENTS?
THERE'S ONLY ONE SUREFIRE WAY TO ACHIEVE IT.

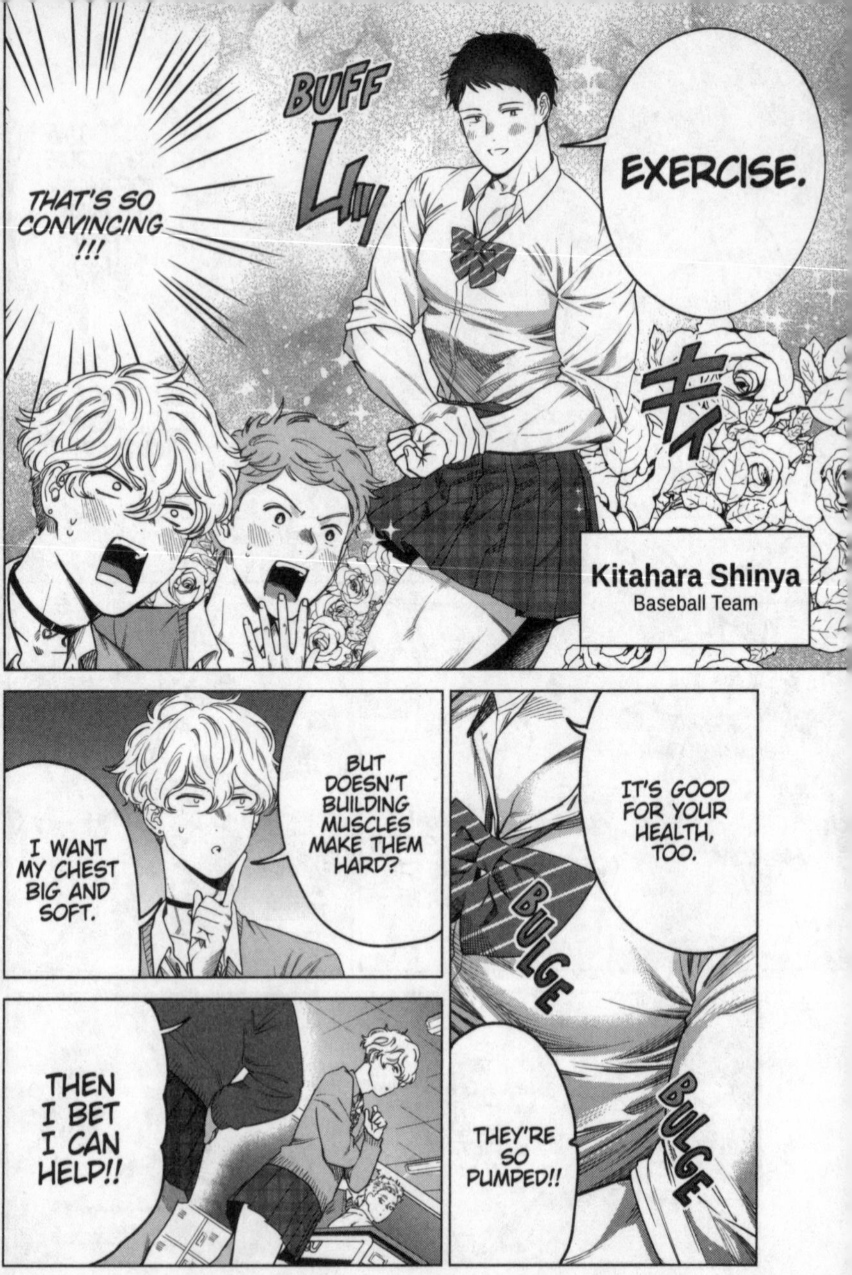
EXERCISE.
BUFF
ムッ
キィ
THAT'S SO CONVINCING !!!
Kitahara Shinya
Baseball Team
IT'S GOOD FOR YOUR HEALTH, TOO.
BULGE
THEY'RE SO PUMPED!!
BULGE
BUT DOESN'T BUILDING MUSCLES MAKE THEM HARD?
I WANT MY CHEST BIG AND SOFT.
THEN I BET I CAN HELP!!

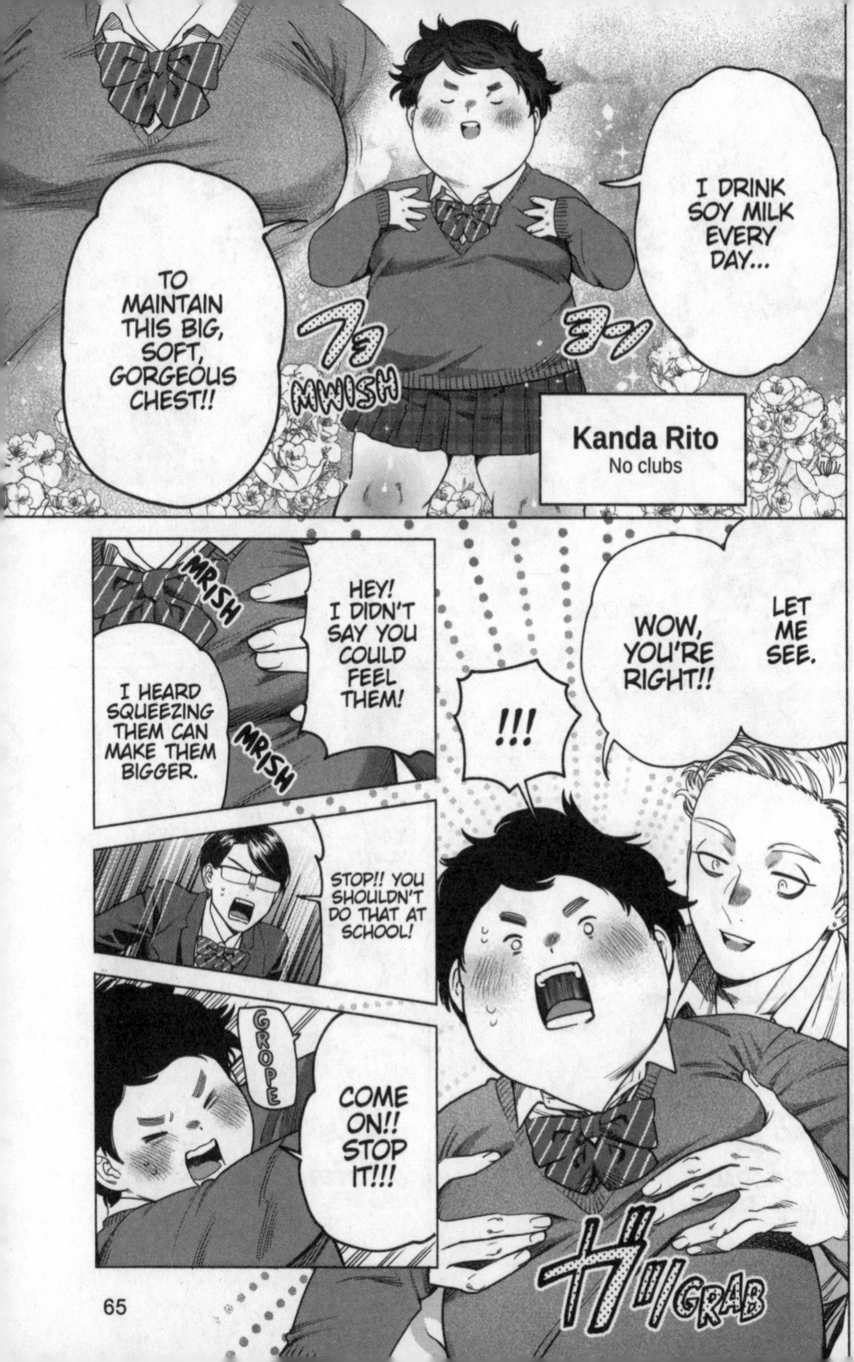
I DRINK SOY MILK EVERY DAY...
TO MAINTAIN THIS BIG, SOFT, GORGEOUS CHEST!!
MWISH
Kanda Rito
No clubs
LET ME SEE.
WOW, YOU'RE RIGHT!!
!!!
GRAB
HEY! I DIDN'T SAY YOU COULD FEEL THEM!
MRISH
I HEARD SQUEEZING THEM CAN MAKE THEM BIGGER.
MRISH
STOP!! YOU SHOULDN'T DO THAT AT SCHOOL!
COME ON!! STOP IT!!!
GROPE

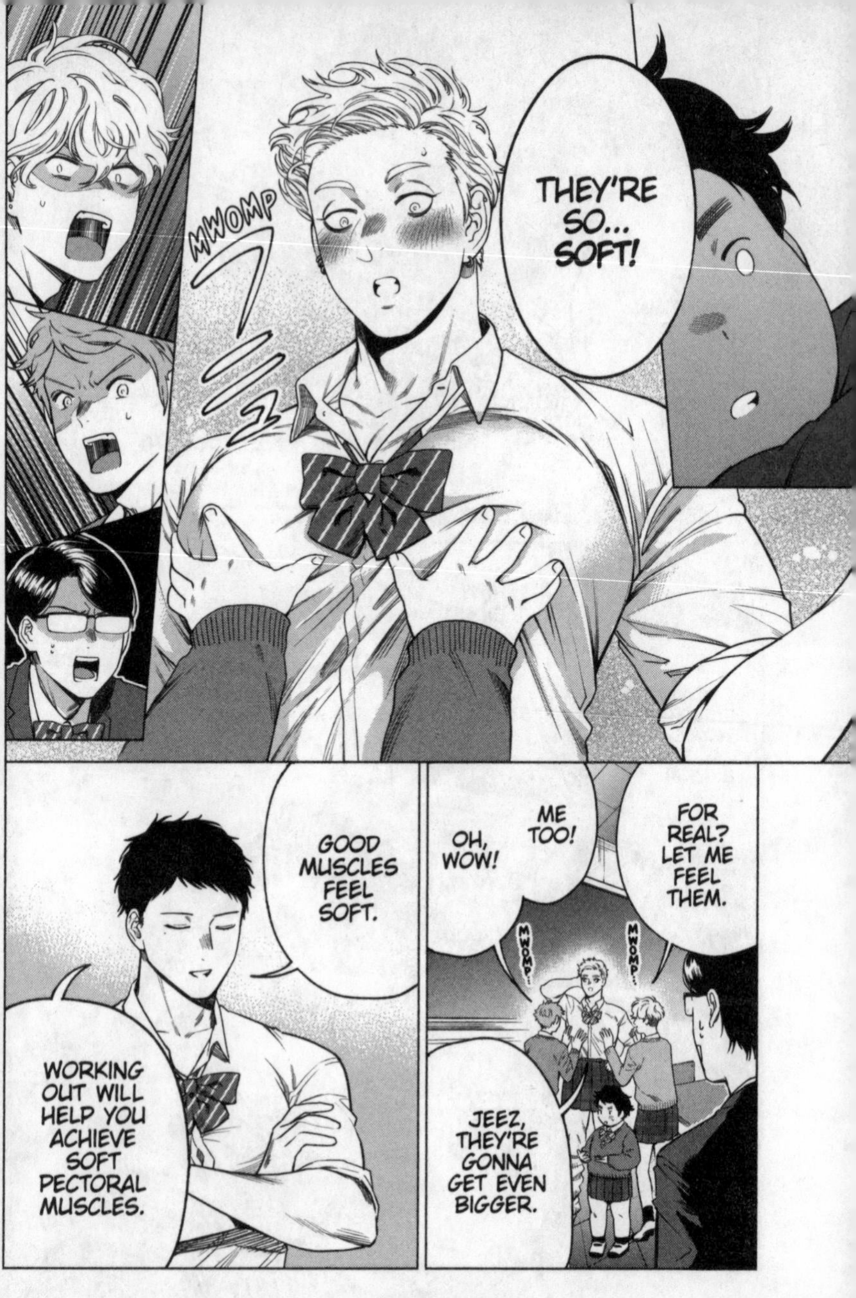

THEY'RE SO... SOFT!
MWOMP
FOR REAL? LET ME FEEL THEM.
ME TOO!
OH, WOW!
MWOMP...
MWOMP...
JEEZ, THEY'RE GONNA GET EVEN BIGGER.
GOOD MUSCLES FEEL SOFT.
WORKING OUT WILL HELP YOU ACHIEVE SOFT PECTORAL MUSCLES.

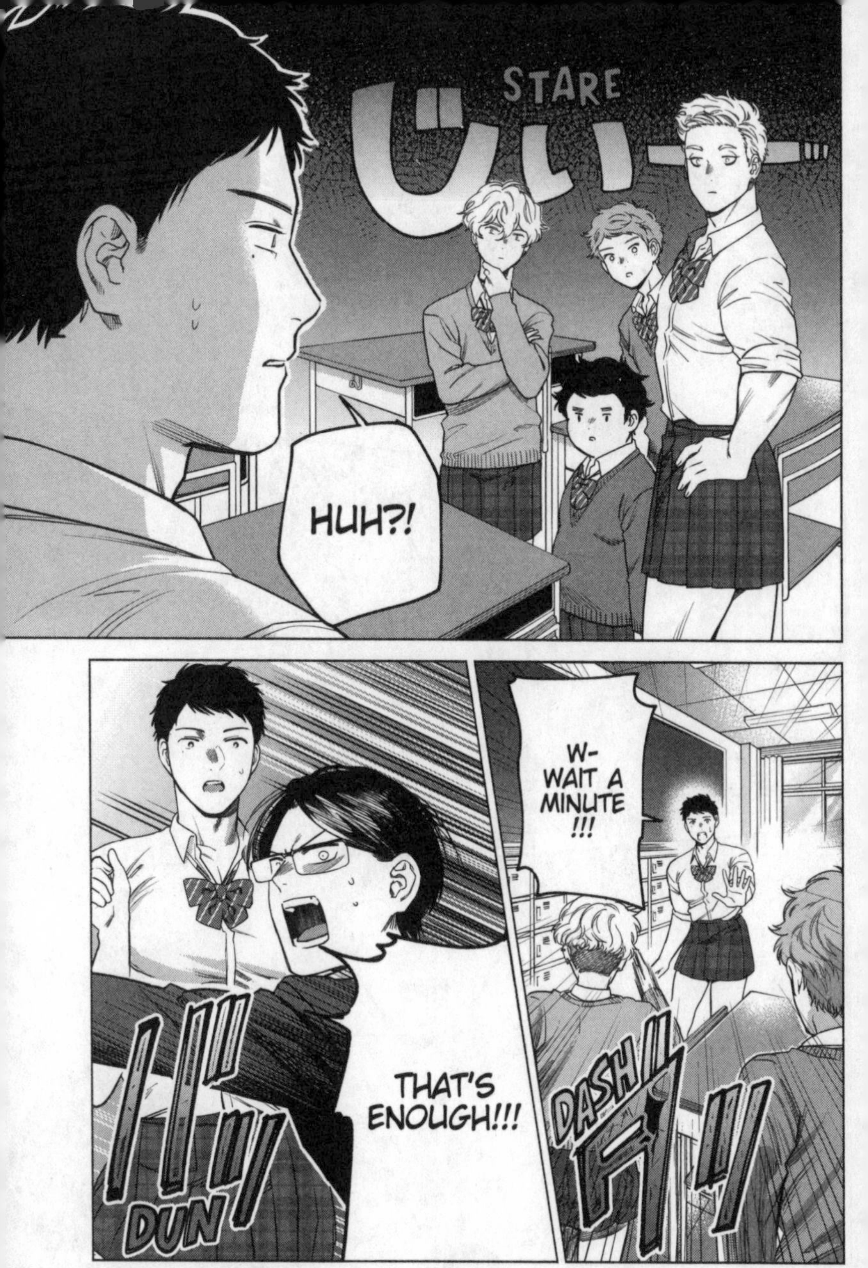
STARE
HUH?!
W- WAIT A MINUTE !!!
DASH
THAT'S ENOUGH!!!
DUN

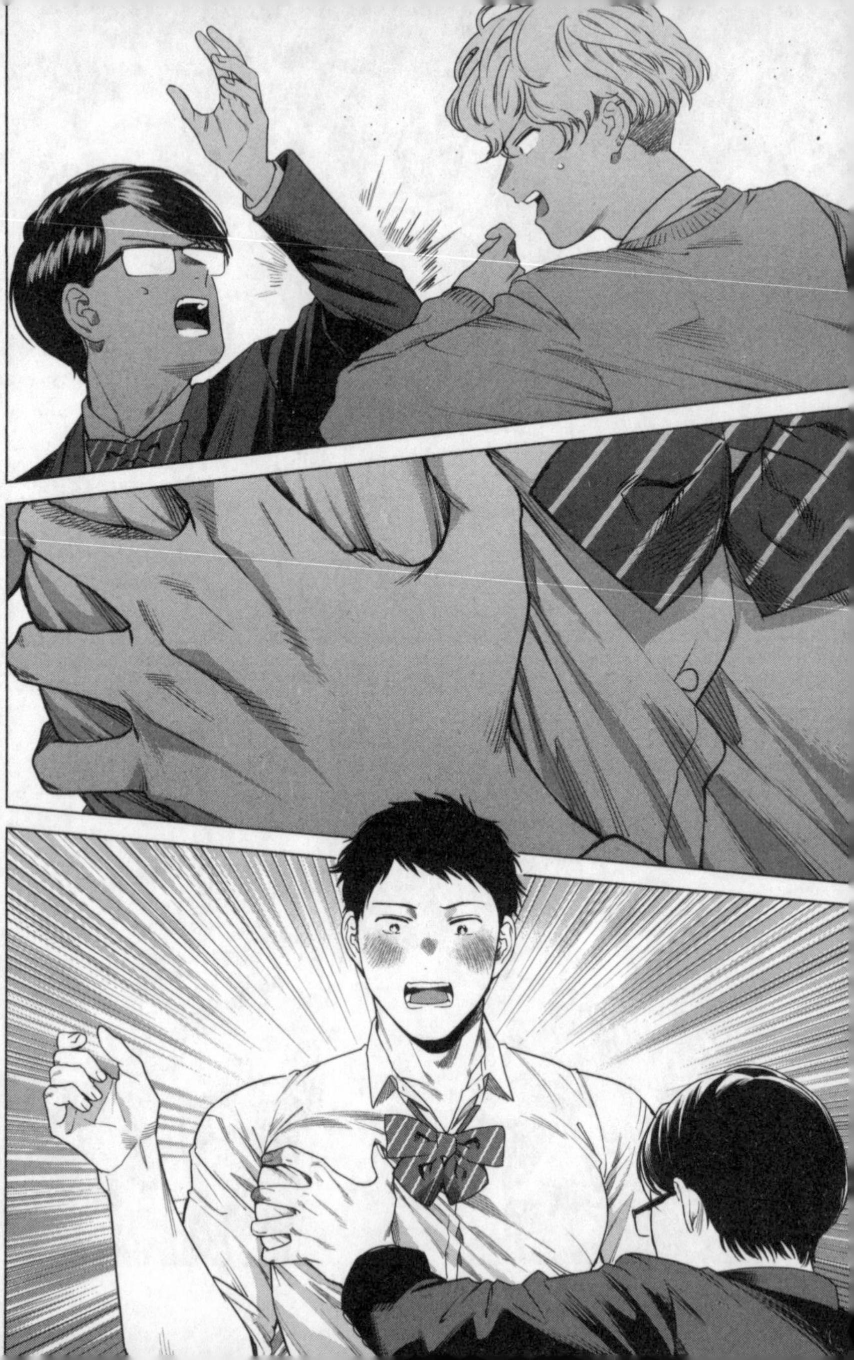

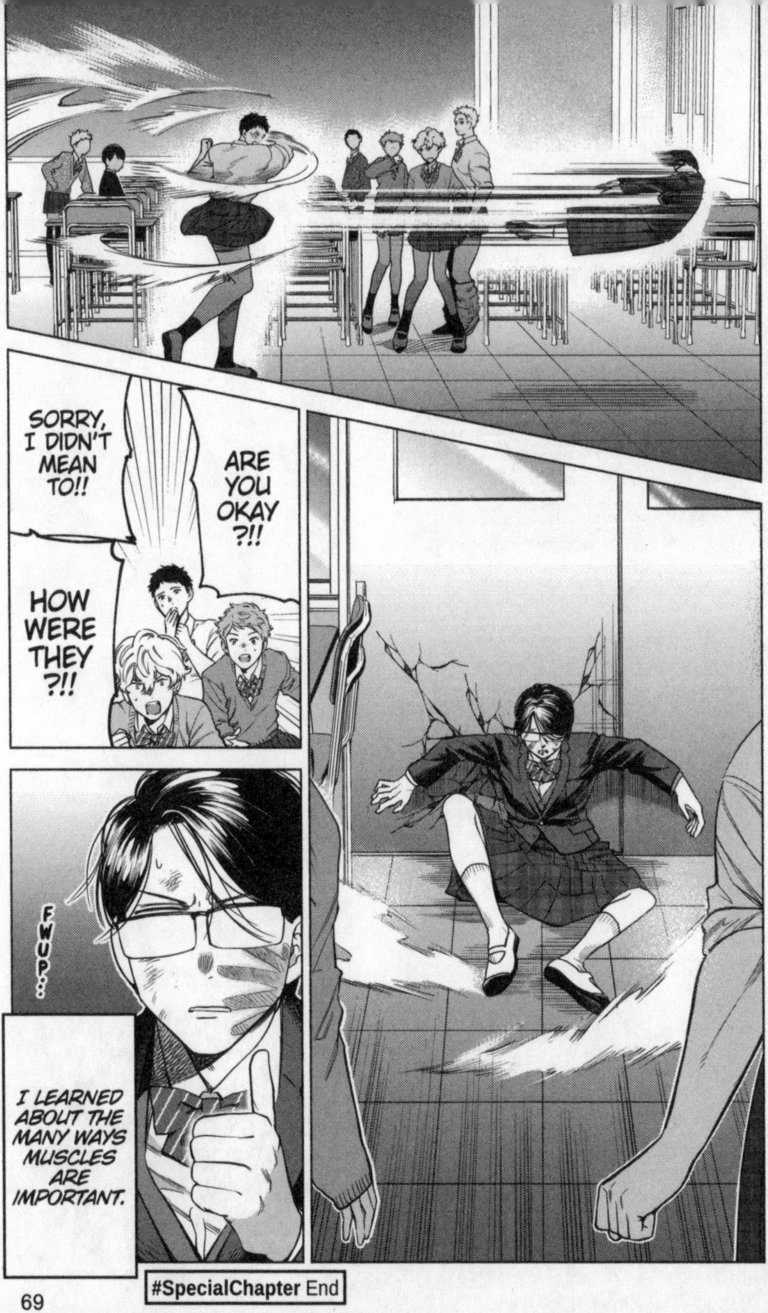
ARE YOU OKAY?!!
SORRY, I DIDN'T MEAN TO!!
HOW WERE THEY?!!
FWUP..
I LEARNED ABOUT THE MANY WAYS MUSCLES ARE IMPORTANT.

#SpecialChapter End

THIGH HIGH
Reiwa Hanamaru Academy

HANAMARU PRIVATE HIGH SCHOOL

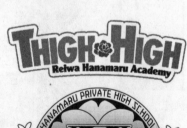

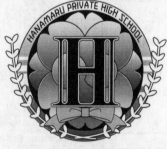

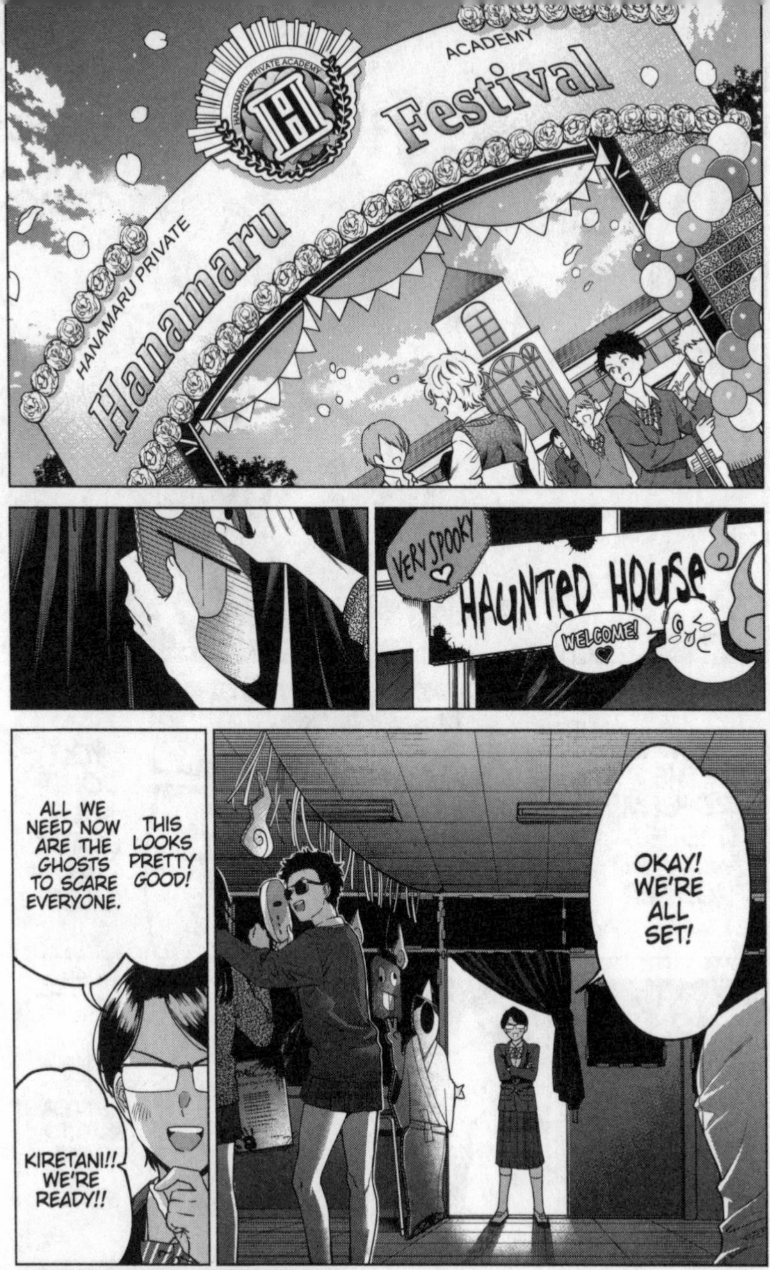
HANAMARU PRIVATE ACADEMY
HANAMARU PRIVATE ACADEMY
Hanamaru Festival
VERY SPOOKY ♥
HAUNTED HOUSE
WELCOME! ♥
OKAY! WE'RE ALL SET!
THIS LOOKS PRETTY GOOD!
ALL WE NEED NOW ARE THE GHOSTS TO SCARE EVERYONE.
KIRETANI!! WE'RE READY!!

#28 #exciting #spookyculturalfestival

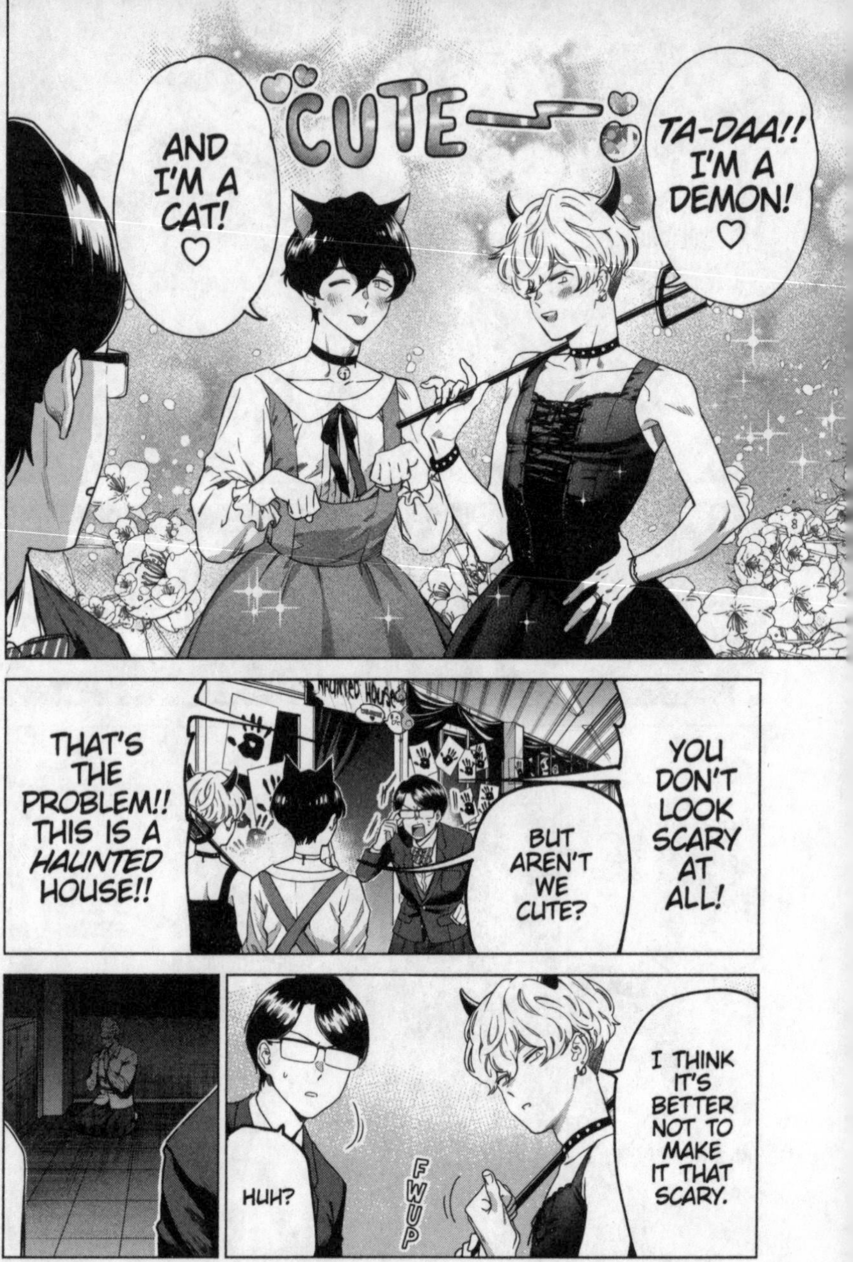
TA-DAA!! I'M A DEMON! ♡
CUTE—
AND I'M A CAT! ♡
YOU DON'T LOOK SCARY AT ALL!
BUT AREN'T WE CUTE?
HAUNTED HOUSE
THAT'S THE PROBLEM!! THIS IS A *HAUNTED* HOUSE!!
I THINK IT'S BETTER NOT TO MAKE IT THAT SCARY.
FWUP
HUH?

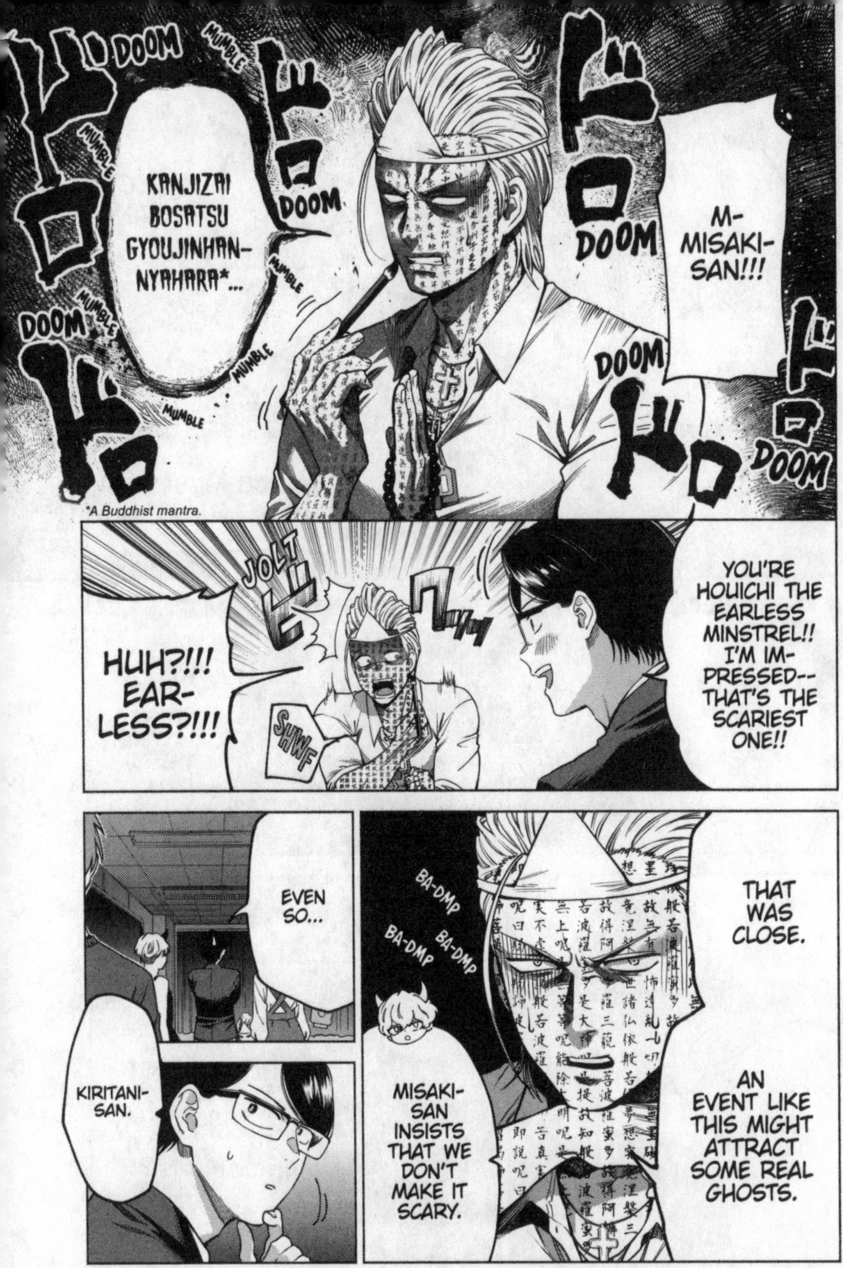
DOOM
MUMBLE
M-MISAKI-SAN!!!
KANJIZAI BOSATSU GYOUJINHAN-NYAHARA*...
DOOM
MUMBLE
YOU'RE HOUICHI THE EARLESS MINSTREL!! I'M IM-PRESSED--THAT'S THE SCARIEST ONE!!
JOLT
HUH?!!! EAR-LESS?!!!
SHWF
THAT WAS CLOSE.
AN EVENT LIKE THIS MIGHT ATTRACT SOME REAL GHOSTS.
BA-DMP BA-DMP BA-DMP
MISAKI-SAN INSISTS THAT WE DON'T MAKE IT SCARY.
EVEN SO...
KIRITANI-SAN.

*A Buddhist mantra.

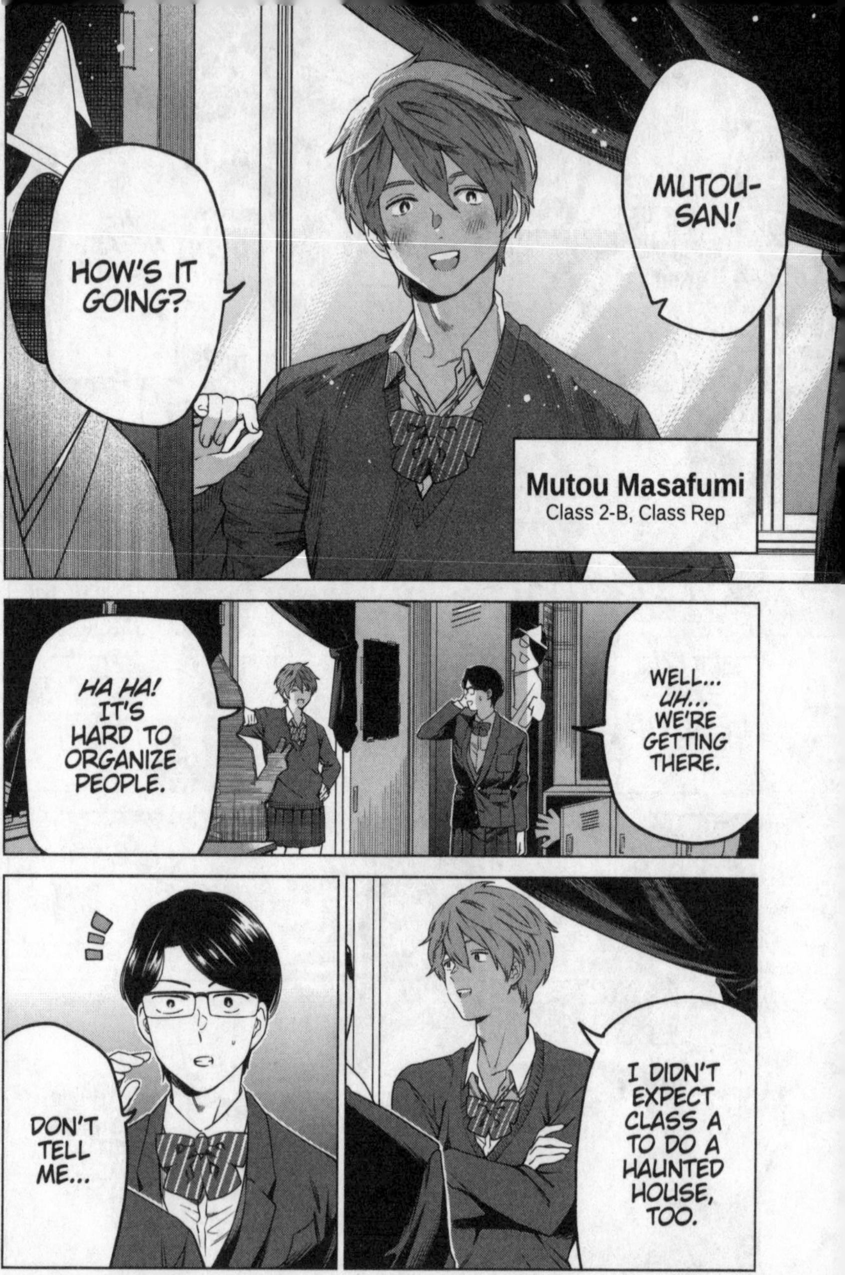
MUTOU-SAN!
HOW'S IT GOING?
Mutou Masafumi
Class 2-B, Class Rep
WELL... *UH...* WE'RE GETTING THERE.
HA HA! IT'S HARD TO ORGANIZE PEOPLE.
I DIDN'T EXPECT CLASS A TO DO A HAUNTED HOUSE, TOO.
DON'T TELL ME...

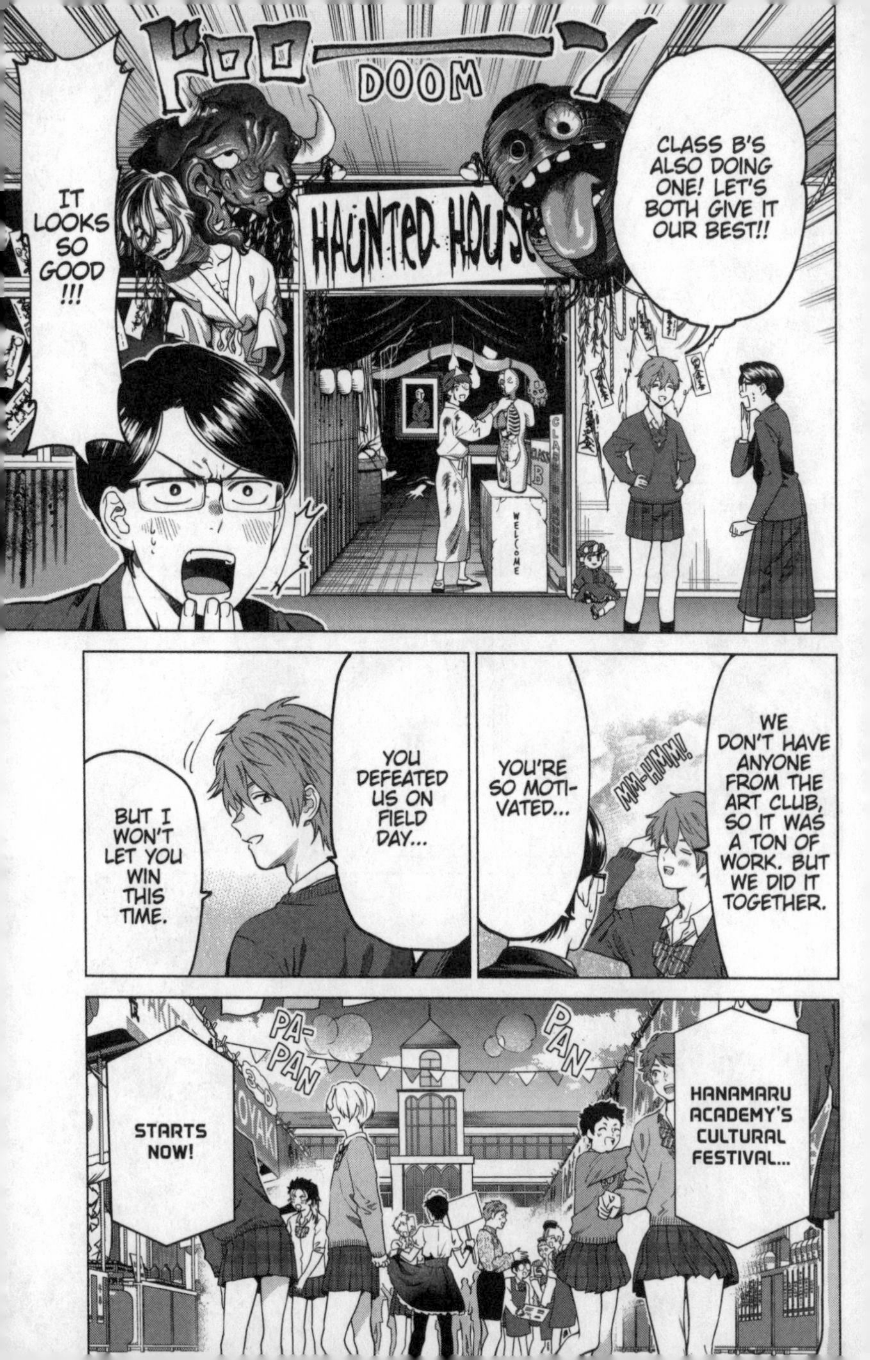
ドロローーン
DOOM
HAUNTED HOUSE
CLASS B'S ALSO DOING ONE! LET'S BOTH GIVE IT OUR BEST!!
IT LOOKS SO GOOD!!!
WE DON'T HAVE ANYONE FROM THE ART CLUB, SO IT WAS A TON OF WORK. BUT WE DID IT TOGETHER.
MM-HMM!
YOU'RE SO MOTI-VATED...
YOU DEFEATED US ON FIELD DAY...
BUT I WON'T LET YOU WIN THIS TIME.
HANAMARU ACADEMY'S CULTURAL FESTIVAL...
PAN
PA-PAN
STARTS NOW!

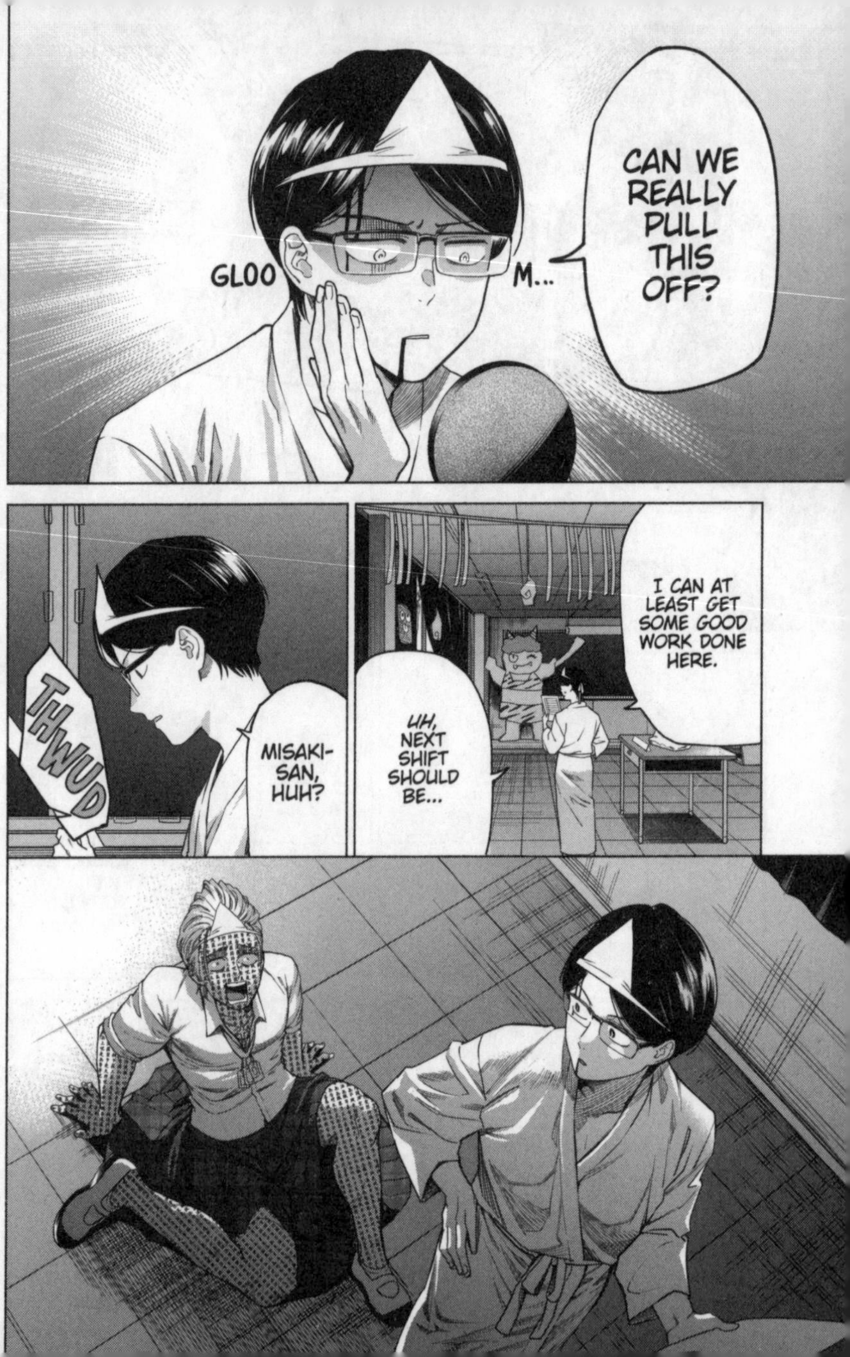
CAN WE REALLY PULL THIS OFF?
GLOOM...
I CAN AT LEAST GET SOME GOOD WORK DONE HERE.
UH, NEXT SHIFT SHOULD BE...
MISAKI-SAN, HUH?
THWUD

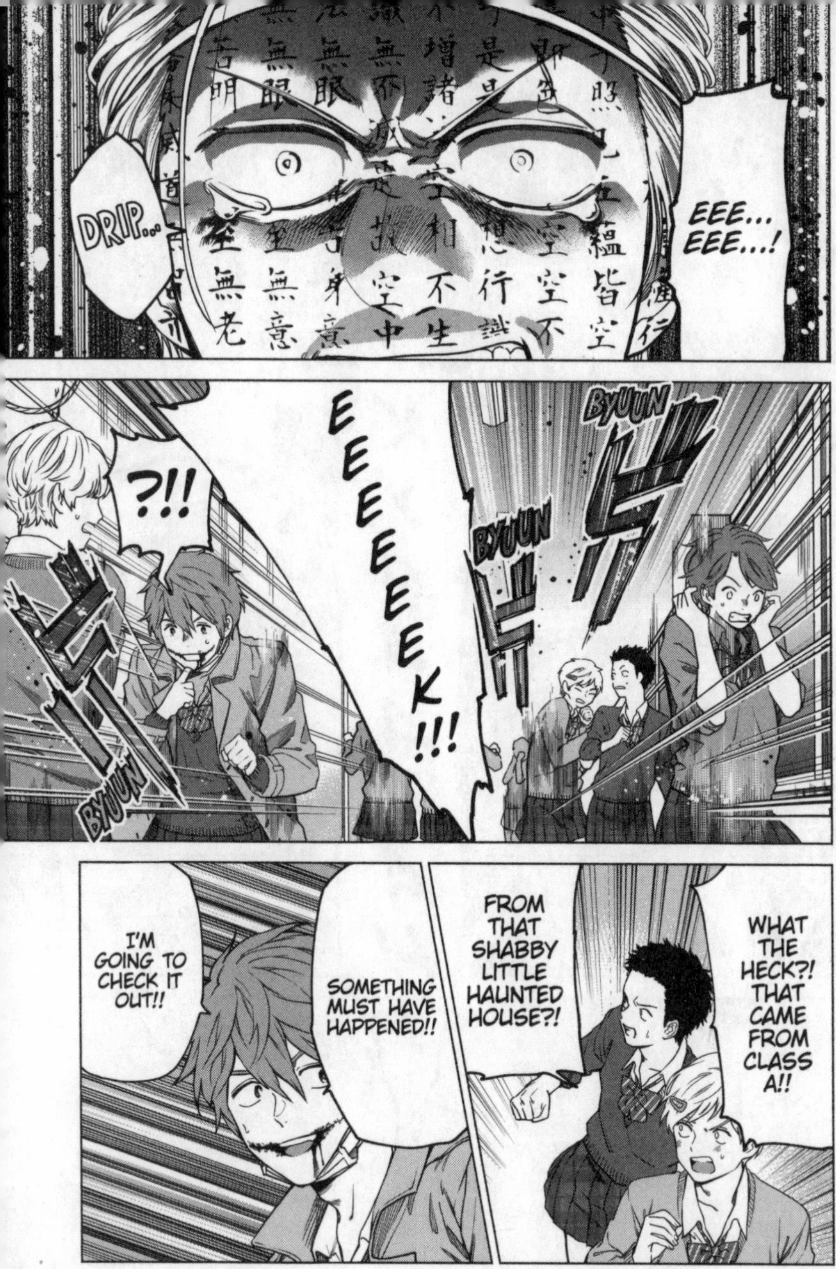
EEE... EEE...!
DRIP...
BYUUN
EEEEEEEK!!!
BYUUN
?!!
BYUUN
WHAT THE HECK?! THAT CAME FROM CLASS A!!
FROM THAT SHABBY LITTLE HAUNTED HOUSE?!
SOMETHING MUST HAVE HAPPENED!!
I'M GOING TO CHECK IT OUT!!

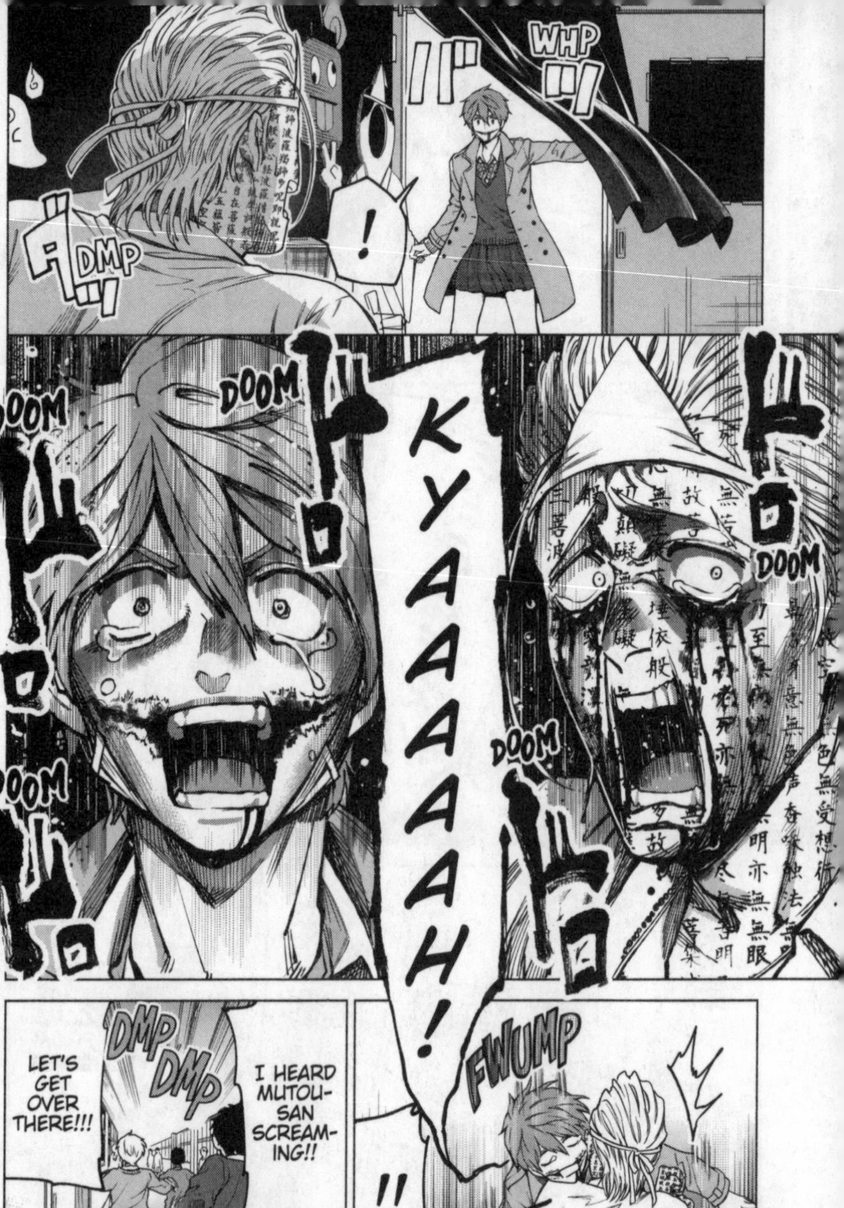
WHP
!
DMP
DOOM
DOOM
KYAAAAAH!
DOOM
DOOM
DOOM
FWUMP
!!
DMP DMP
I HEARD MUTOU-SAN SCREAMING!!
LET'S GET OVER THERE!!!

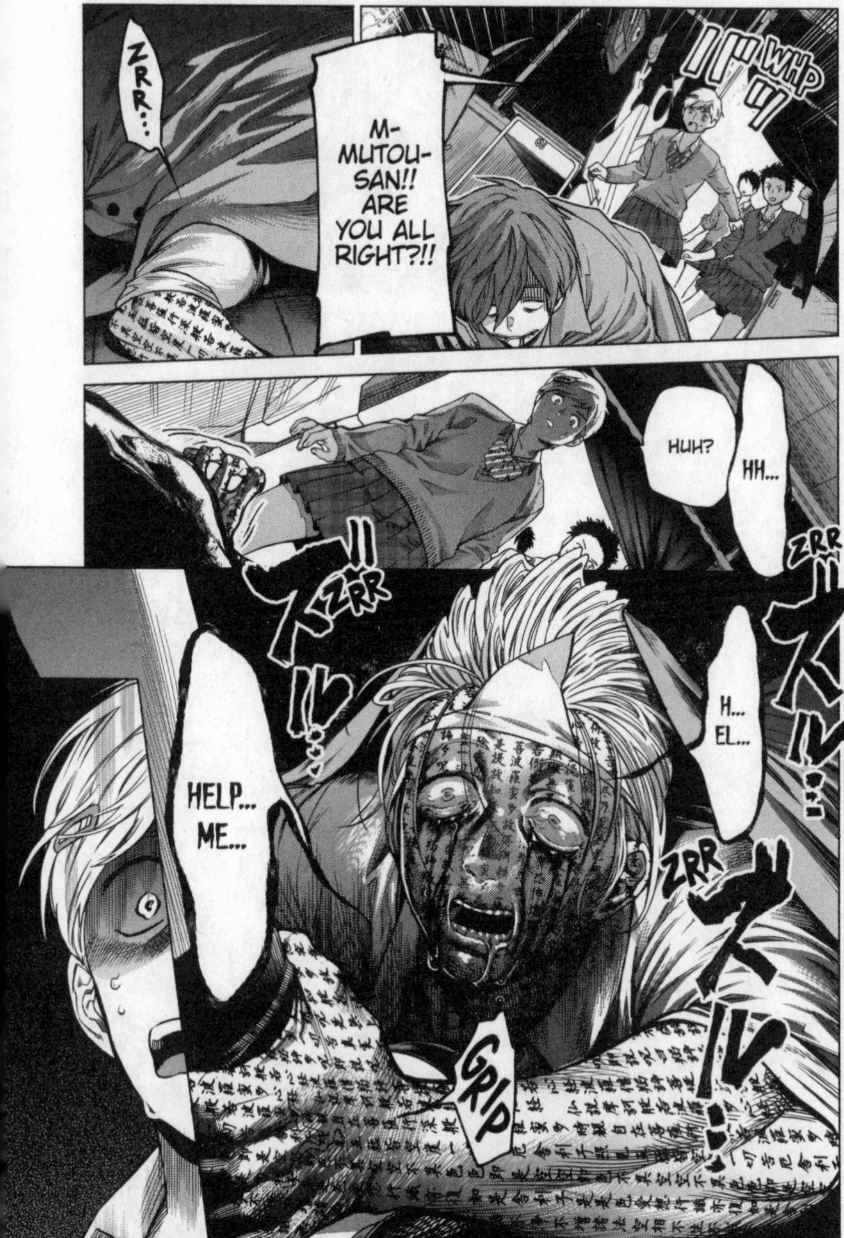
WHP
M-MUTOU-SAN!! ARE YOU ALL RIGHT?!!
ZRR...
HH...
HUH?
ZRR
H... EL...
ZRR
ZRR
HELP... ME...
GRIP

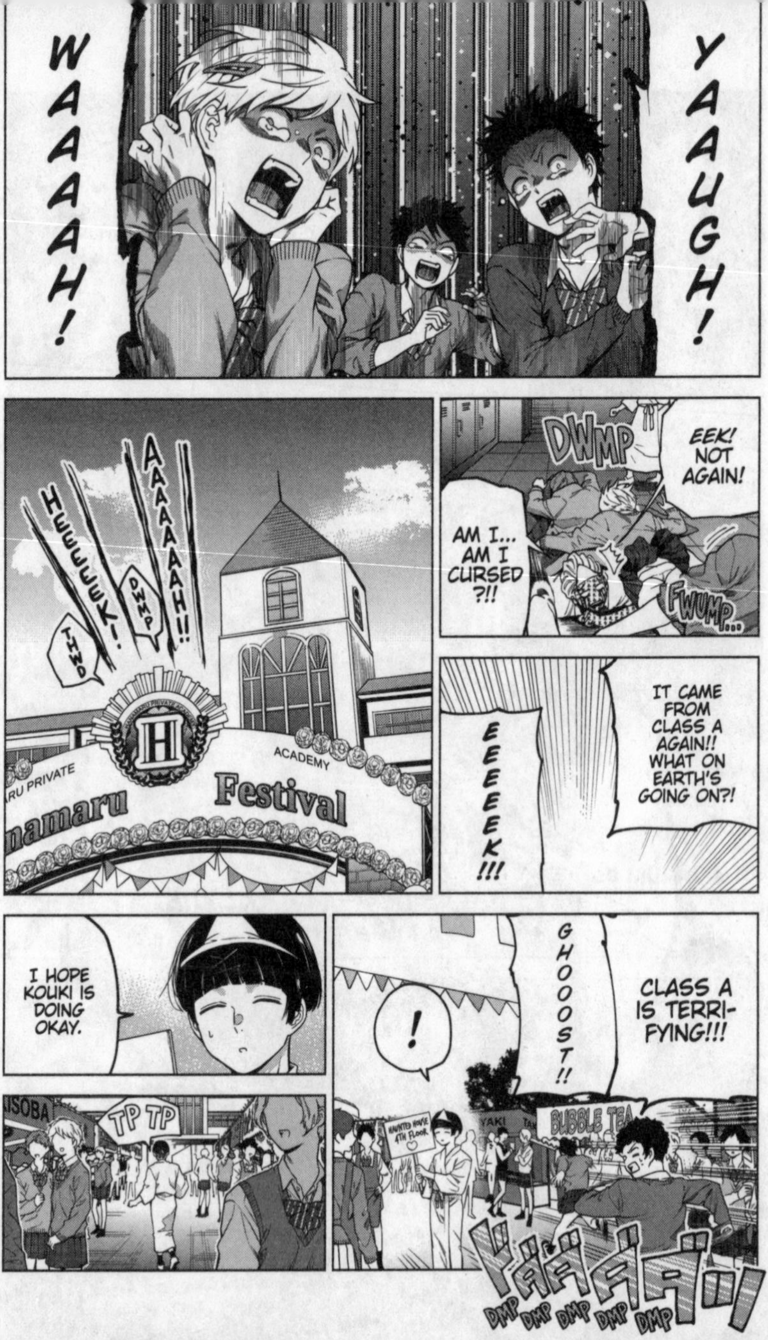
YAAAUGH!
WAAAAAAH!
DWMP
EEK! NOT AGAIN!
AM I... AM I CURSED?!!
FWUMP...
IT CAME FROM CLASS A AGAIN!! WHAT ON EARTH'S GOING ON?!
EEEEEEK!!!
AAAAAAAAH!!
HEEEEEEK!
DWMP
THWD
ACADEMY
Festival
CLASS A IS TERRI-FYING!!!
GHOOOOST!!
!
I HOPE KOUKI IS DOING OKAY.
BUBBLE TEA
HAUNTED HOUSE 4TH FLOOR
DMP DMP DMP DMP DMP
TP TP

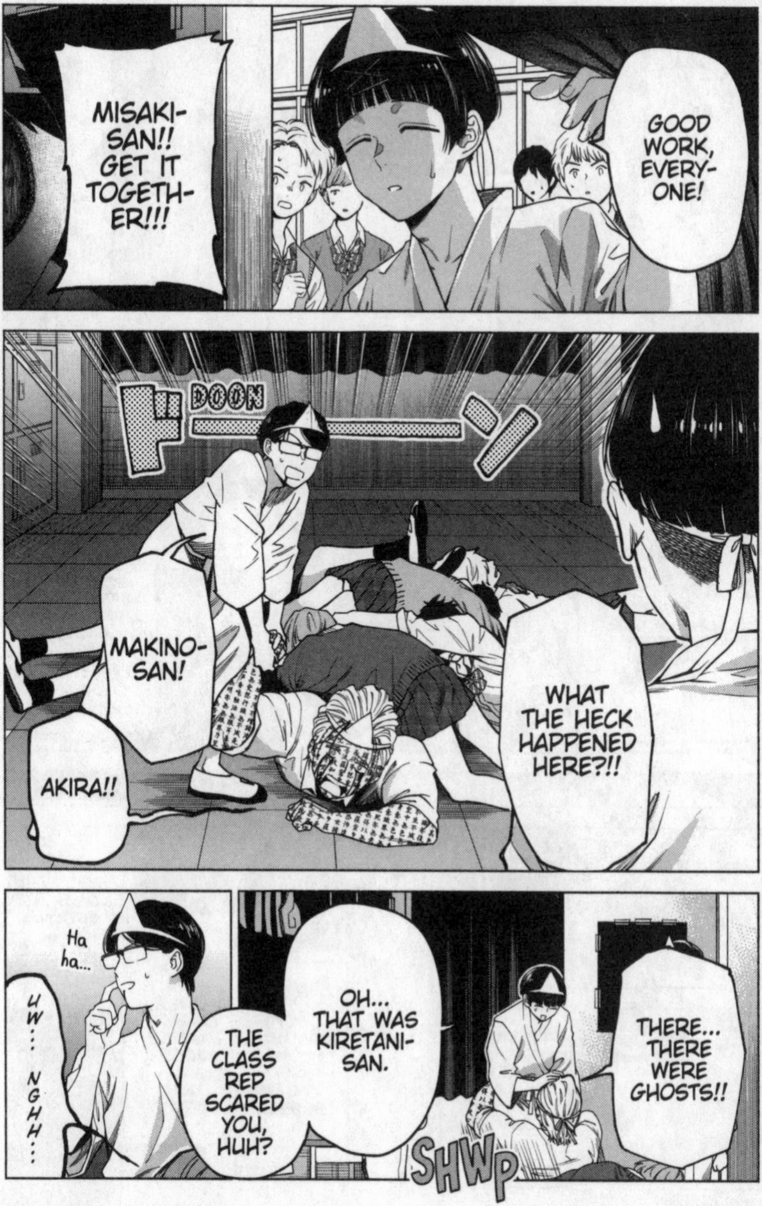
GOOD WORK, EVERY-ONE!
MISAKI-SAN!! GET IT TOGETH-ER!!!
DOOON
WHAT THE HECK HAPPENED HERE?!!
MAKINO-SAN!
AKIRA!!
THERE... THERE WERE GHOSTS!!
SHWP
OH... THAT WAS KIRETANI-SAN.
THE CLASS REP SCARED YOU, HUH?
Ha ha...
UW... NGHH...

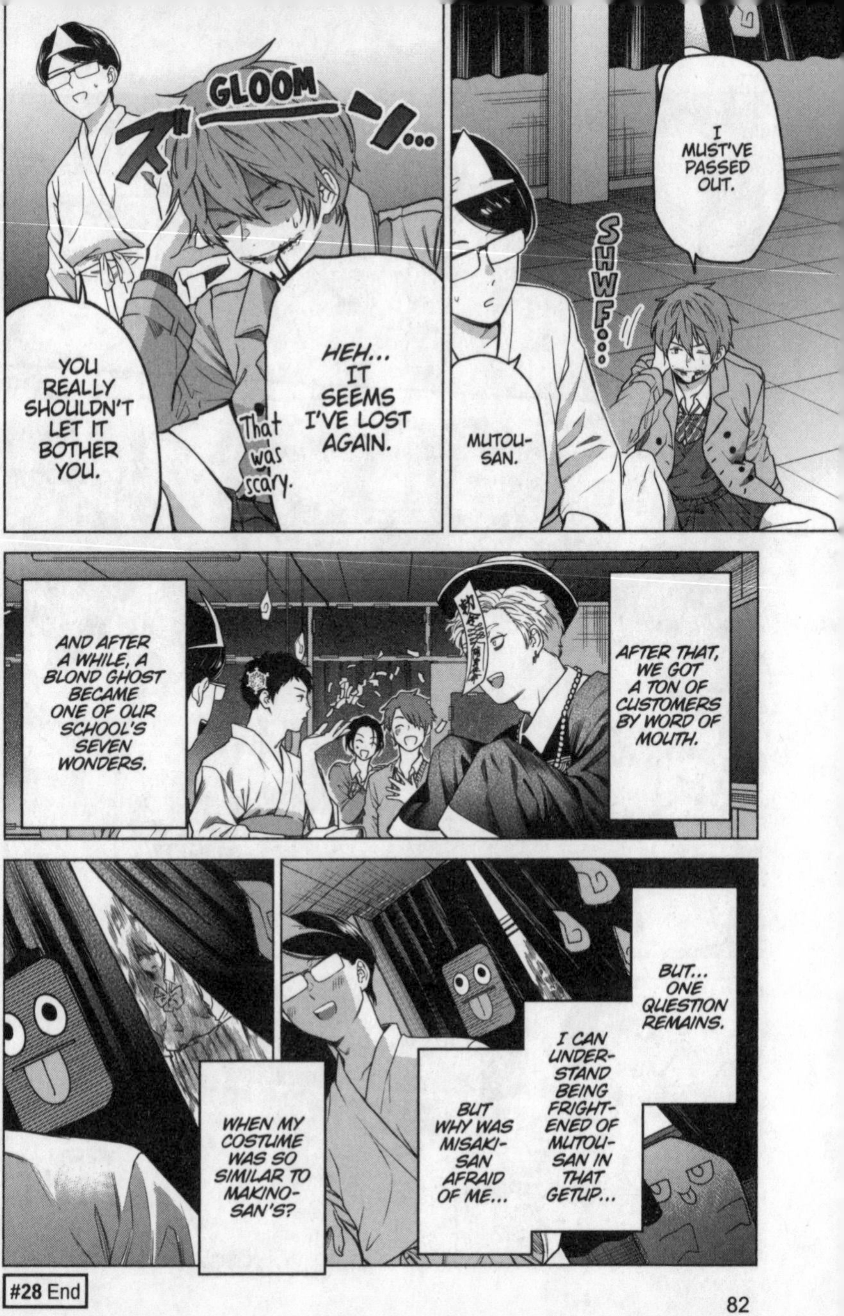
I MUST'VE PASSED OUT.
SHWF...
MUTOU-SAN.
GLOOM
HEH... IT SEEMS I'VE LOST AGAIN.
That was scary.
YOU REALLY SHOULDN'T LET IT BOTHER YOU.
AFTER THAT, WE GOT A TON OF CUSTOMERS BY WORD OF MOUTH.
AND AFTER A WHILE, A BLOND GHOST BECAME ONE OF OUR SCHOOL'S SEVEN WONDERS.
BUT... ONE QUESTION REMAINS.
I CAN UNDERSTAND BEING FRIGHTENED OF MUTOU-SAN IN THAT GETUP...
BUT WHY WAS MISAKI-SAN AFRAID OF ME...
WHEN MY COSTUME WAS SO SIMILAR TO MAKINO-SAN'S?

#28 End

Possibly a Real-Life Horror Story

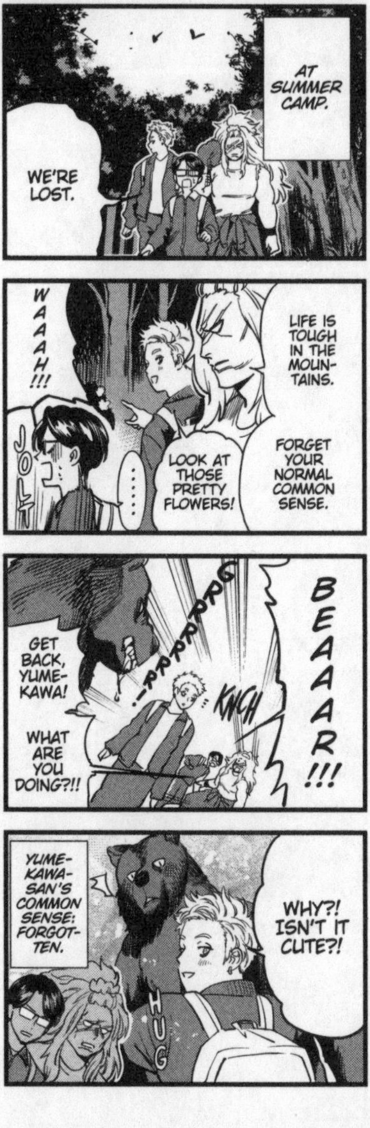
AT SUMMER CAMP.
WE'RE LOST.
LIFE IS TOUGH IN THE MOUNTAINS.
FORGET YOUR NORMAL COMMON SENSE.
LOOK AT THOSE PRETTY FLOWERS!
WAAAAH!!!
JOLT
......
BEAAAAR!!!
KNCH
RRRRRRRG!
GET BACK, YUME-KAWA!
WHAT ARE YOU DOING?!!
WHY?! ISN'T IT CUTE?!
HUG
YUME-KAWA-SAN'S COMMON SENSE: FORGOT-TEN.

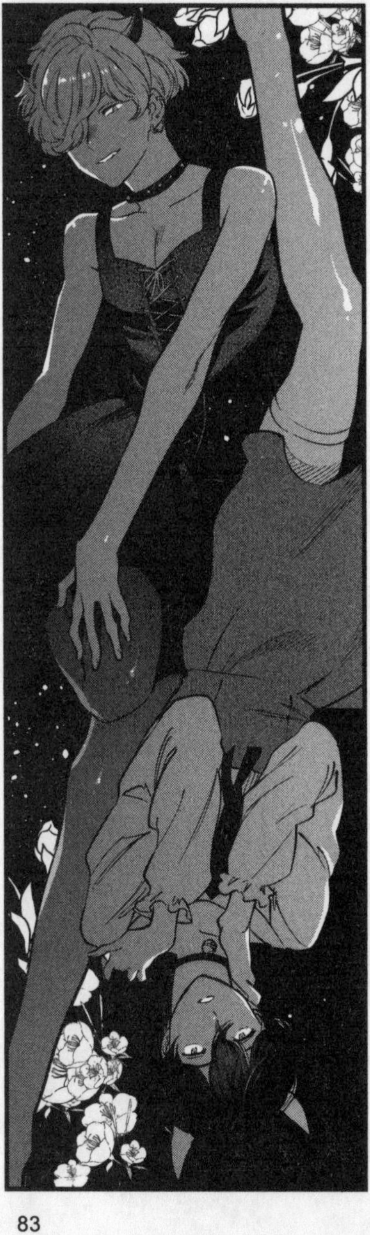

THIGH HIGH
Reiwa Hanamaru Academy

HANAMARU PRIVATE HIGH SCHOOL

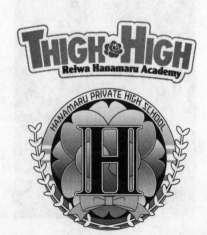

#29 #Kiretani #and #thereversesurprise

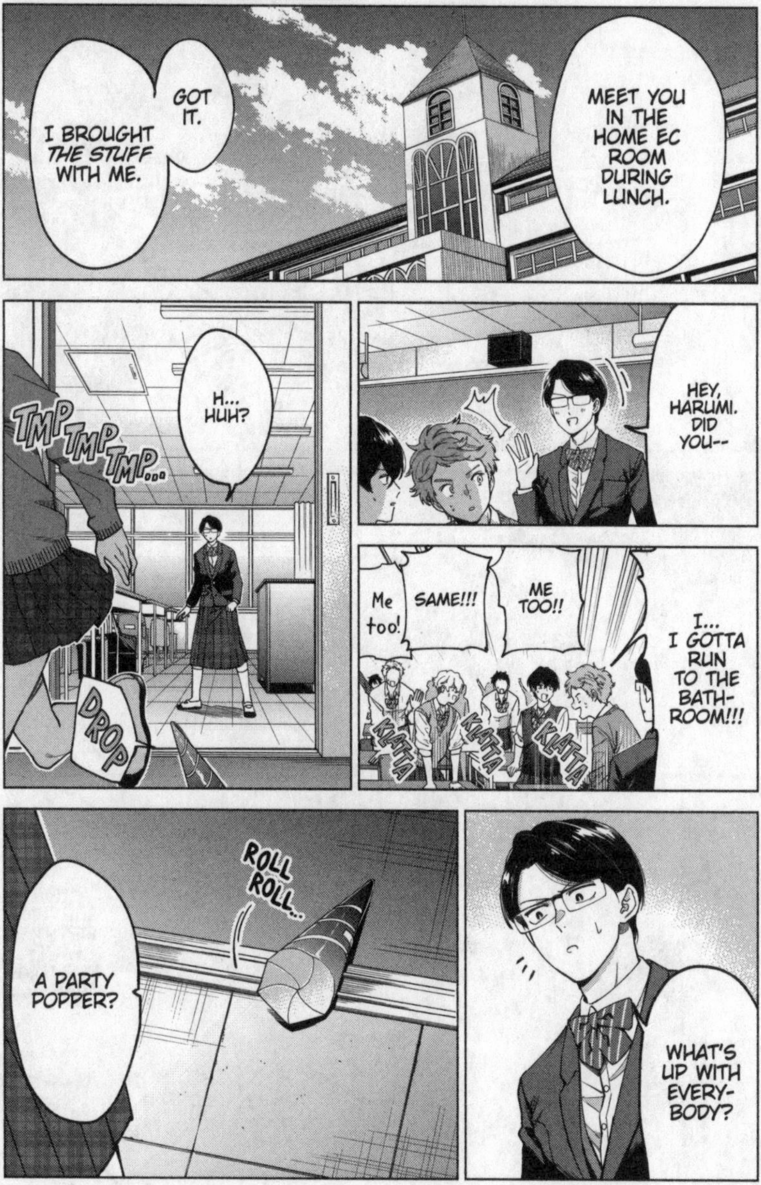
MEET YOU IN THE HOME EC ROOM DURING LUNCH.
GOT IT.
I BROUGHT *THE STUFF* WITH ME.
HEY, HARUMI. DID YOU--
I... I GOTTA RUN TO THE BATH-ROOM!!!
ME TOO!!
SAME!!!
Me too!
KLATTA
KLATTA
KLATTA
H... HUH?
TMP TMP TMP...
DROP
WHAT'S UP WITH EVERY-BODY?
ROLL ROLL...
A PARTY POPPER?

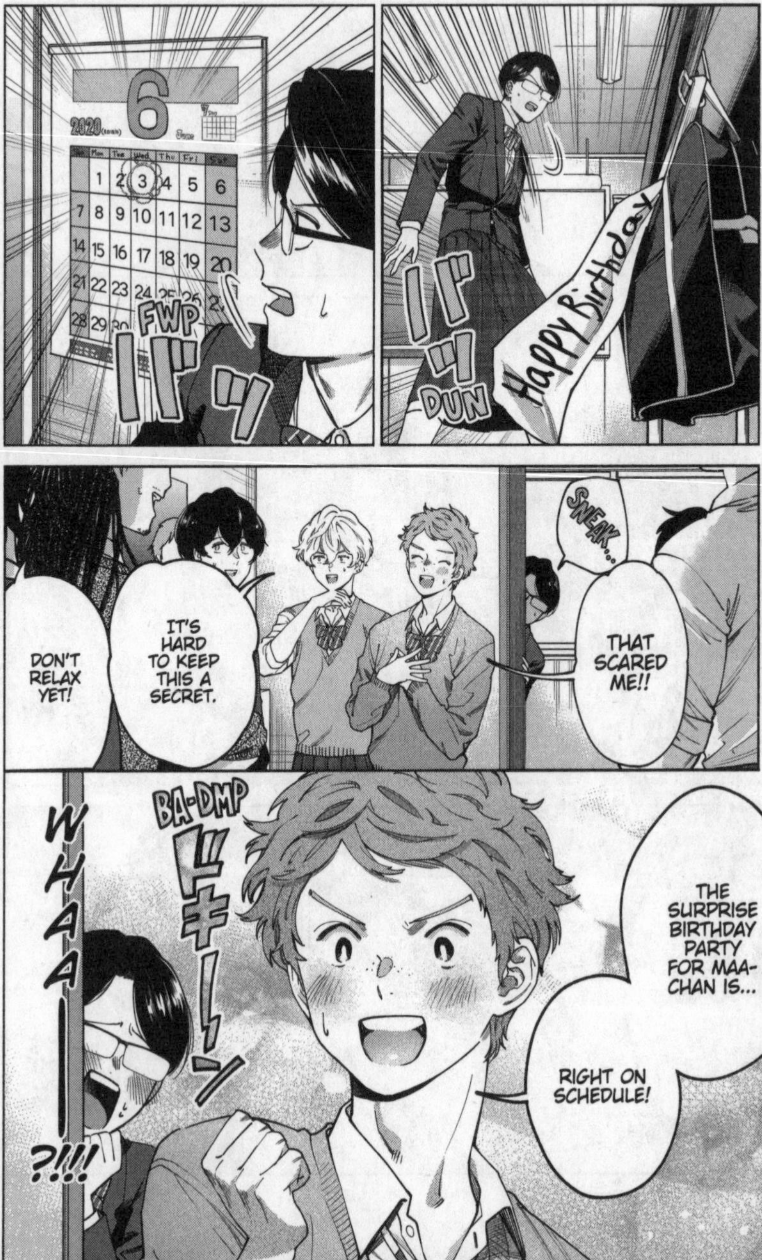

Happy Birthday
DUN
FWP
SNEAK...
THAT SCARED ME!!
IT'S HARD TO KEEP THIS A SECRET.
DON'T RELAX YET!
THE SURPRISE BIRTHDAY PARTY FOR MAA-CHAN IS...
RIGHT ON SCHEDULE!
BA-DMP
WHAAA—?!!!

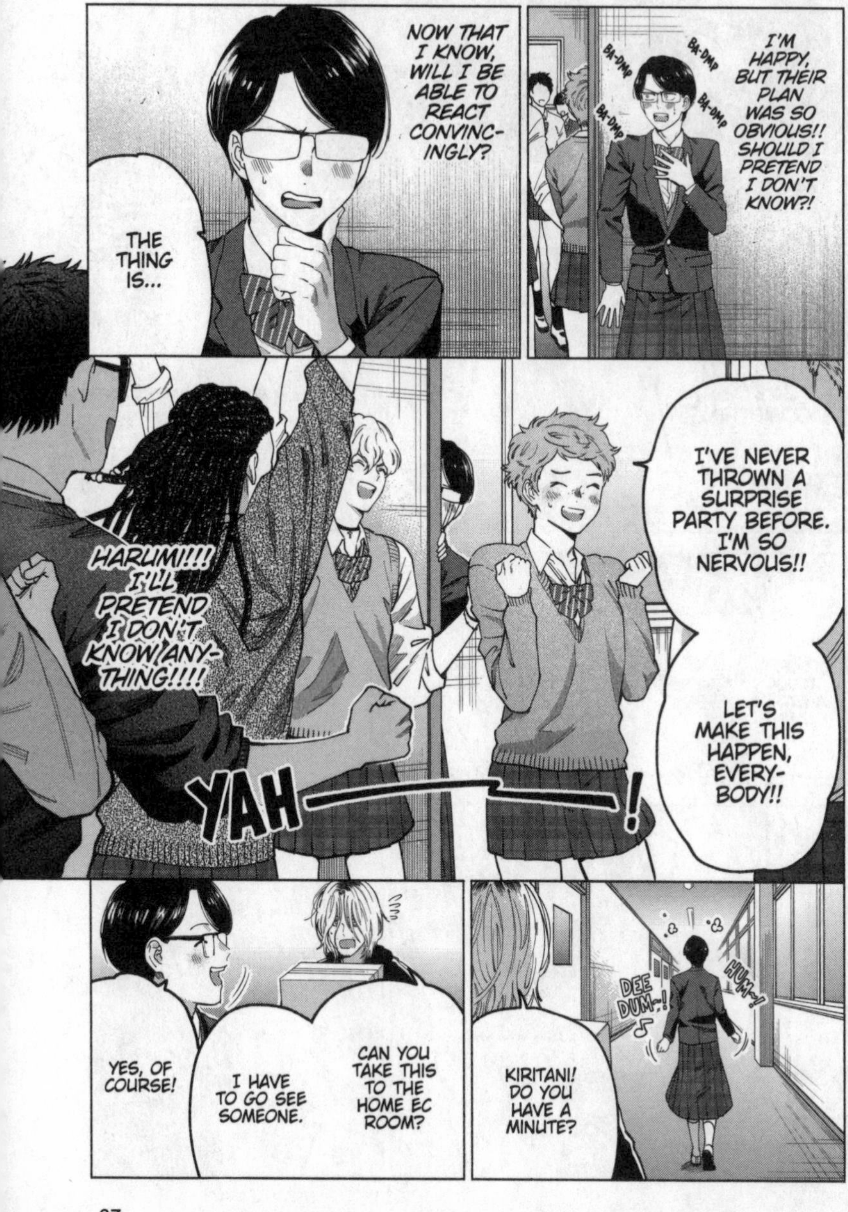
BA-DMP
BA-DMP
BA-DMP
BA-DMP
I'M HAPPY, BUT THEIR PLAN WAS SO OBVIOUS!! SHOULD I PRETEND I DON'T KNOW?!
NOW THAT I KNOW, WILL I BE ABLE TO REACT CONVINC-INGLY?
THE THING IS...
I'VE NEVER THROWN A SURPRISE PARTY BEFORE. I'M SO NERVOUS!!
LET'S MAKE THIS HAPPEN, EVERY-BODY!!
HARUMI!!! I'LL PRETEND I DON'T KNOW ANY-THING!!!!
YAH—!
HUM~!
DEE DUM~!
KIRITANI! DO YOU HAVE A MINUTE?
CAN YOU TAKE THIS TO THE HOME EC ROOM?
I HAVE TO GO SEE SOMEONE.
YES, OF COURSE!

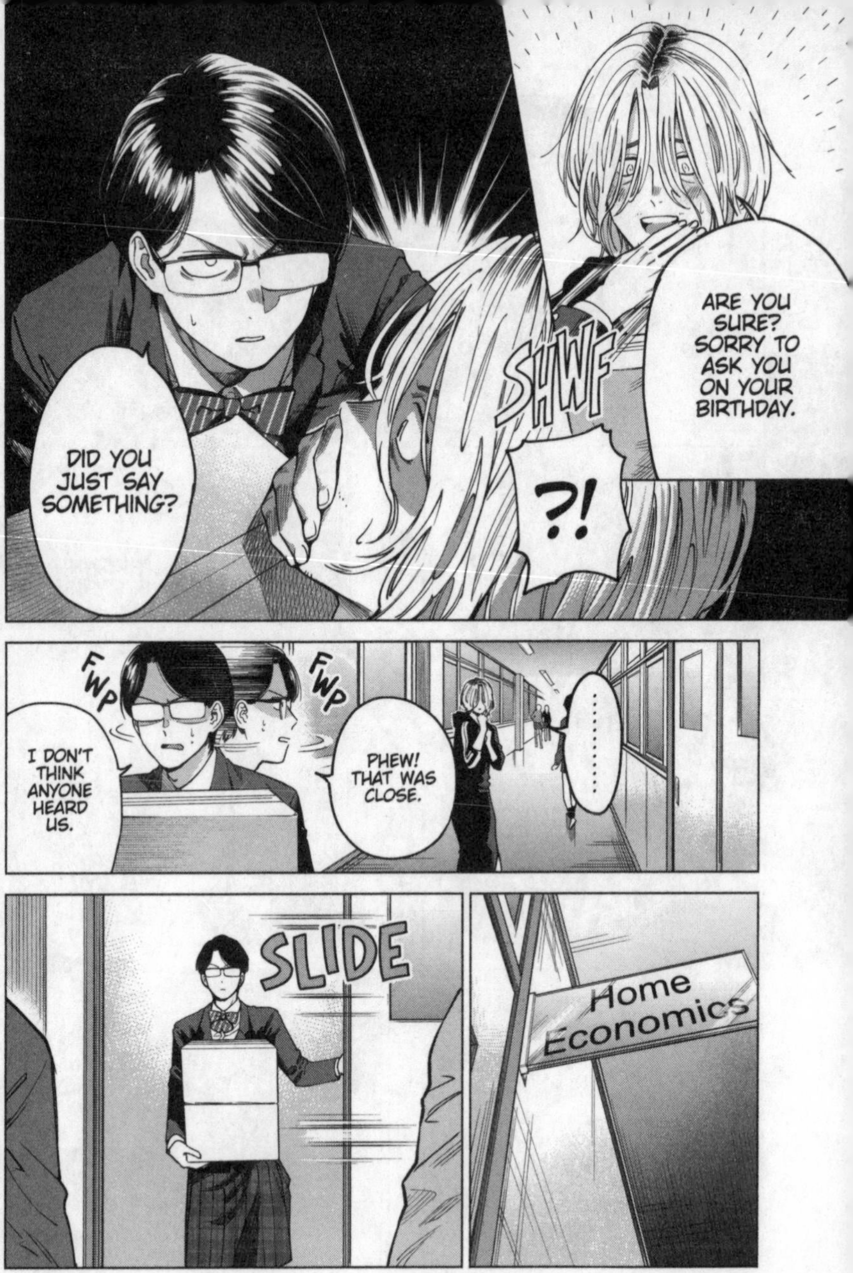
ARE YOU SURE? SORRY TO ASK YOU ON YOUR BIRTHDAY.
SHWF
?!
DID YOU JUST SAY SOMETHING?
......
FWP
PHEW! THAT WAS CLOSE.
FWP
I DON'T THINK ANYONE HEARD US.
Home Economics
SLIDE

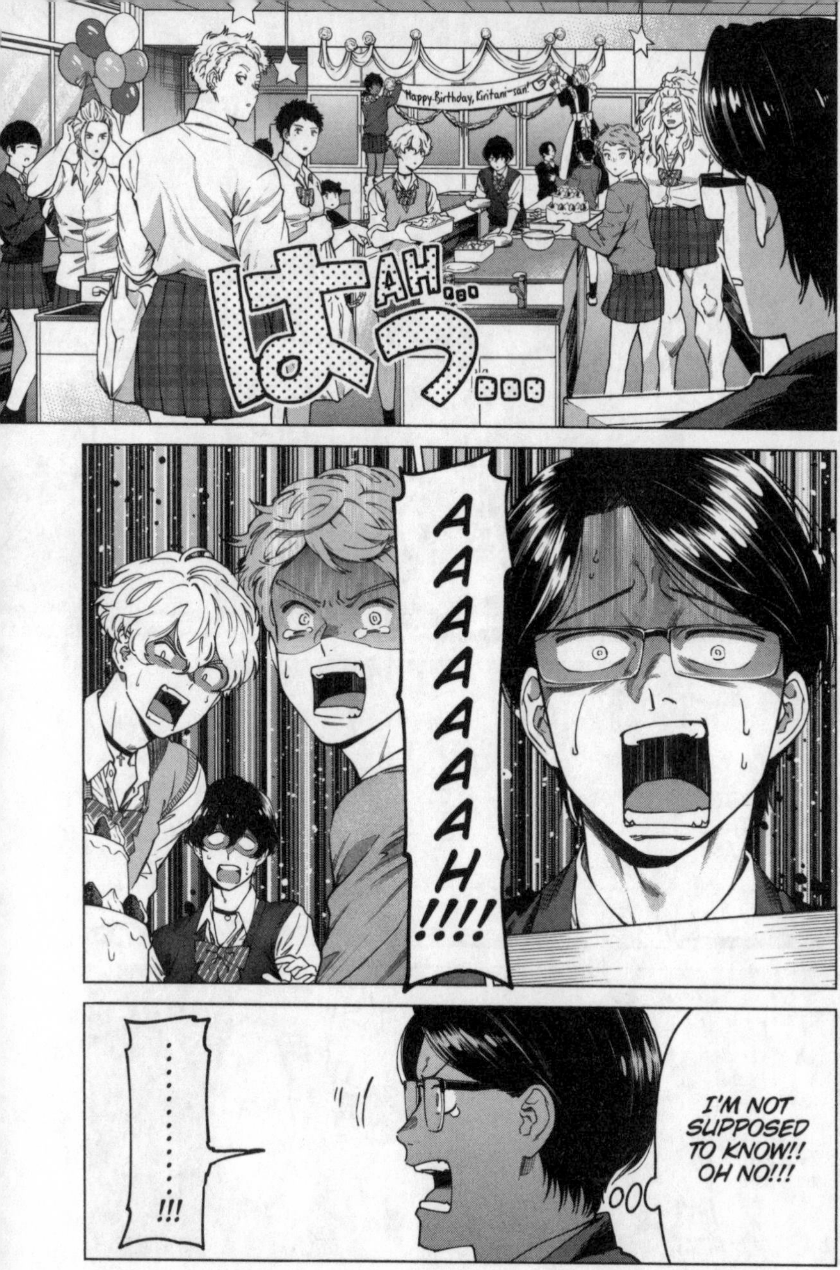
Happy Birthday, Kiritani-san!
はっ…
AH…
AAAAAAAAH!!!!
I'M NOT SUPPOSED TO KNOW!! OH NO!!!
……!!!

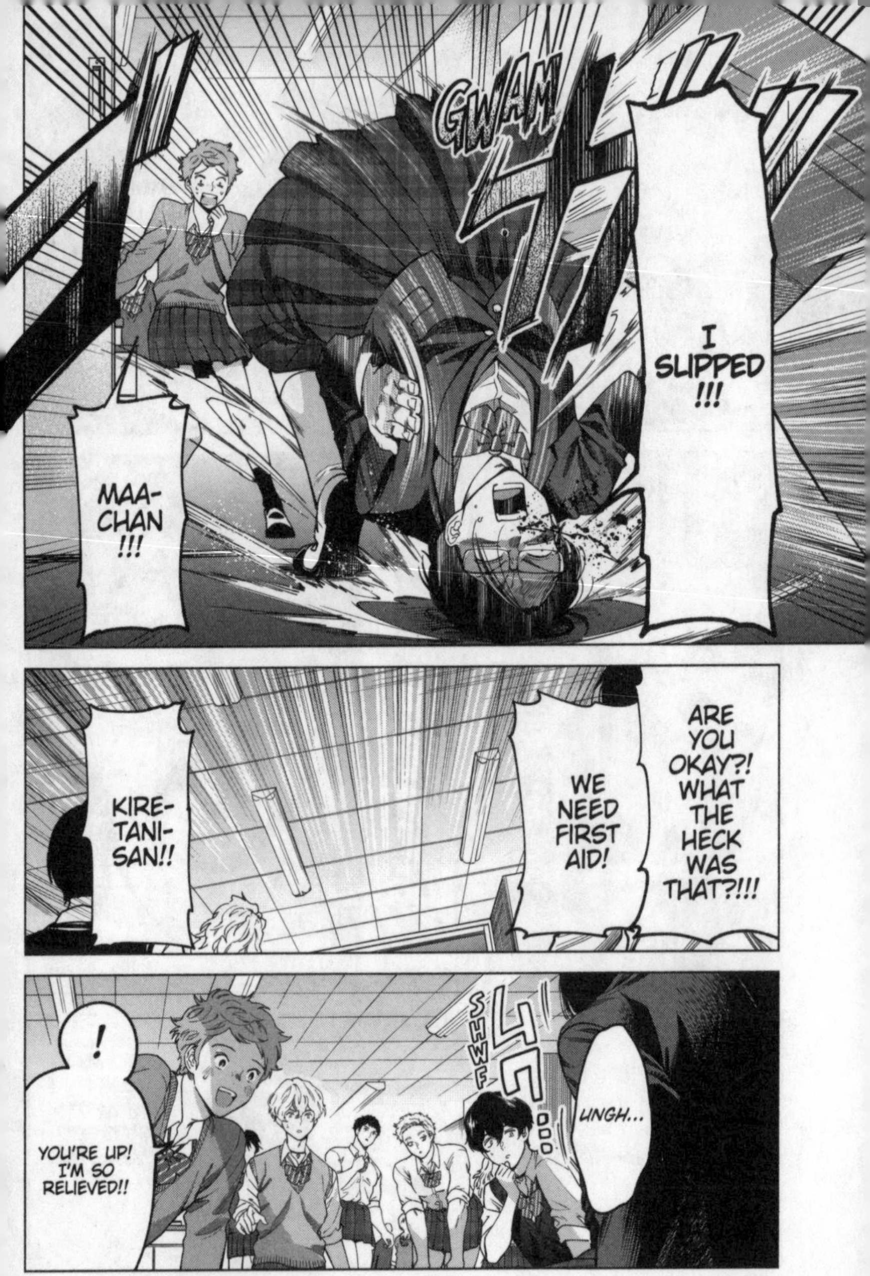
GWAM
I SLIPPED!!!
MAA-CHAN!!!
ARE YOU OKAY?! WHAT THE HECK WAS THAT?!!!
WE NEED FIRST AID!
KIRE-TANI-SAN!!
UNGH...
SHWF
!
YOU'RE UP! I'M SO RELIEVED!!

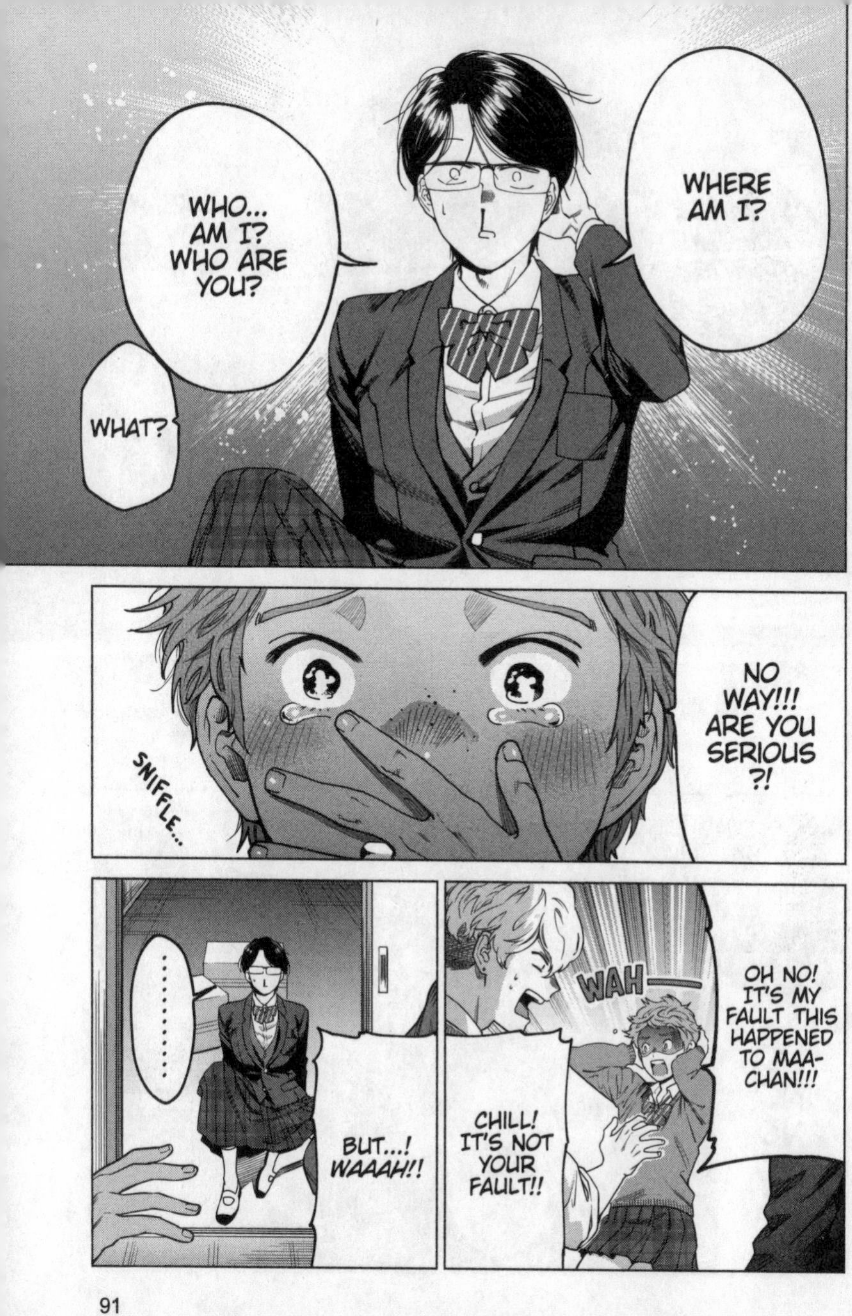
WHERE AM I?
WHO... AM I? WHO ARE YOU?
WHAT?
NO WAY!!! ARE YOU SERIOUS ?!
SNIFFLE...
OH NO! IT'S MY FAULT THIS HAPPENED TO MAA-CHAN!!!
WAH—
CHILL! IT'S NOT YOUR FAULT!!
BUT...! WAAAH!!
....

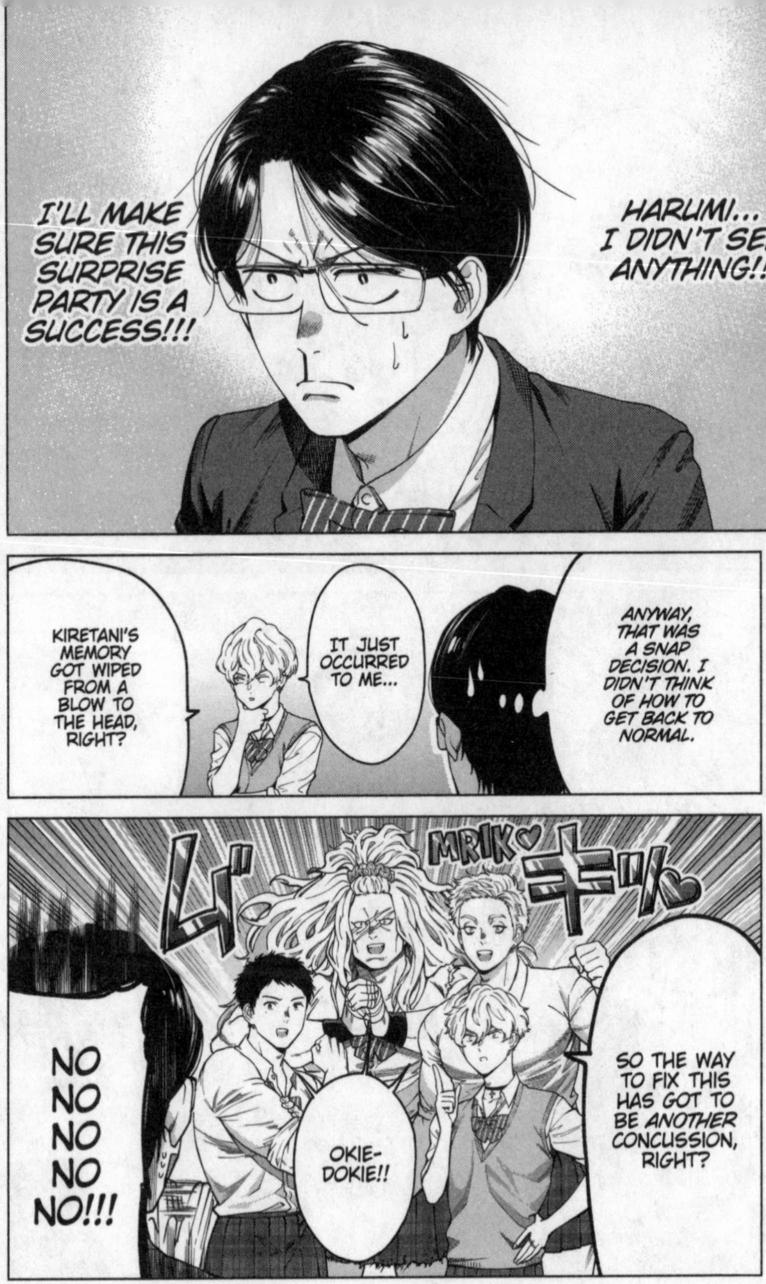
HARUMI... I DIDN'T SEE ANYTHING!!
I'LL MAKE SURE THIS SURPRISE PARTY IS A SUCCESS!!!
ANYWAY, THAT WAS A SNAP DECISION. I DIDN'T THINK OF HOW TO GET BACK TO NORMAL.
IT JUST OCCURRED TO ME...
KIRETANI'S MEMORY GOT WIPED FROM A BLOW TO THE HEAD, RIGHT?
MRIK♥
SO THE WAY TO FIX THIS HAS GOT TO BE *ANOTHER* CONCUSSION, RIGHT?
OKIE-DOKIE!!
NO NO NO NO NO!!!

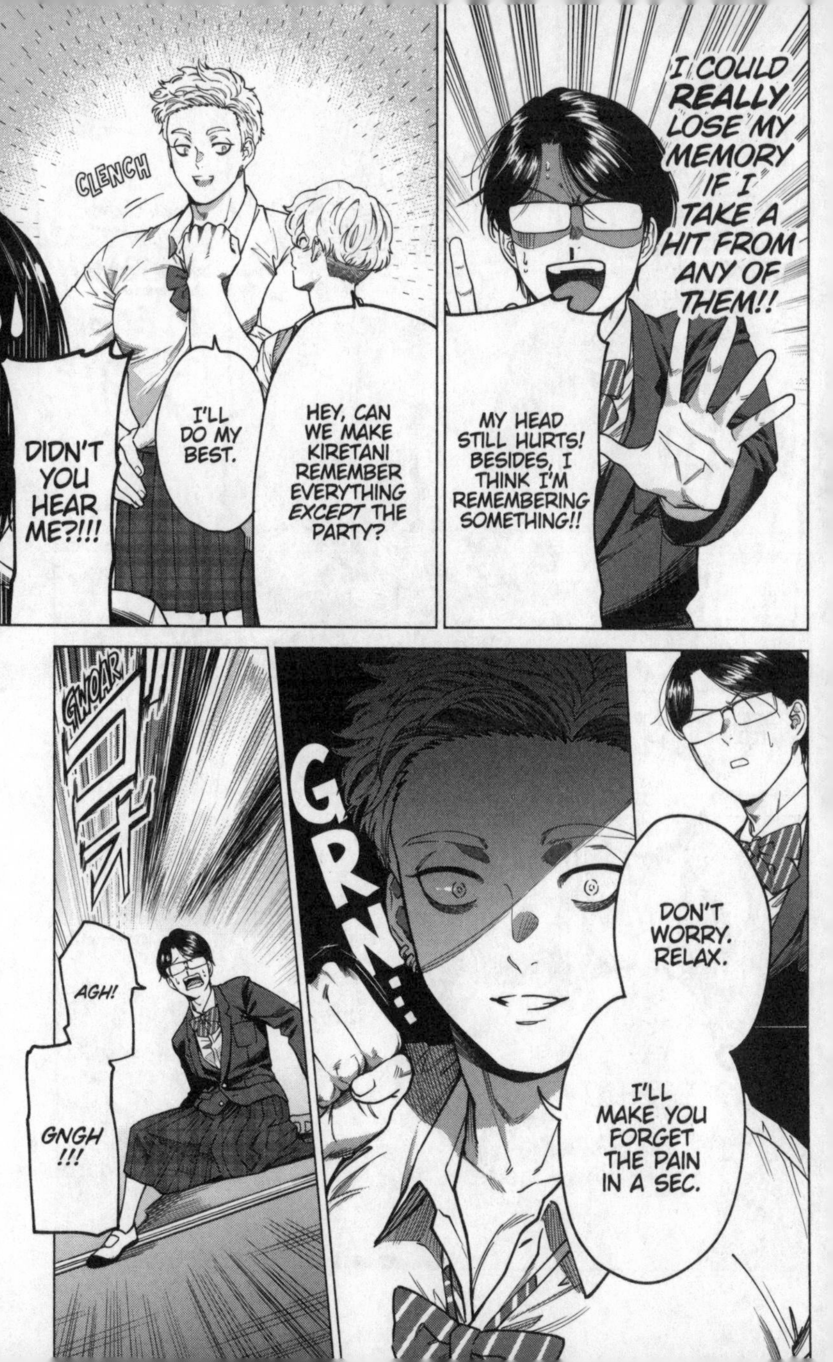

I COULD REALLY LOSE MY MEMORY IF I TAKE A HIT FROM ANY OF THEM!!
MY HEAD STILL HURTS! BESIDES, I THINK I'M REMEMBERING SOMETHING!!
CLENCH
HEY, CAN WE MAKE KIRETANI REMEMBER EVERYTHING *EXCEPT* THE PARTY?
I'LL DO MY BEST.
DIDN'T YOU HEAR ME?!!!
DON'T WORRY. RELAX.
GRN...
I'LL MAKE YOU FORGET THE PAIN IN A SEC.
GWOAR
AGH!
GNGH !!!

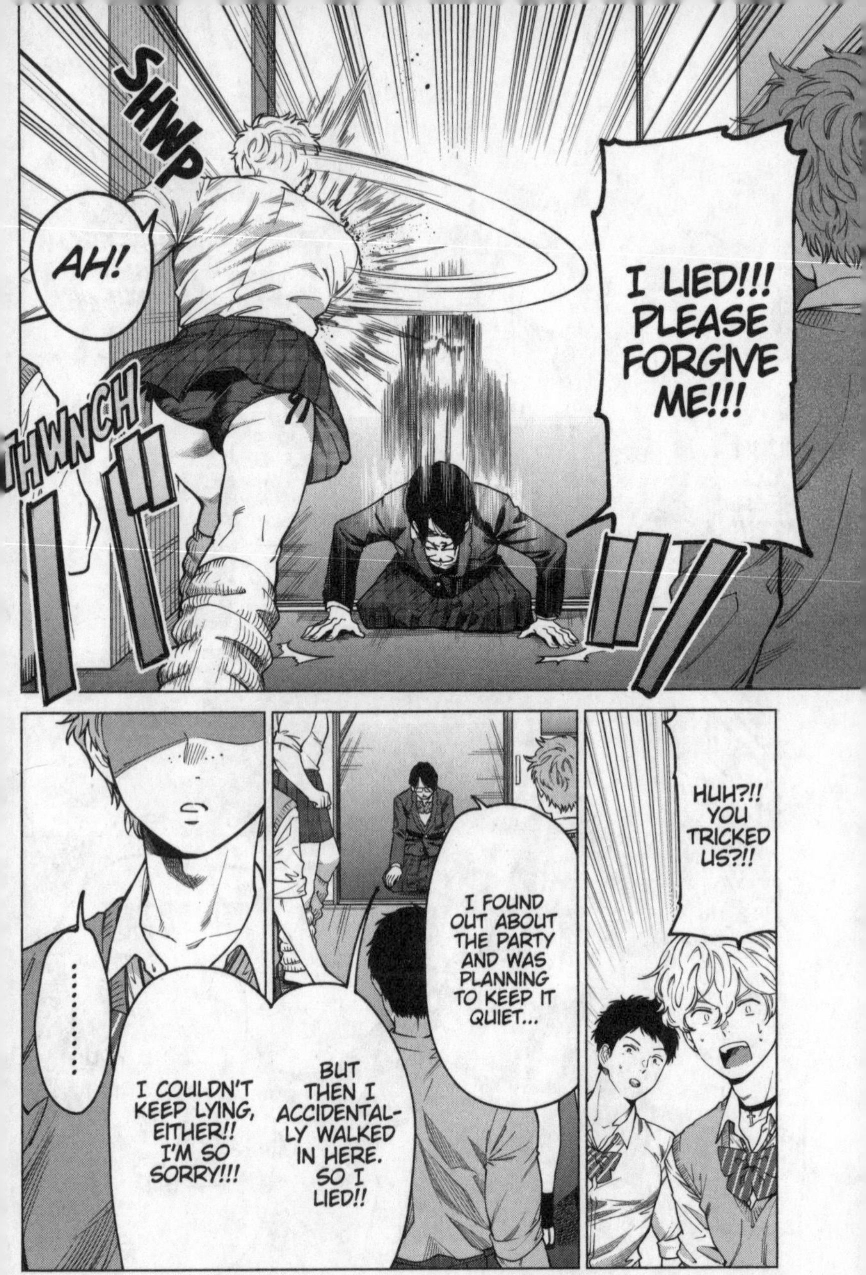
I LIED!!! PLEASE FORGIVE ME!!!
SHWP
AH!
THWNCH
HUH?!! YOU TRICKED US?!!
I FOUND OUT ABOUT THE PARTY AND WAS PLANNING TO KEEP IT QUIET...
BUT THEN I ACCIDENTAL-LY WALKED IN HERE. SO I LIED!!
......
I COULDN'T KEEP LYING, EITHER!! I'M SO SORRY!!!

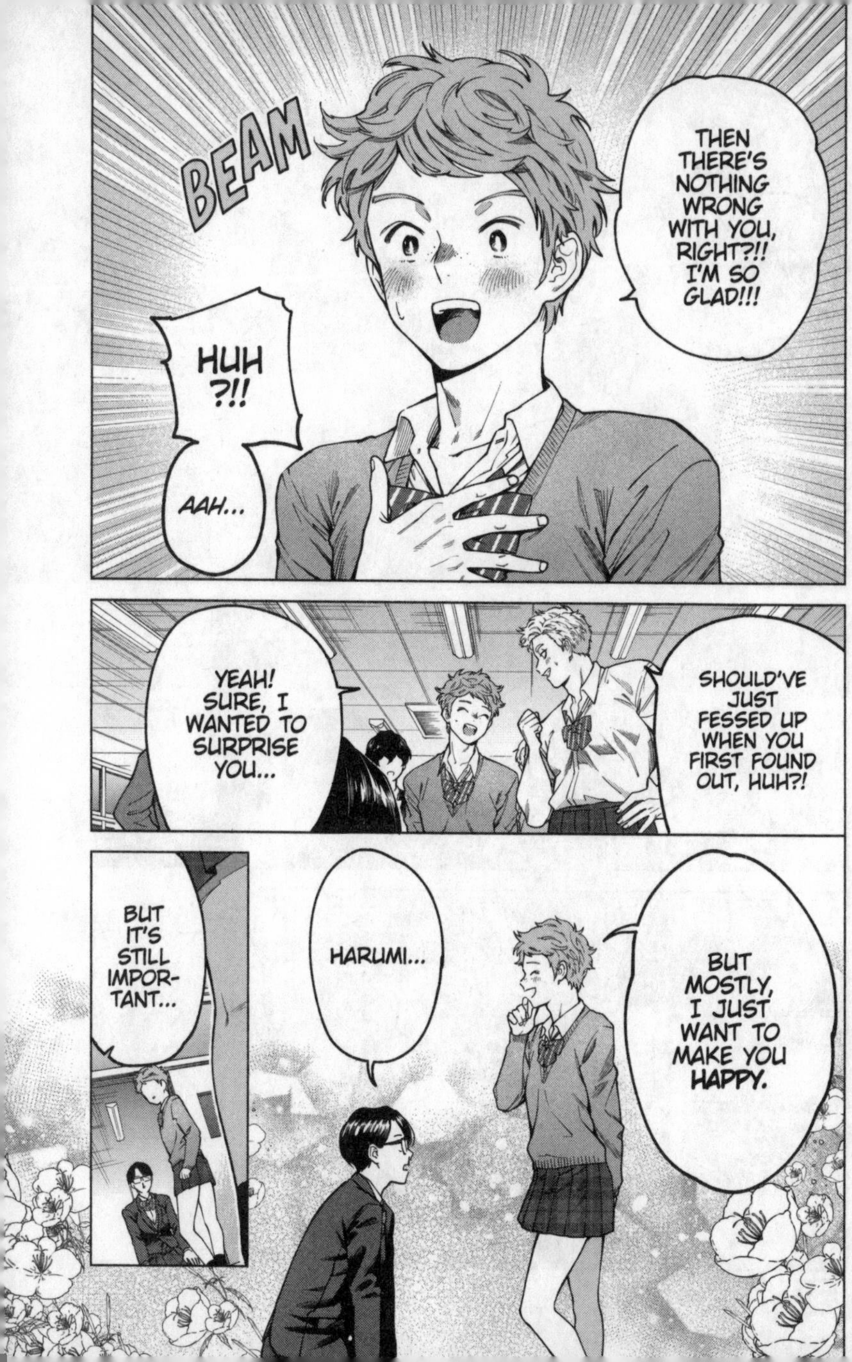

THEN THERE'S NOTHING WRONG WITH YOU, RIGHT?!! I'M SO GLAD!!!
BEAM
HUH ?!!
AAH...
SHOULD'VE JUST FESSED UP WHEN YOU FIRST FOUND OUT, HUH?!
YEAH! SURE, I WANTED TO SURPRISE YOU...
BUT MOSTLY, I JUST WANT TO MAKE YOU **HAPPY.**
HARUMI...
BUT IT'S STILL IMPOR-TANT...

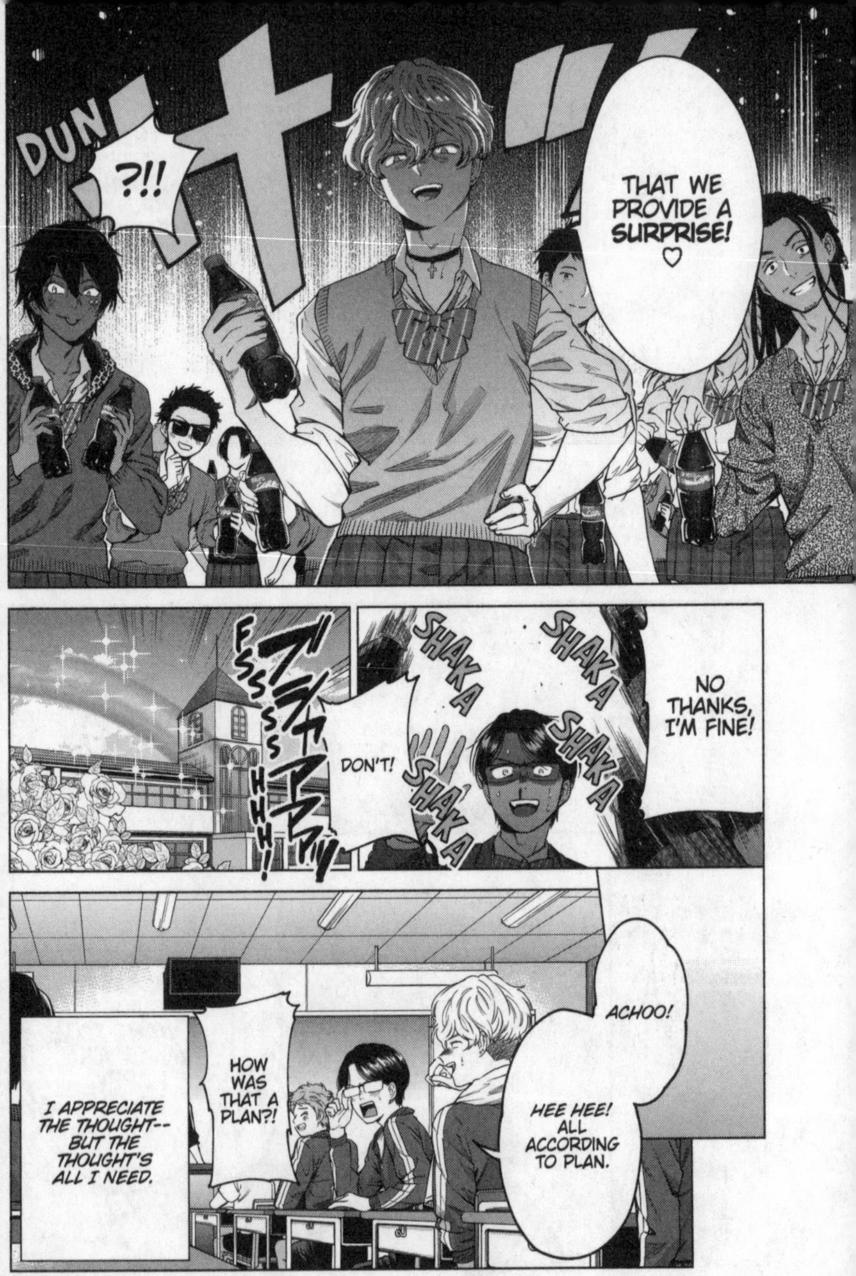
THAT WE PROVIDE A SURPRISE! ♡
?!!
DUN
NO THANKS, I'M FINE!
SHAKA SHAKA SHAKA
SHAKA SHAKA
SHAKA
DON'T!
FSSSSSHHH!
ACHOO!
HEE HEE! ALL ACCORDING TO PLAN.
HOW WAS THAT A PLAN?!
I APPRECIATE THE THOUGHT-- BUT THE THOUGHT'S ALL I NEED.

#29 End

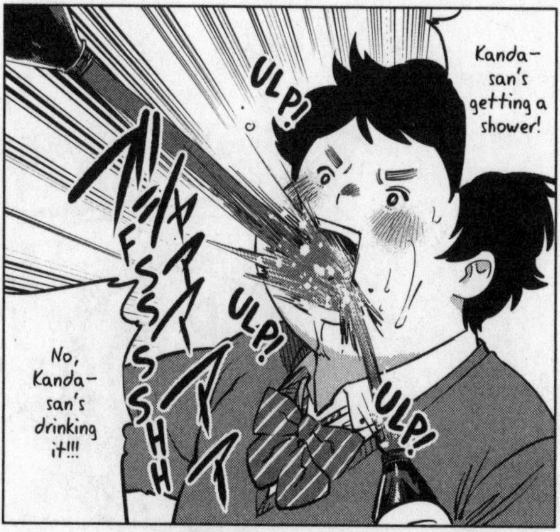
Kanda-san's getting a shower!
ULP!
FSSSSHH
ULP!
ULP!
No, Kanda-san's drinking it!!!

THIGH HIGH
Reiwa Hanamaru Academy

HANAMARU PRIVATE HIGH SCHOOL

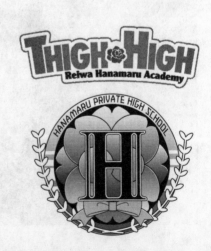

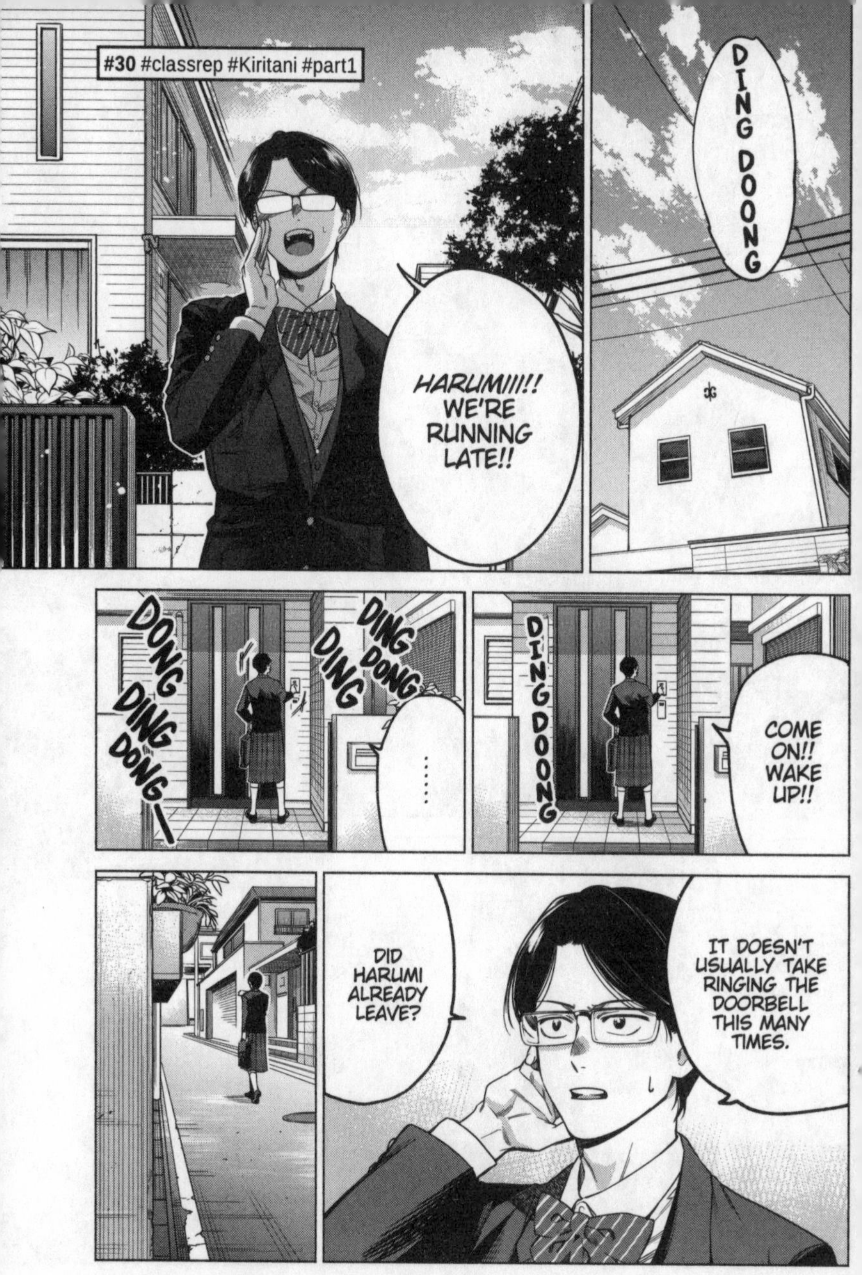
DING DOONG
#30 #classrep #Kiritani #part1
HARUMI!!!! WE'RE RUNNING LATE!!
DING DOONG
COME ON!! WAKE UP!!
DING DONG DING
DONG DING DONG—
......
IT DOESN'T USUALLY TAKE RINGING THE DOORBELL THIS MANY TIMES.
DID HARUMI ALREADY LEAVE?

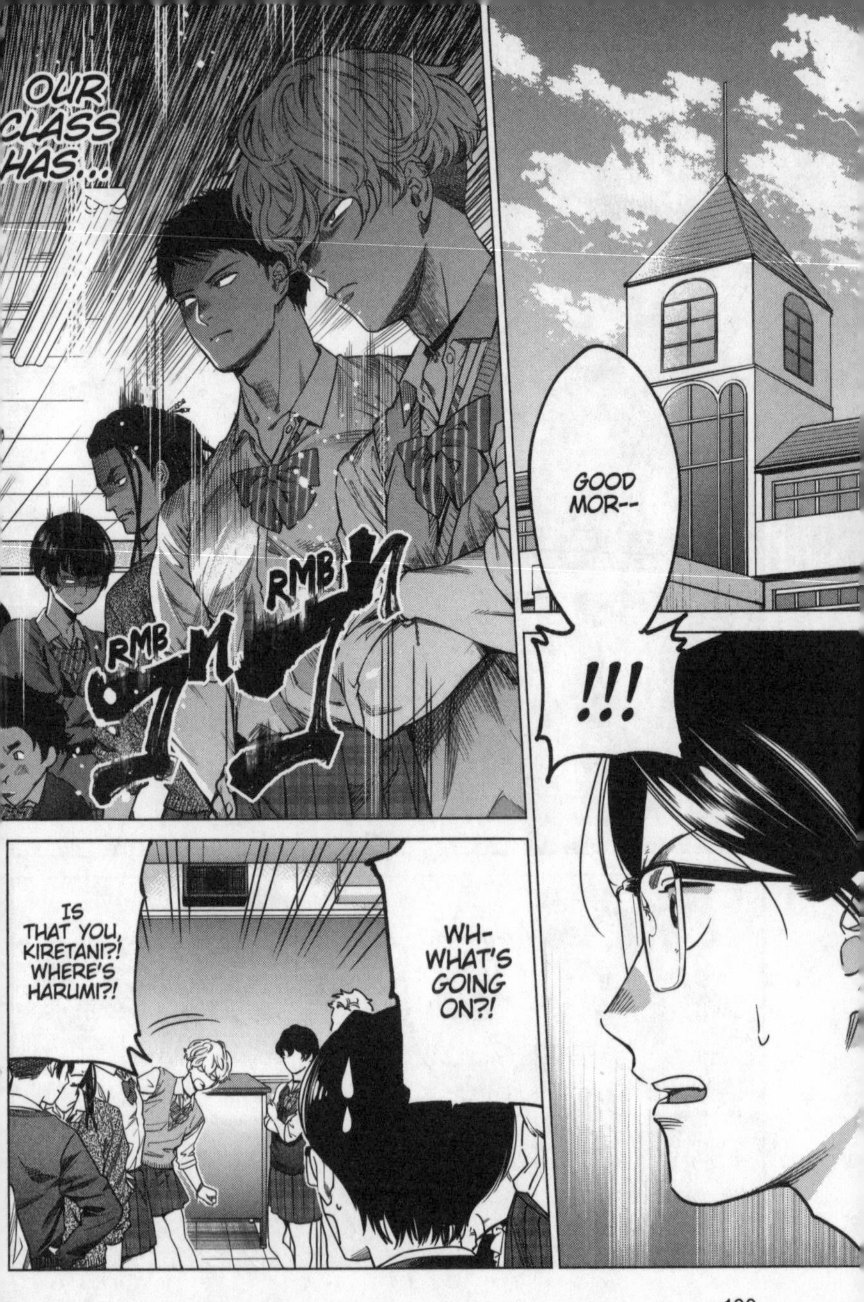
GOOD MOR--
!!!
OUR CLASS HAS...
RMB
RMB
WH-WHAT'S GOING ON?!
IS THAT YOU, KIRETANI?! WHERE'S HARUMI?!

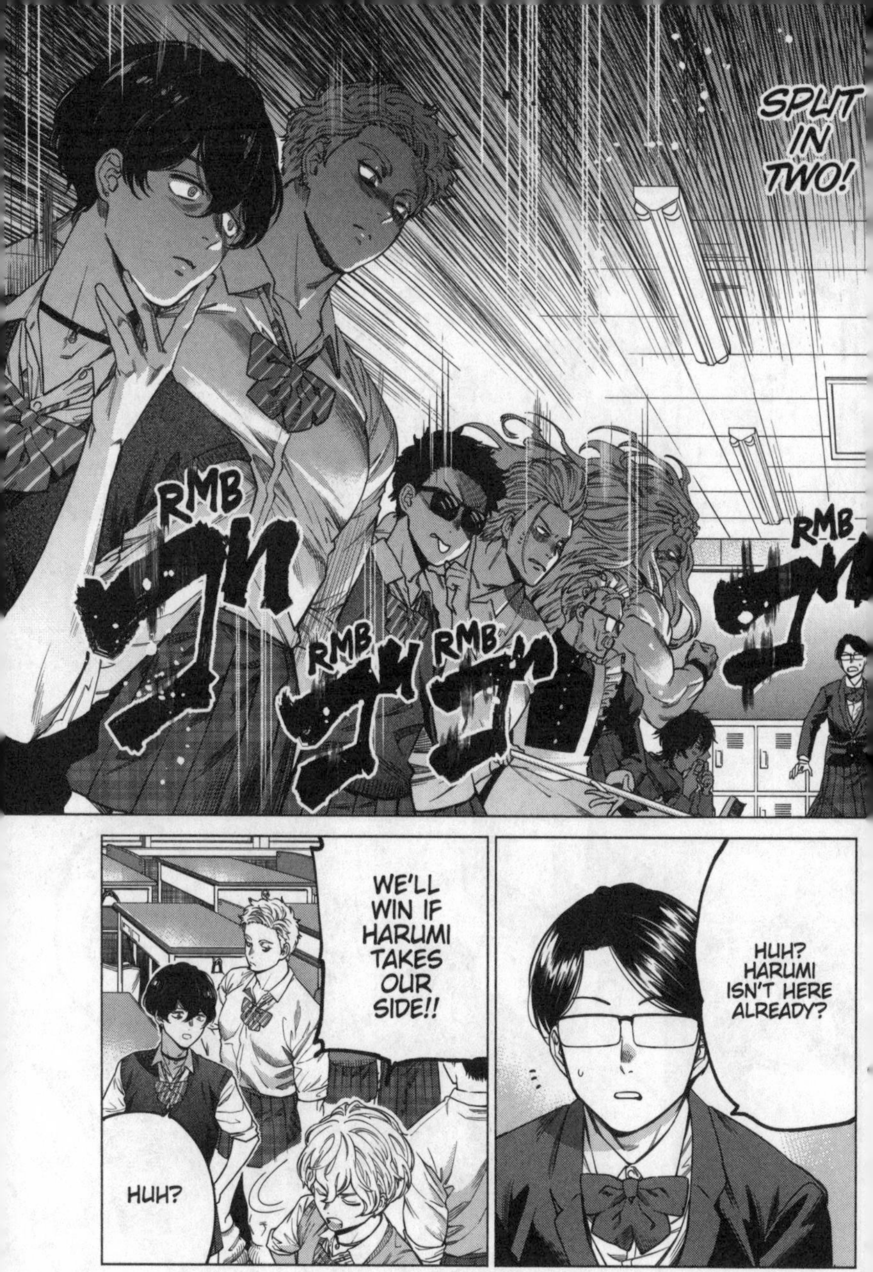
SPLIT IN TWO!
RMB
RMB
RMB
RMB
HUH? HARUMI ISN'T HERE ALREADY?
WE'LL WIN IF HARUMI TAKES OUR SIDE!!
HUH?

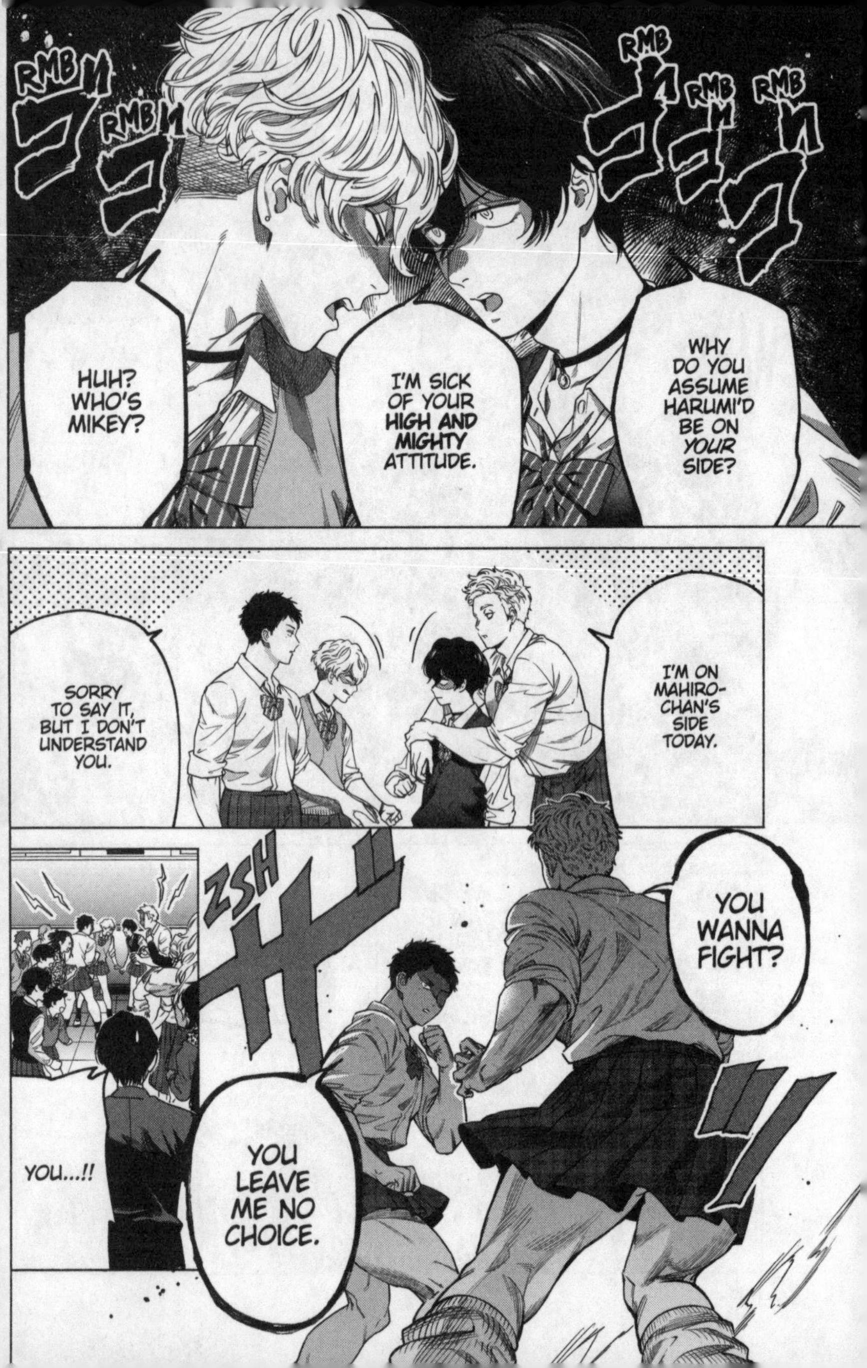
RMB N
RMB N
RMB N
RMB N
RMB N
WHY DO YOU ASSUME HARUMI'D BE ON YOUR SIDE?
I'M SICK OF YOUR HIGH AND MIGHTY ATTITUDE.
HUH? WHO'S MIKEY?
I'M ON MAHIRO-CHAN'S SIDE TODAY.
SORRY TO SAY IT, BUT I DON'T UNDERSTAND YOU.
YOU WANNA FIGHT?
ZSH
YOU LEAVE ME NO CHOICE.
YOU...!!

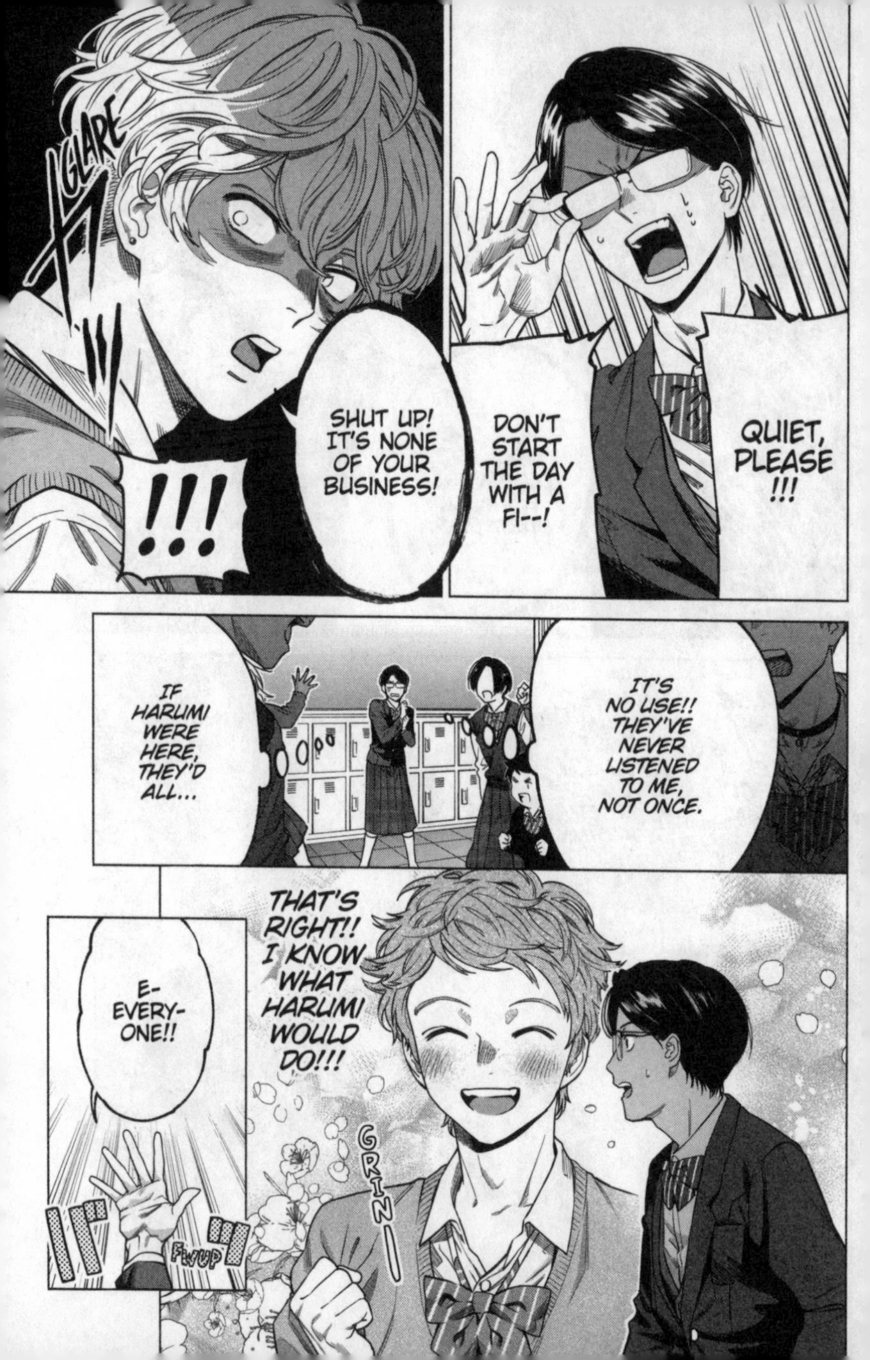
QUIET, PLEASE!!!
DON'T START THE DAY WITH A FI--!
SHUT UP! IT'S NONE OF YOUR BUSINESS!
!!!
GLARE
IT'S NO USE!! THEY'VE NEVER LISTENED TO ME, NOT ONCE.
IF HARUMI WERE HERE, THEY'D ALL...
THAT'S RIGHT!! I KNOW WHAT HARUMI WOULD DO!!!
GRIN
E-EVERYONE!!
FWUP

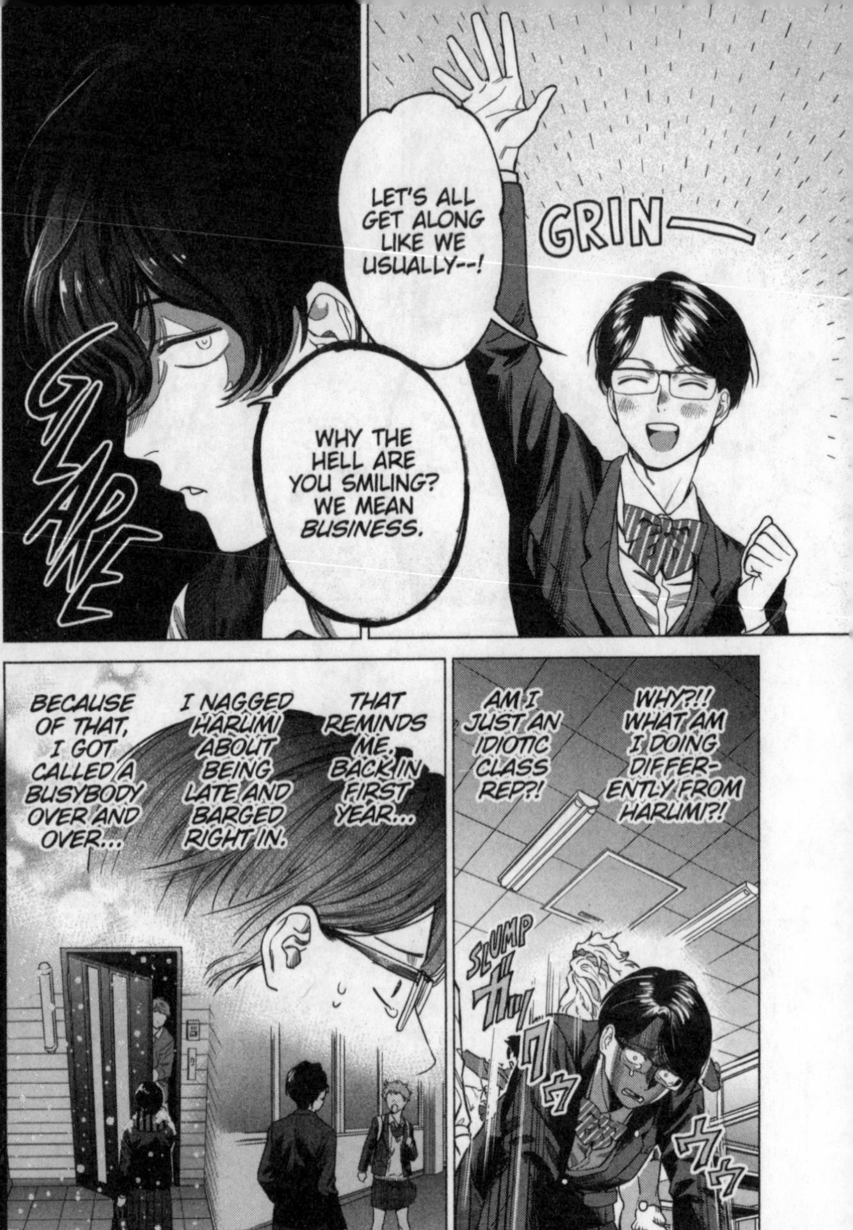
LET'S ALL GET ALONG LIKE WE USUALLY--!
GRIN—
WHY THE HELL ARE YOU SMILING? WE MEAN *BUSINESS.*
GLARE
WHY?!! WHAT AM I DOING DIFFER-ENTLY FROM HARUMI?!
AM I JUST AN IDIOTIC CLASS REP?!
SLUMP
THAT REMINDS ME, BACK IN FIRST YEAR...
I NAGGED HARUMI ABOUT BEING LATE AND BARGED RIGHT IN.
BECAUSE OF THAT, I GOT CALLED A BUSYBODY OVER AND OVER...

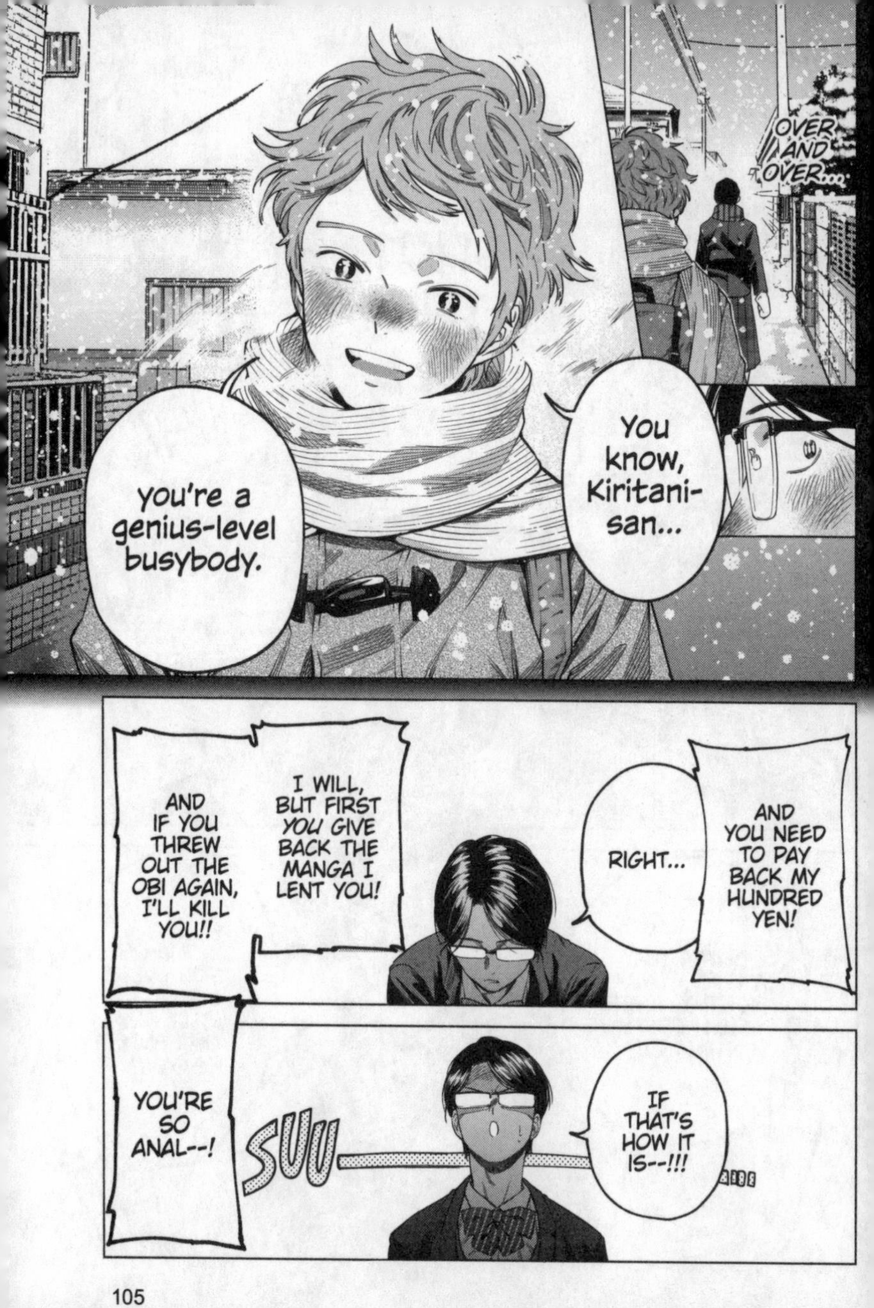
OVER AND OVER...
You know, Kiritani-san...
you're a genius-level busybody.
AND YOU NEED TO PAY BACK MY HUNDRED YEN!
RIGHT...
I WILL, BUT FIRST *YOU* GIVE BACK THE MANGA I LENT YOU!
AND IF YOU THREW OUT THE OBI AGAIN, I'LL KILL YOU!!
IF THAT'S HOW IT IS--!!!
SUU
YOU'RE SO ANAL--!

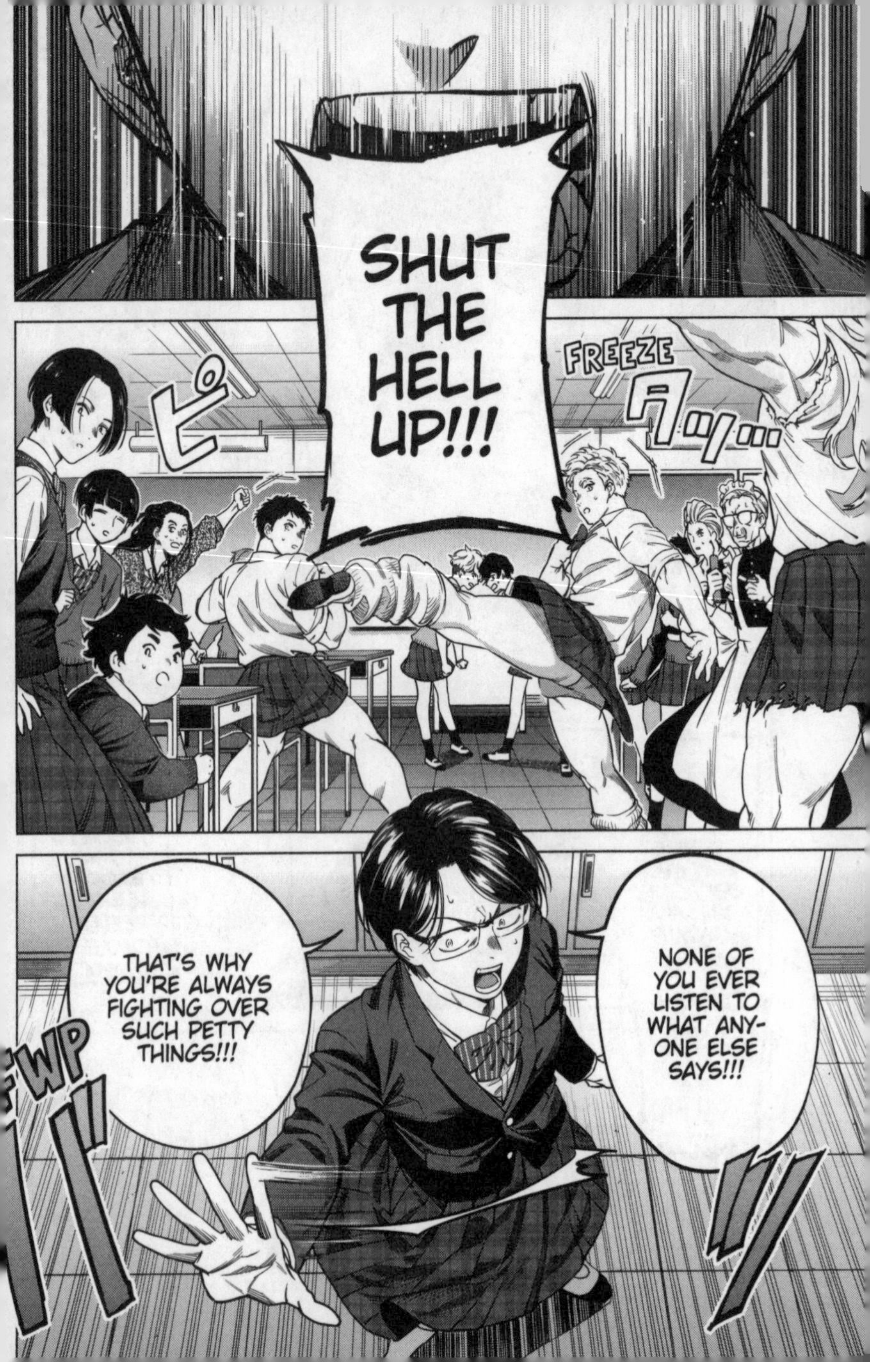
SHUT THE HELL UP!!!
FREEZE
タッ…
ピ
NONE OF YOU EVER LISTEN TO WHAT ANY-ONE ELSE SAYS!!!
THAT'S WHY YOU'RE ALWAYS FIGHTING OVER SUCH PETTY THINGS!!!
FWP

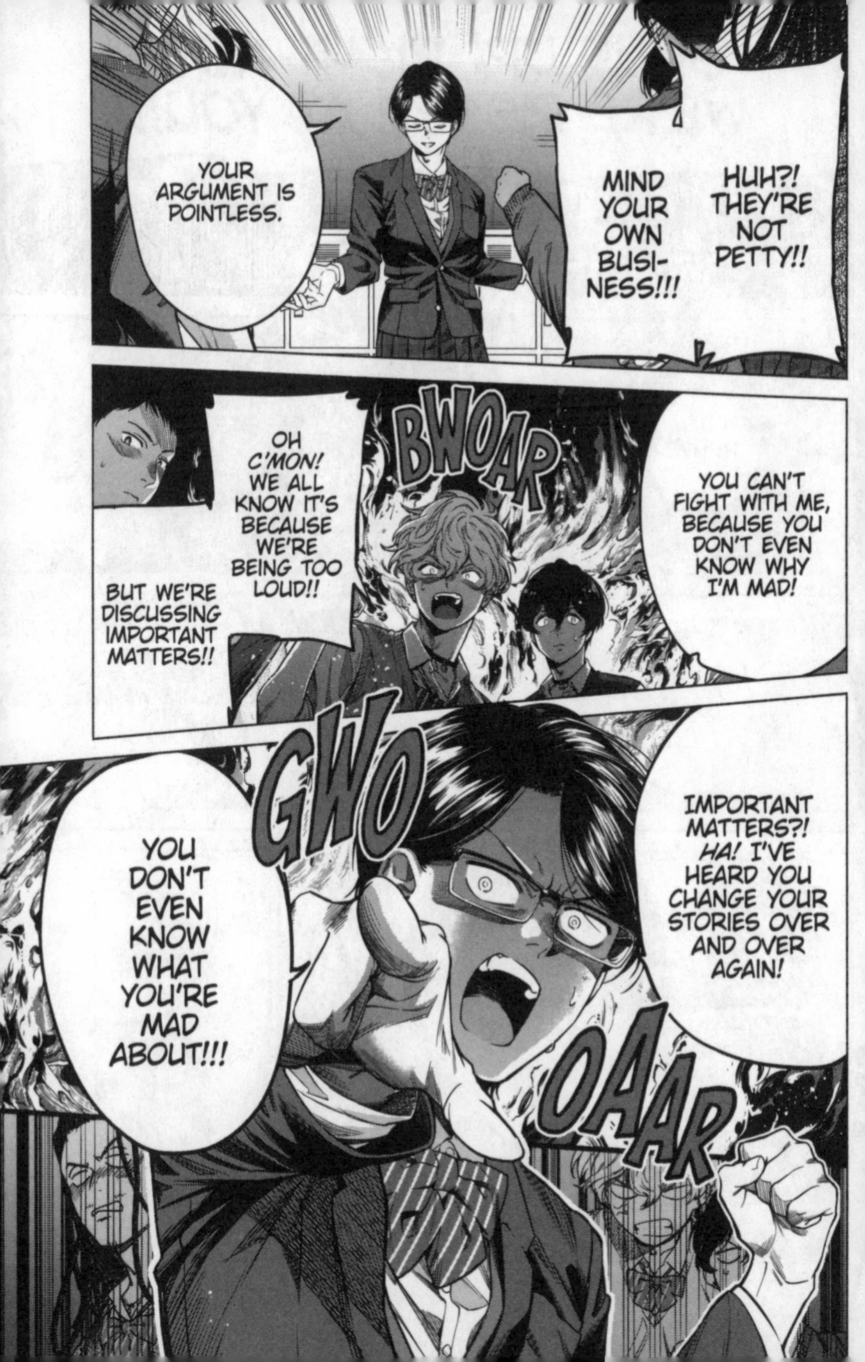
HUH?! THEY'RE NOT PETTY!!
MIND YOUR OWN BUSI-NESS!!!
YOUR ARGUMENT IS POINTLESS.
YOU CAN'T FIGHT WITH ME, BECAUSE YOU DON'T EVEN KNOW WHY I'M MAD!
BWOAR
OH C'MON! WE ALL KNOW IT'S BECAUSE WE'RE BEING TOO LOUD!!
BUT WE'RE DISCUSSING IMPORTANT MATTERS!!
IMPORTANT MATTERS?! HA! I'VE HEARD YOU CHANGE YOUR STORIES OVER AND OVER AGAIN!
GWO
OAAR
YOU DON'T EVEN KNOW WHAT YOU'RE MAD ABOUT!!!

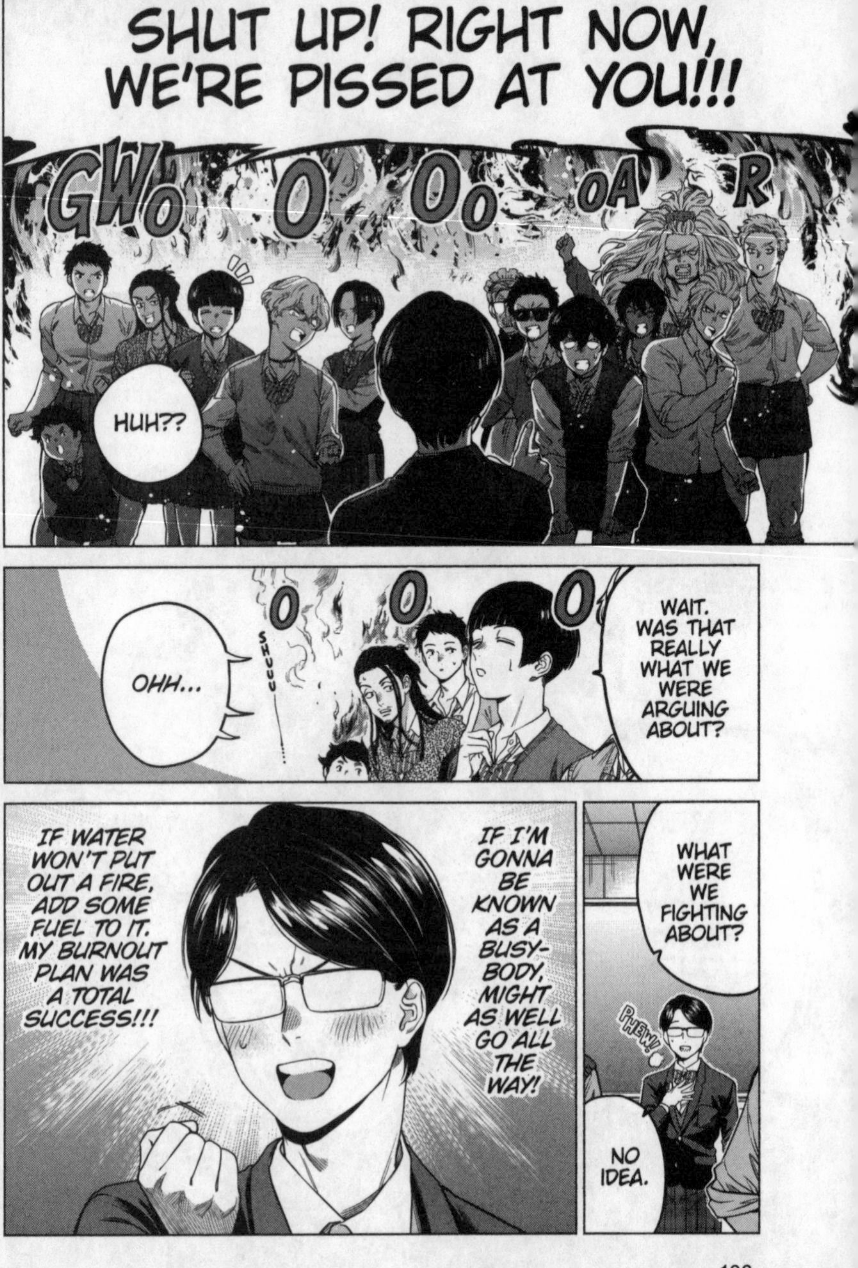
SHUT UP! RIGHT NOW, WE'RE PISSED AT YOU!!!
GWOOOOOOAR
HUH??
WAIT. WAS THAT REALLY WHAT WE WERE ARGUING ABOUT?
OOO
SHUUU
OHH...
WHAT WERE WE FIGHTING ABOUT?
PHEW!
NO IDEA.
IF I'M GONNA BE KNOWN AS A BUSY-BODY, MIGHT AS WELL GO ALL THE WAY!
IF WATER WON'T PUT OUT A FIRE, ADD SOME FUEL TO IT. MY BURNOUT PLAN WAS A TOTAL SUCCESS!!!

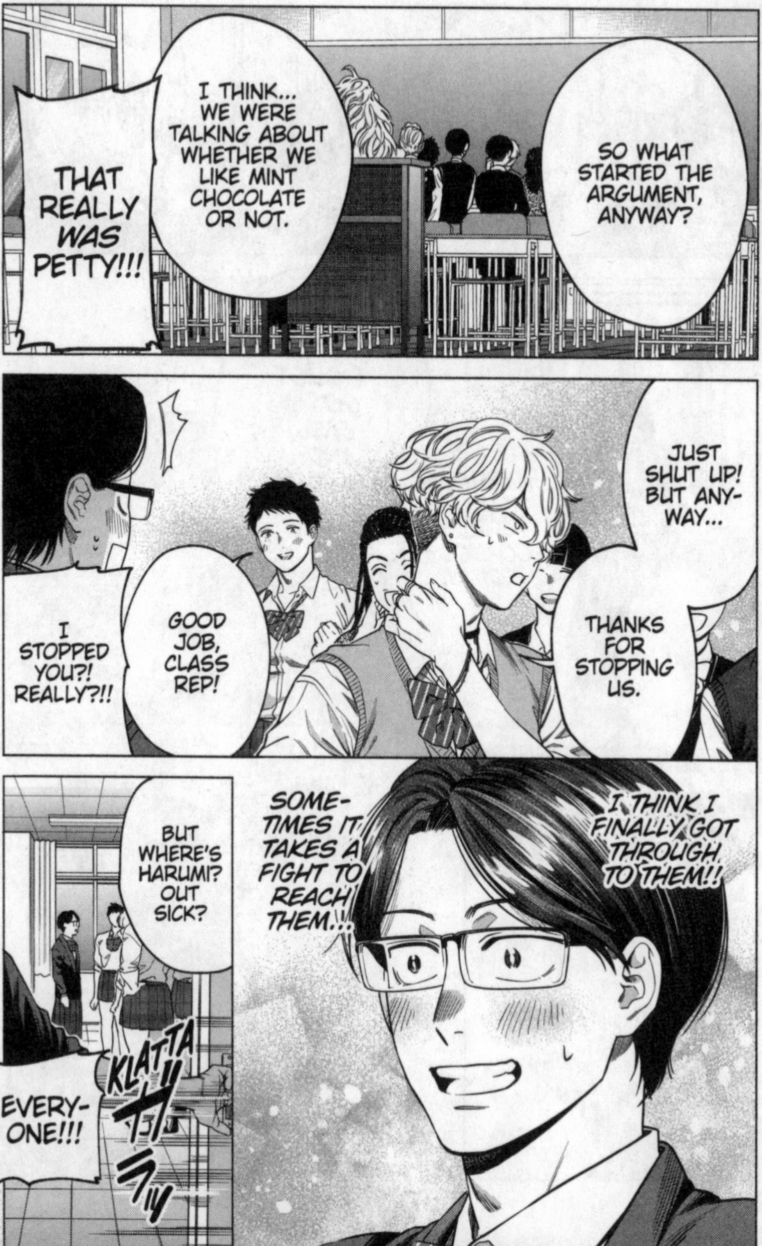
SO WHAT STARTED THE ARGUMENT, ANYWAY?
I THINK... WE WERE TALKING ABOUT WHETHER WE LIKE MINT CHOCOLATE OR NOT.
THAT REALLY WAS PETTY!!!
JUST SHUT UP! BUT ANY-WAY...
THANKS FOR STOPPING US.
GOOD JOB, CLASS REP!
I STOPPED YOU?! REALLY?!!
I THINK I FINALLY GOT THROUGH TO THEM!!
SOME-TIMES IT TAKES A FIGHT TO REACH THEM...!!
BUT WHERE'S HARUMI? OUT SICK?
KLATTA
EVERY-ONE!!!

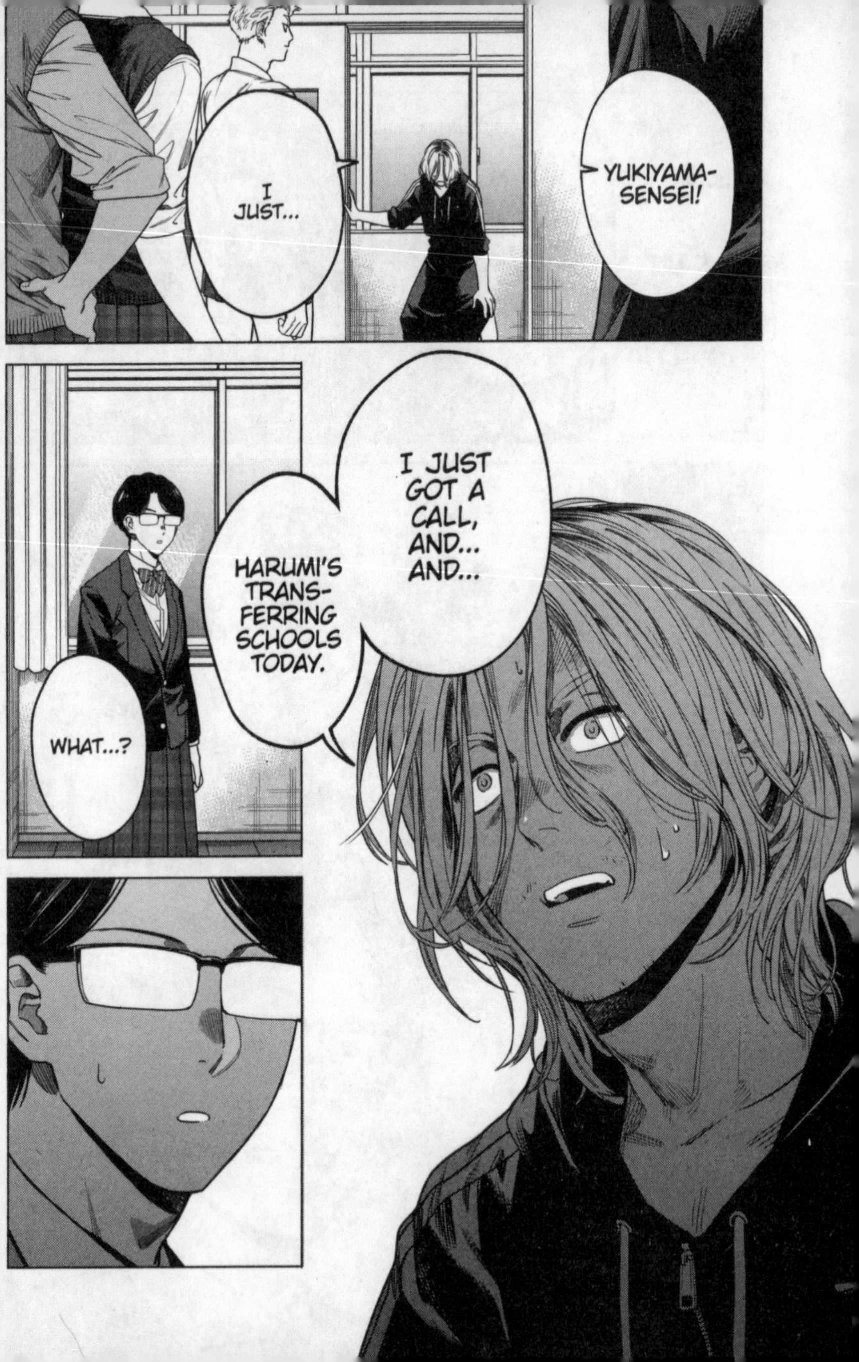
YUKIYAMA-SENSEI!
I JUST...
I JUST GOT A CALL, AND... AND...
HARUMI'S TRANS-FERRING SCHOOLS TODAY.
WHAT...?

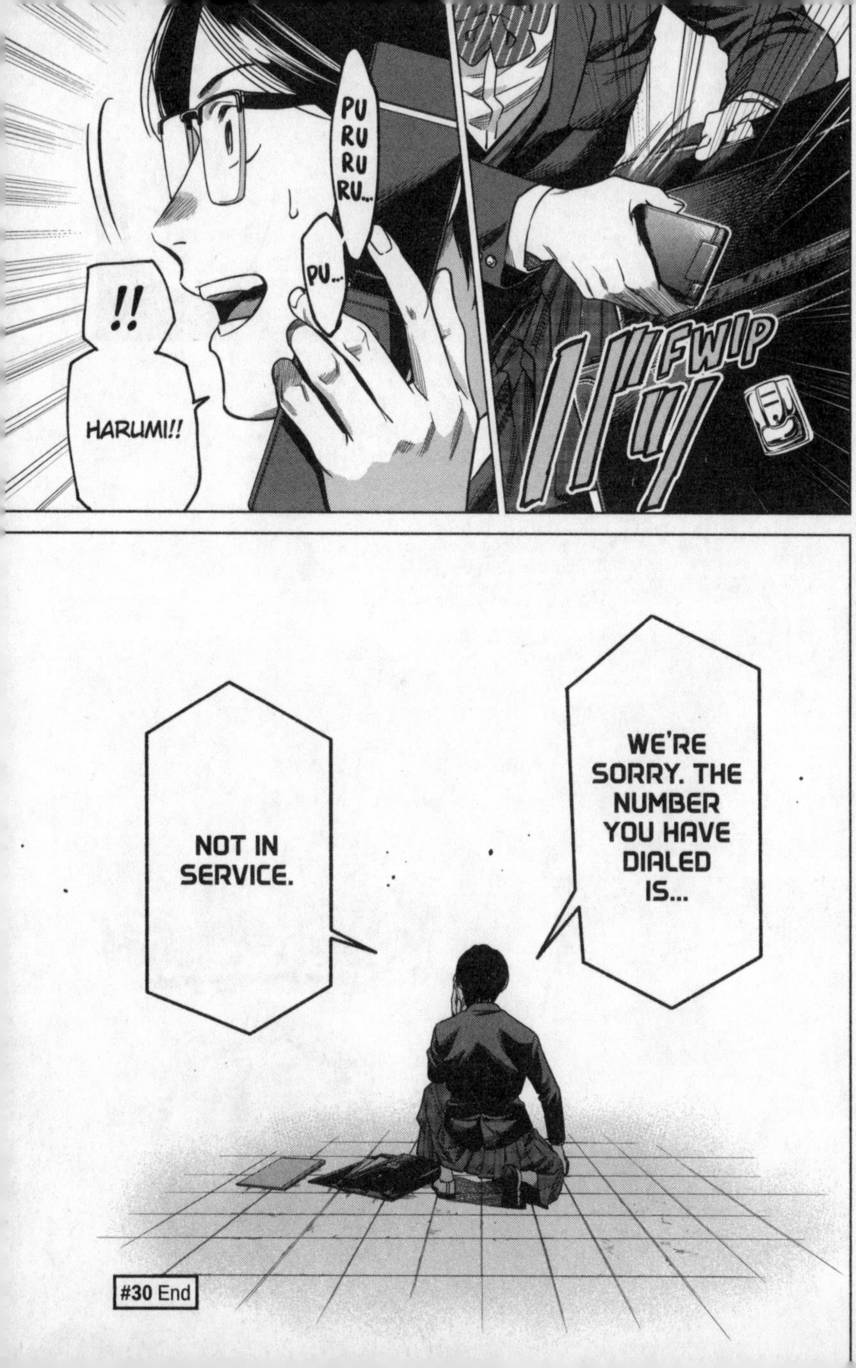
FWIP
PU RU RU RU...
PU...
!!
HARUMI!!
WE'RE SORRY. THE NUMBER YOU HAVE DIALED IS...
NOT IN SERVICE.
#30 End

THIGH HIGH
Reiwa Hanamaru Academy

HANAMARU PRIVATE HIGH SCHOOL

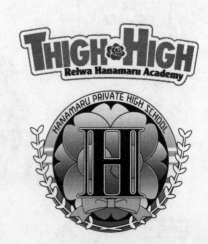

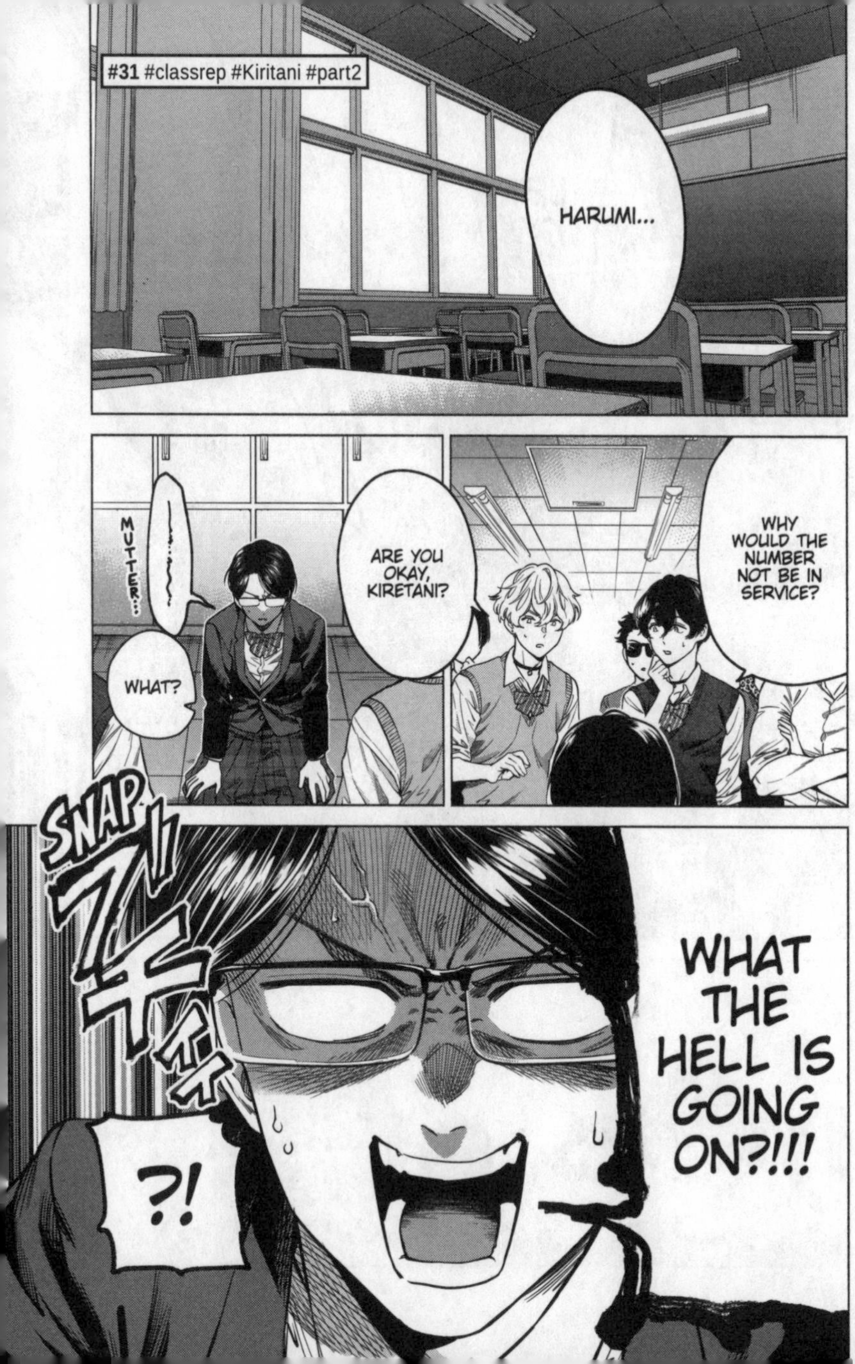
#31 #classrep #Kiritani #part2
HARUMI...
WHY WOULD THE NUMBER NOT BE IN SERVICE?
ARE YOU OKAY, KIRETANI?
MUTTER...
WHAT?
WHAT THE HELL IS GOING ON?!!!
SNAP
?!

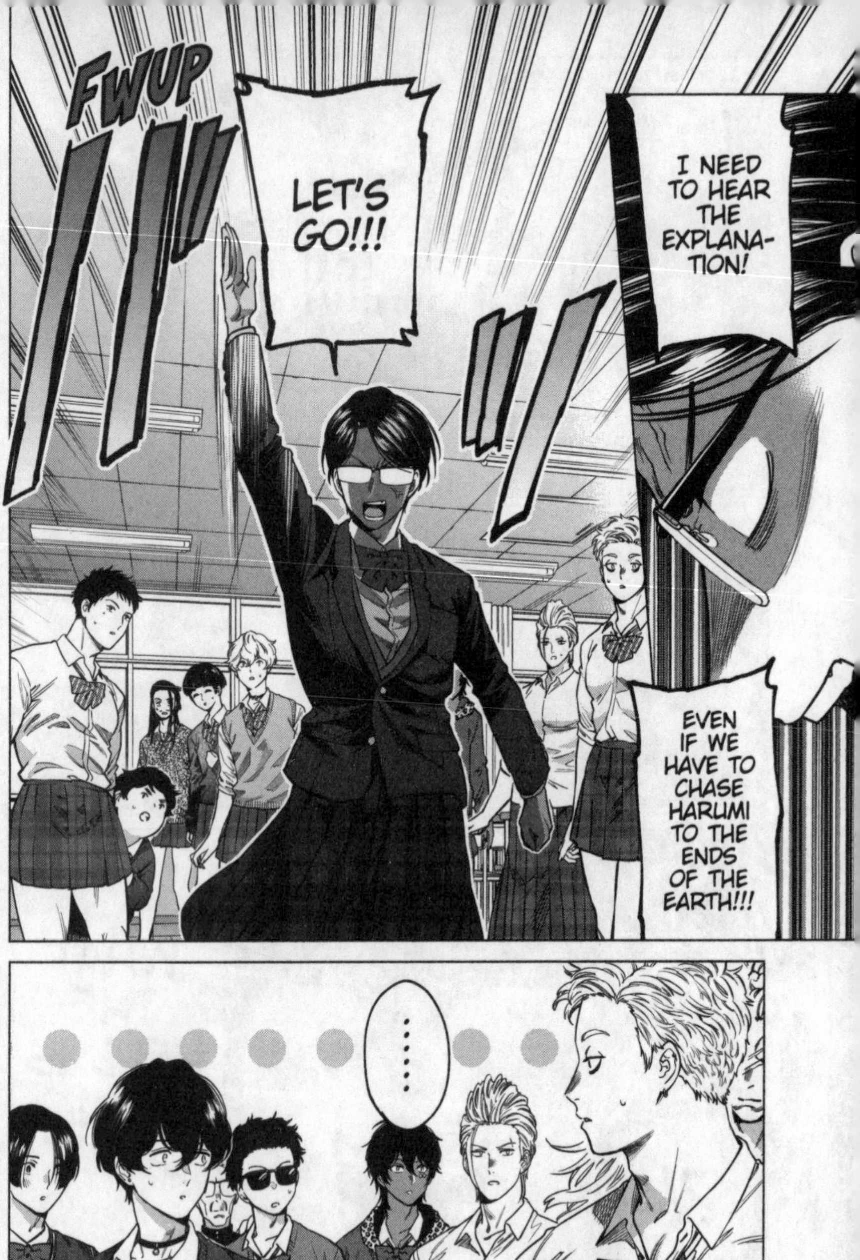
I NEED TO HEAR THE EXPLANATION!
EVEN IF WE HAVE TO CHASE HARUMI TO THE ENDS OF THE EARTH!!!
LET'S GO!!!
FWUP
......

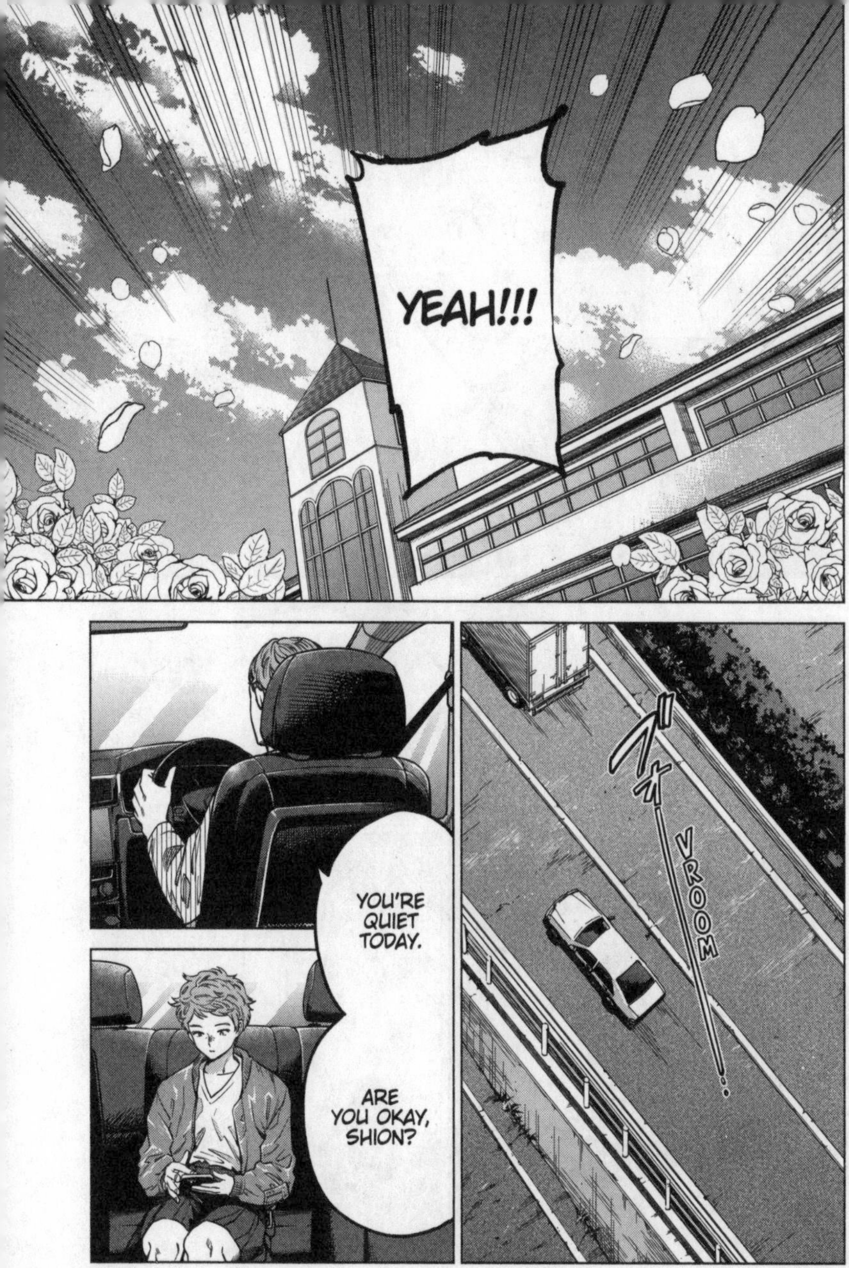
YEAH!!!
VROOM
YOU'RE QUIET TODAY.
ARE YOU OKAY, SHION?

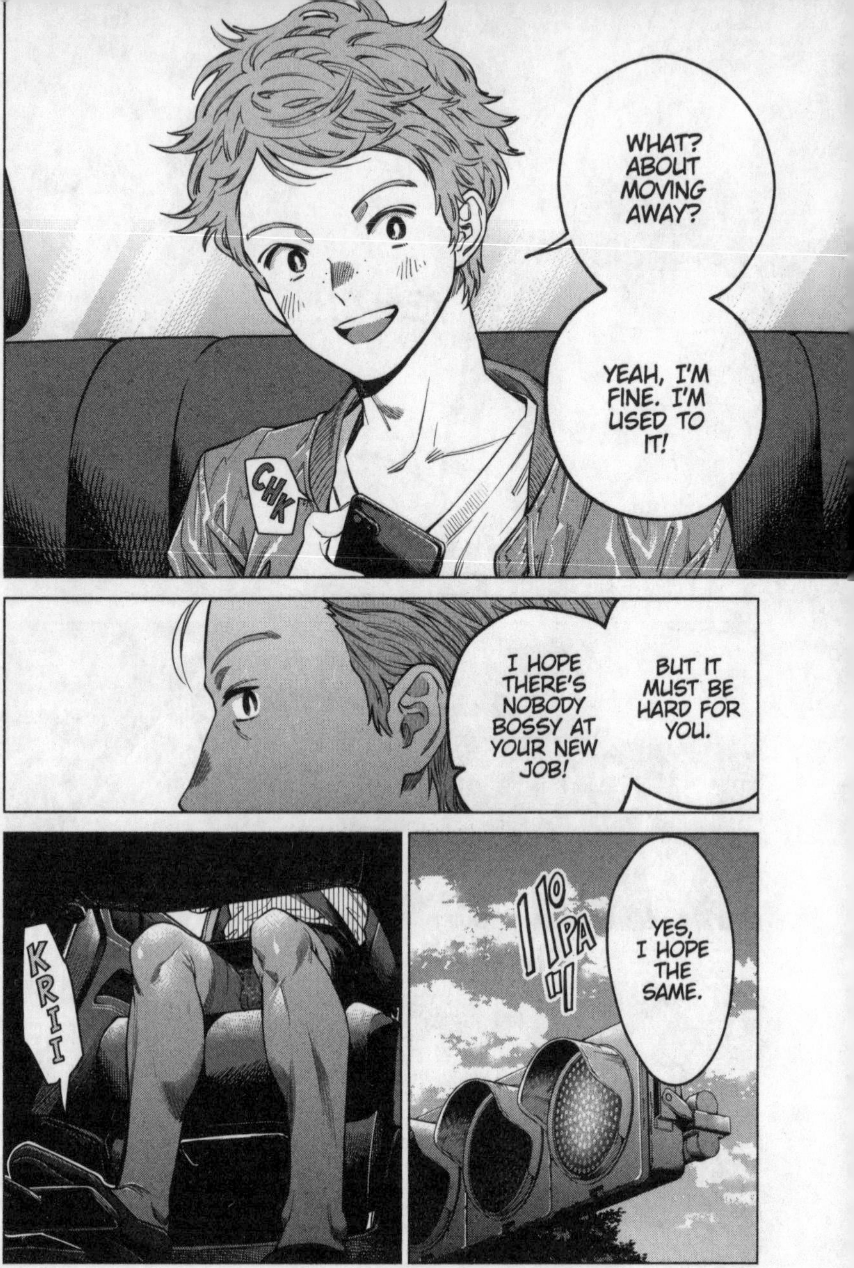
WHAT? ABOUT MOVING AWAY?
YEAH, I'M FINE. I'M USED TO IT!
CHK
BUT IT MUST BE HARD FOR YOU.
I HOPE THERE'S NOBODY BOSSY AT YOUR NEW JOB!
PA
YES, I HOPE THE SAME.
KRIII

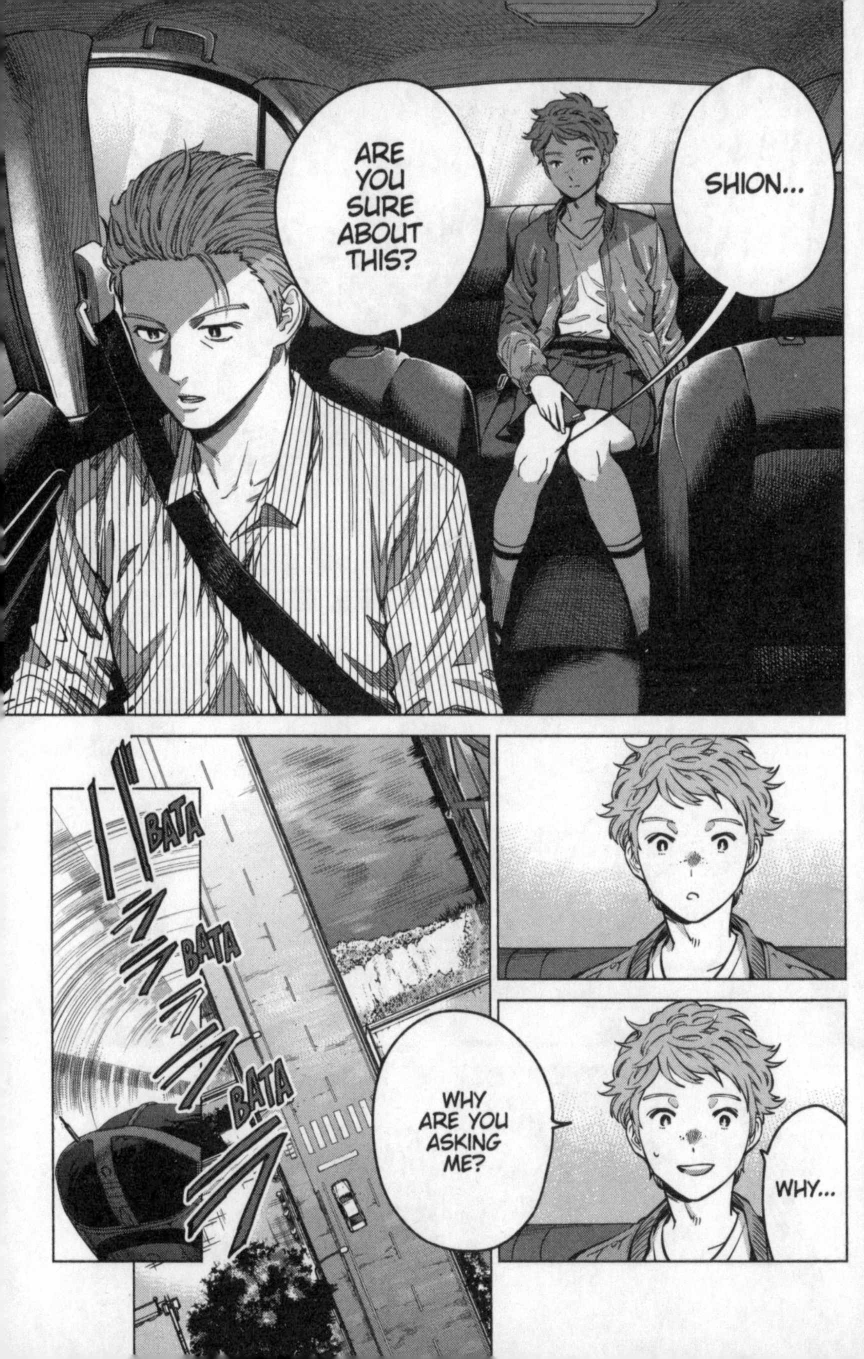
SHION...
ARE YOU SURE ABOUT THIS?
WHY...
WHY ARE YOU ASKING ME?
BATA
BATA
BATA

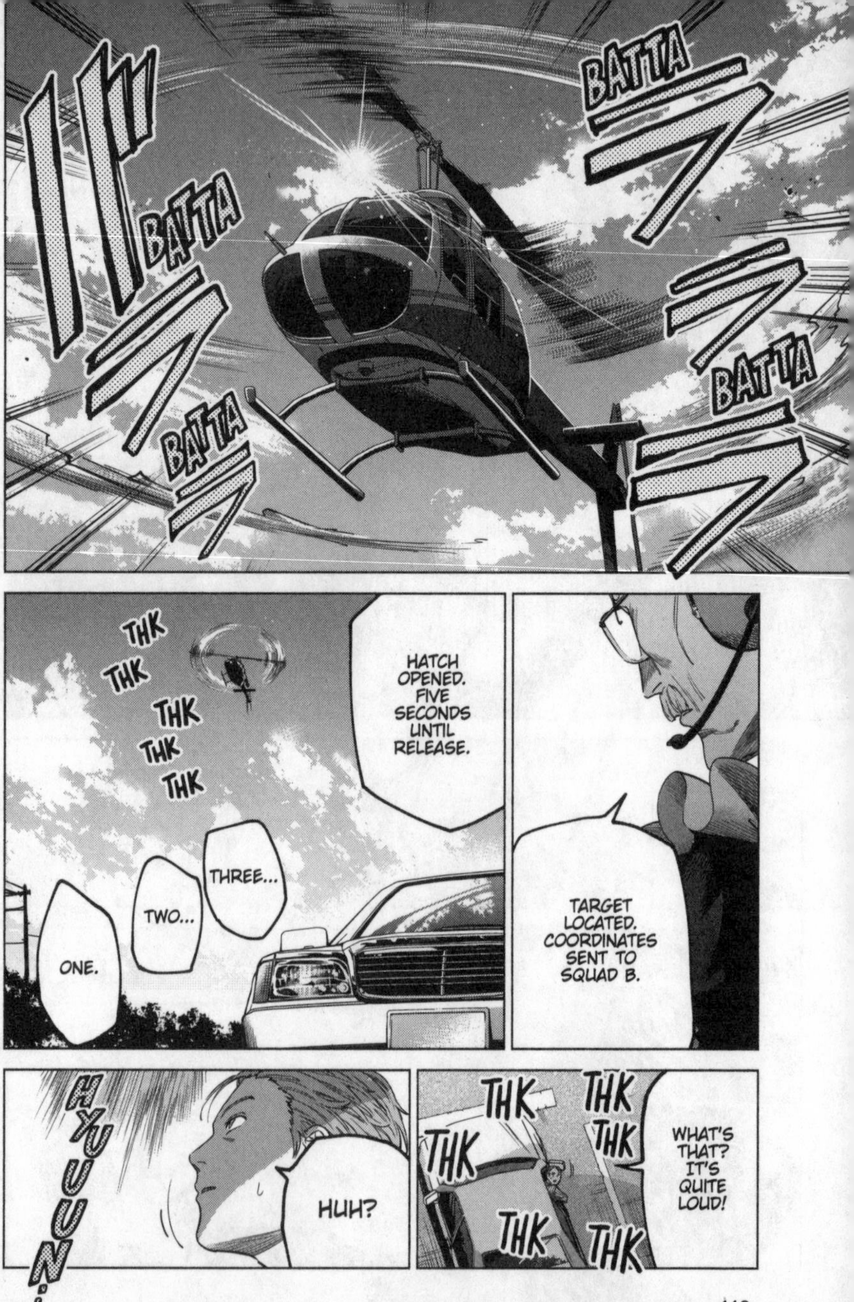

BATTA
BATTA
BATTA
BATTA
TARGET LOCATED. COORDINATES SENT TO SQUAD B.
HATCH OPENED. FIVE SECONDS UNTIL RELEASE.
THK THK THK THK THK
THREE...
TWO...
ONE.
THK THK THK THK THK THK
WHAT'S THAT? IT'S QUITE LOUD!
HUH?
HYUUUN...

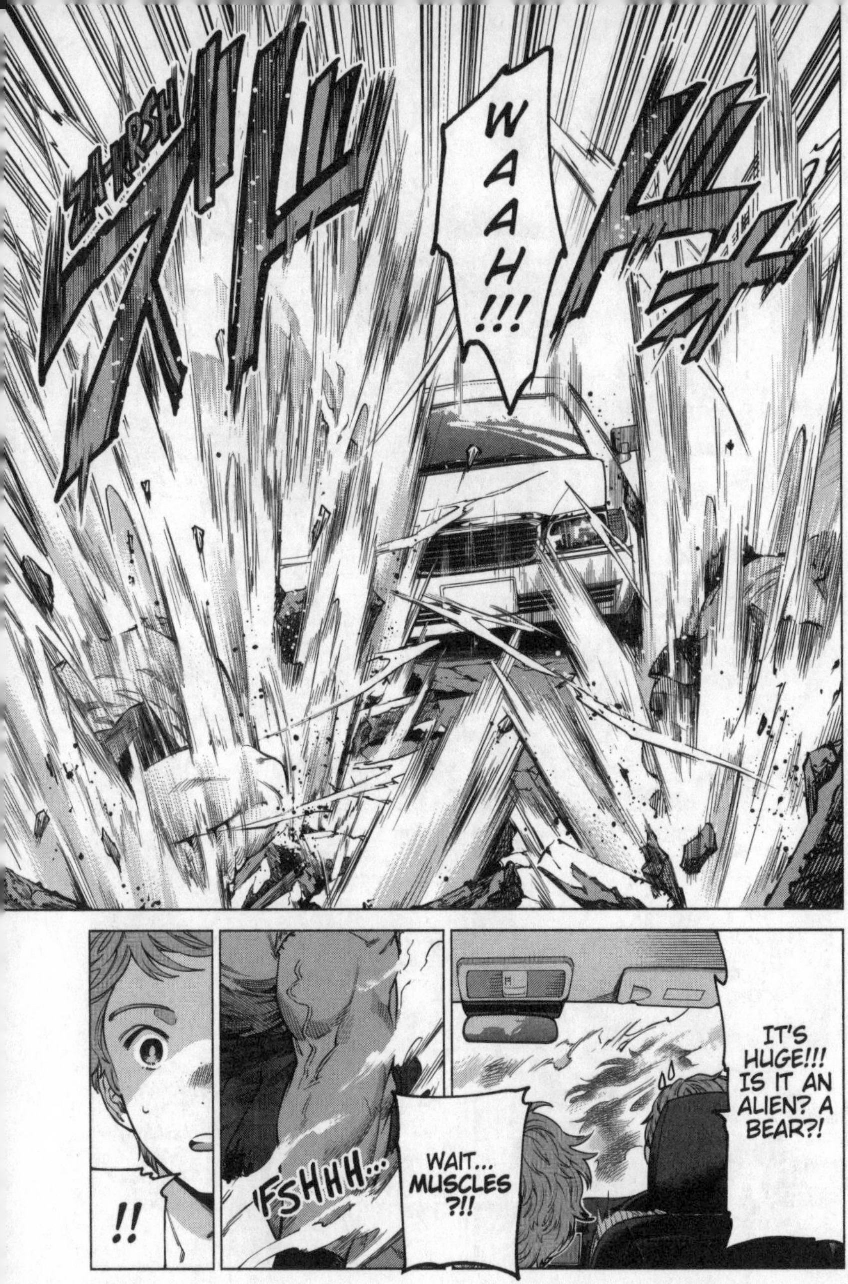
WAAH!!!
ZA-RRSH
IT'S HUGE!!! IS IT AN ALIEN? A BEAR?!
WAIT... MUSCLES?!!
FSHHH...
!!

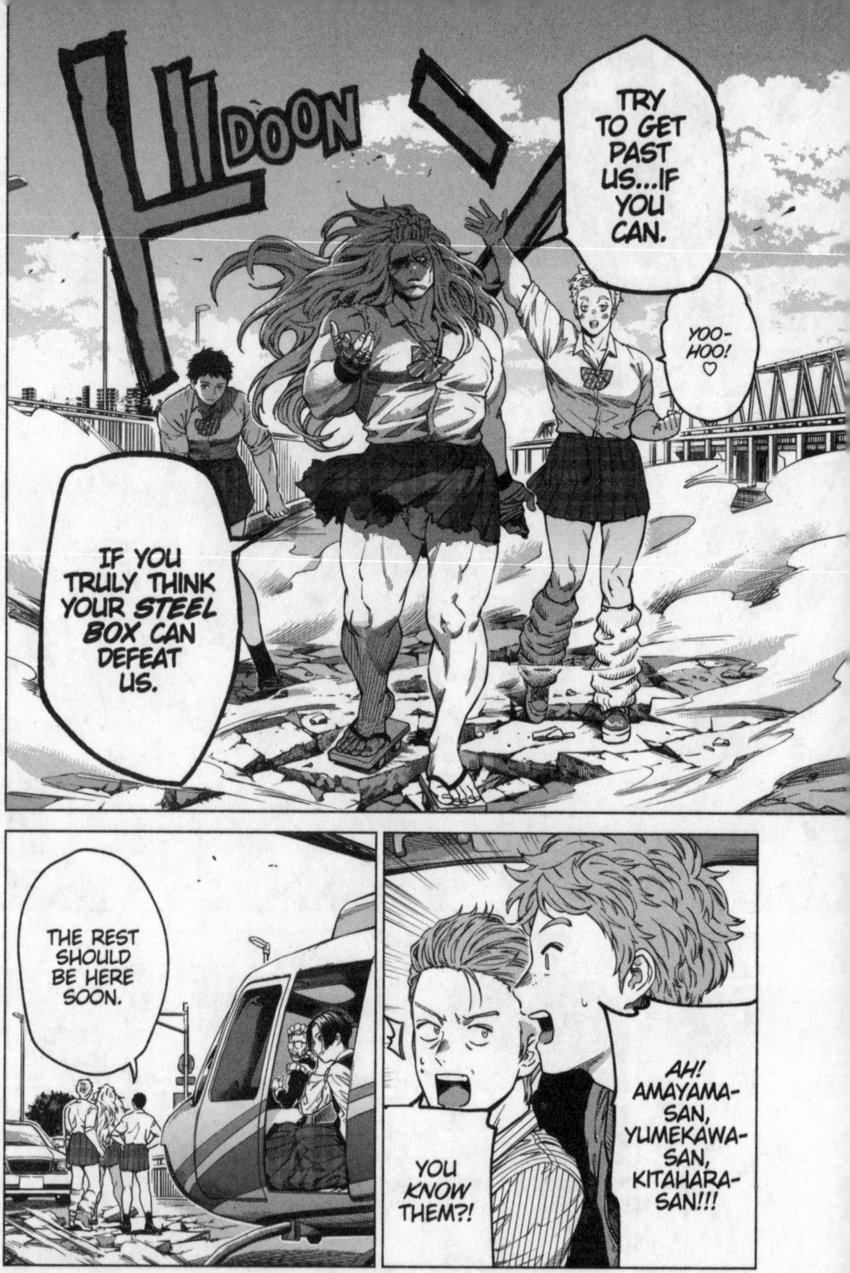
TRY TO GET PAST US...IF YOU CAN.
DOON
YOO-HOO! ♡
IF YOU TRULY THINK YOUR STEEL BOX CAN DEFEAT US.
AH! AMAYAMA-SAN, YUMEKAWA-SAN, KITAHARA-SAN!!!
YOU KNOW THEM?!
THE REST SHOULD BE HERE SOON.

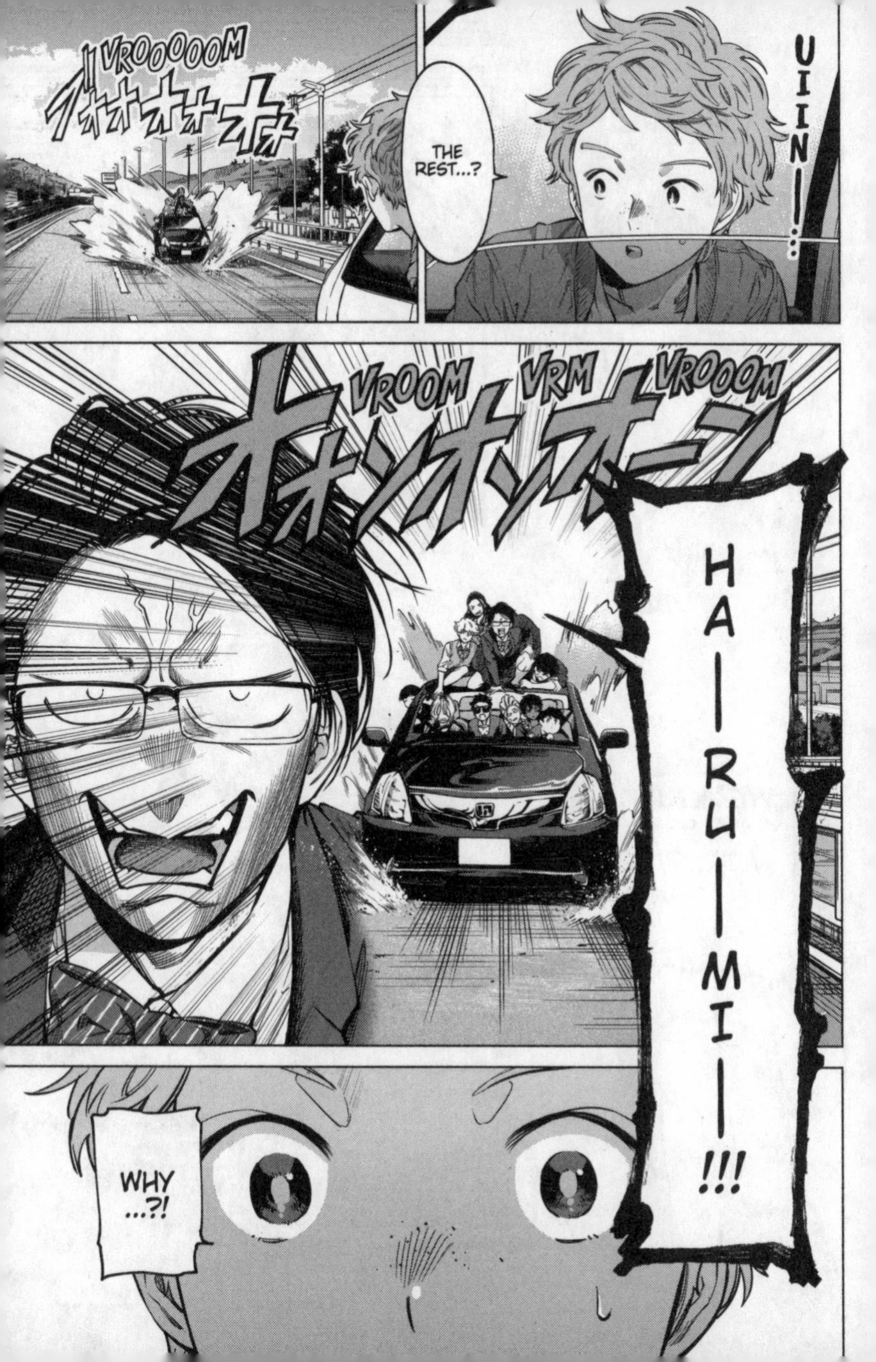
UIIN—!..
THE REST...?
VROOOOOM
VROOM VRM VROOOM
HA—RU——MI——!!!
WHY ...?!

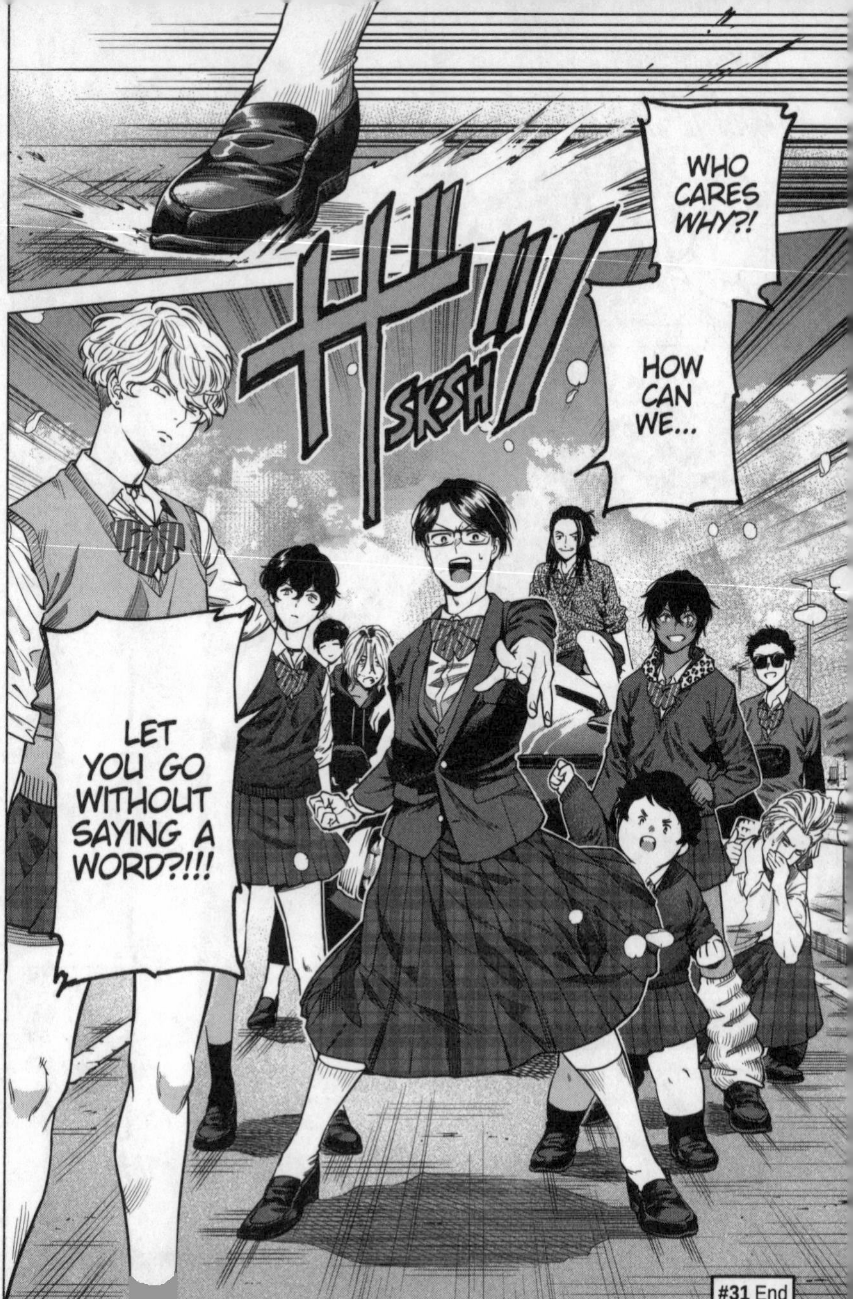
SKSH
WHO CARES WHY?!
HOW CAN WE...
LET YOU GO WITHOUT SAYING A WORD?!!!
#31 End

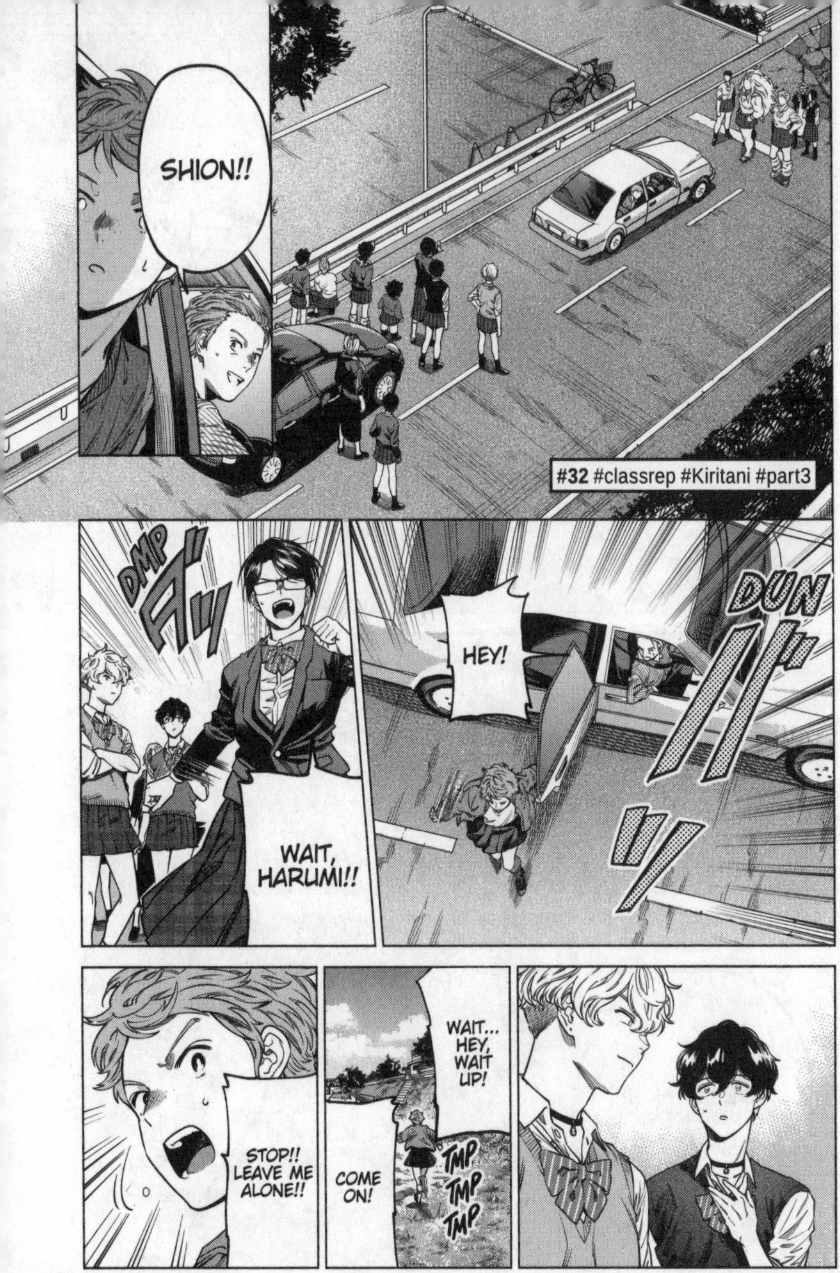
#32 #classrep #Kiritani #part3
SHION!!
DUN
HEY!
DMP
WAIT, HARUMI!!
WAIT... HEY, WAIT UP!
COME ON!
TMP TMP TMP
STOP!! LEAVE ME ALONE!!

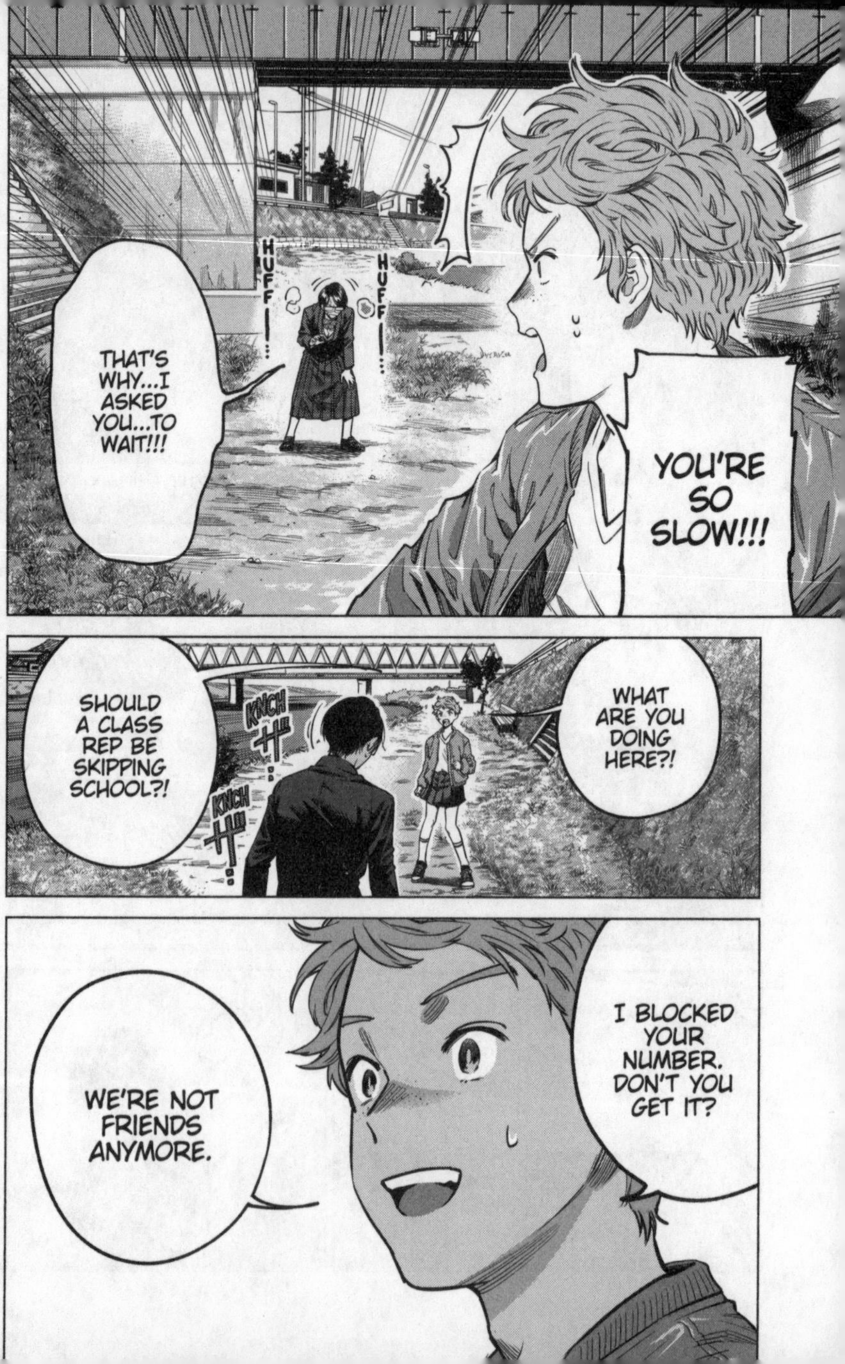
YOU'RE SO SLOW!!!
HUFF...!!
HUFF...!!
THAT'S WHY...I ASKED YOU...TO WAIT!!!
WHAT ARE YOU DOING HERE?!
KNCH!!
KNCH!!
SHOULD A CLASS REP BE SKIPPING SCHOOL?!
I BLOCKED YOUR NUMBER. DON'T YOU GET IT?
WE'RE NOT FRIENDS ANYMORE.

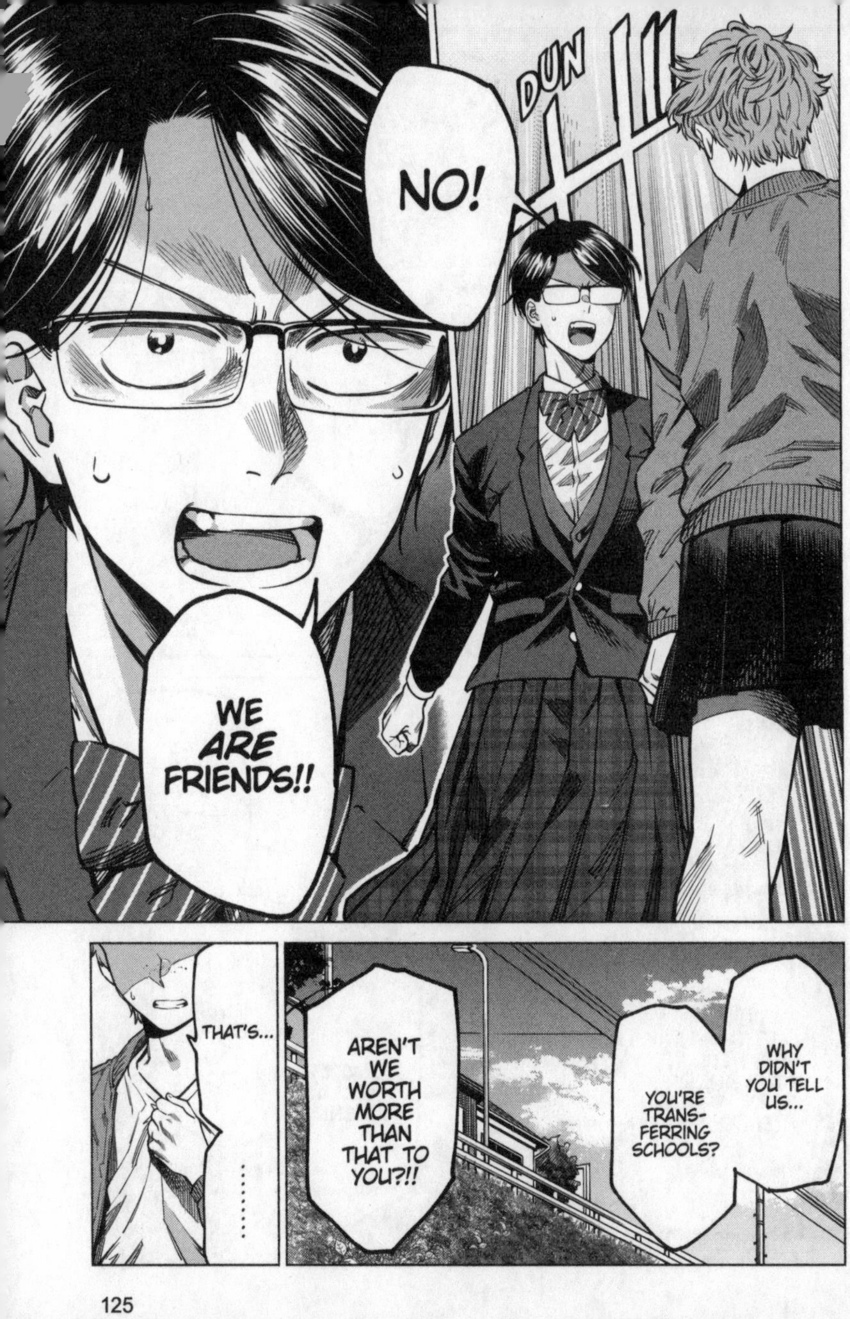
DUN
NO!
WE ARE FRIENDS!!
WHY DIDN'T YOU TELL US...
YOU'RE TRANS-FERRING SCHOOLS?
AREN'T WE WORTH MORE THAN THAT TO YOU?!!
THAT'S...
......

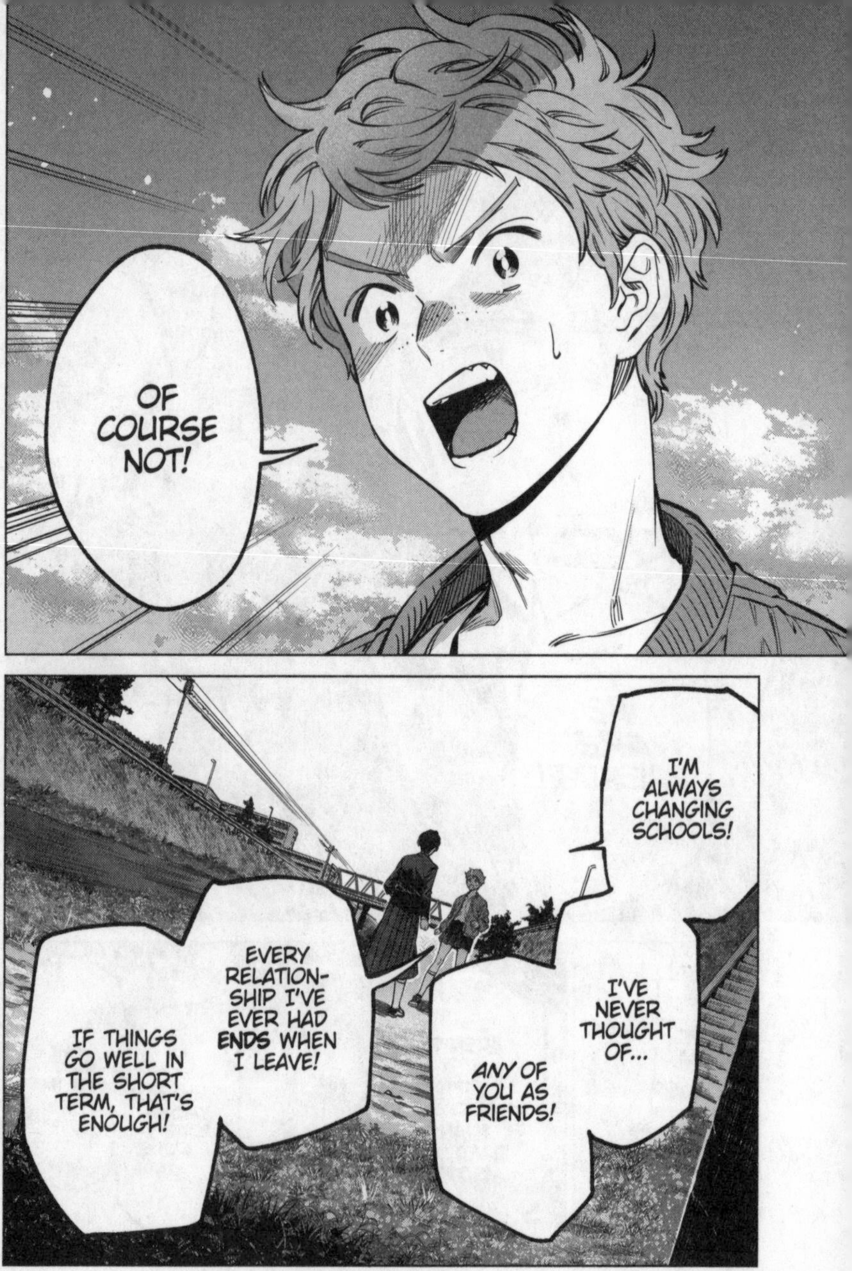
OF COURSE NOT!
I'M ALWAYS CHANGING SCHOOLS!
I'VE NEVER THOUGHT OF...
ANY OF YOU AS FRIENDS!
EVERY RELATION-SHIP I'VE EVER HAD **ENDS** WHEN I LEAVE!
IF THINGS GO WELL IN THE SHORT TERM, THAT'S ENOUGH!

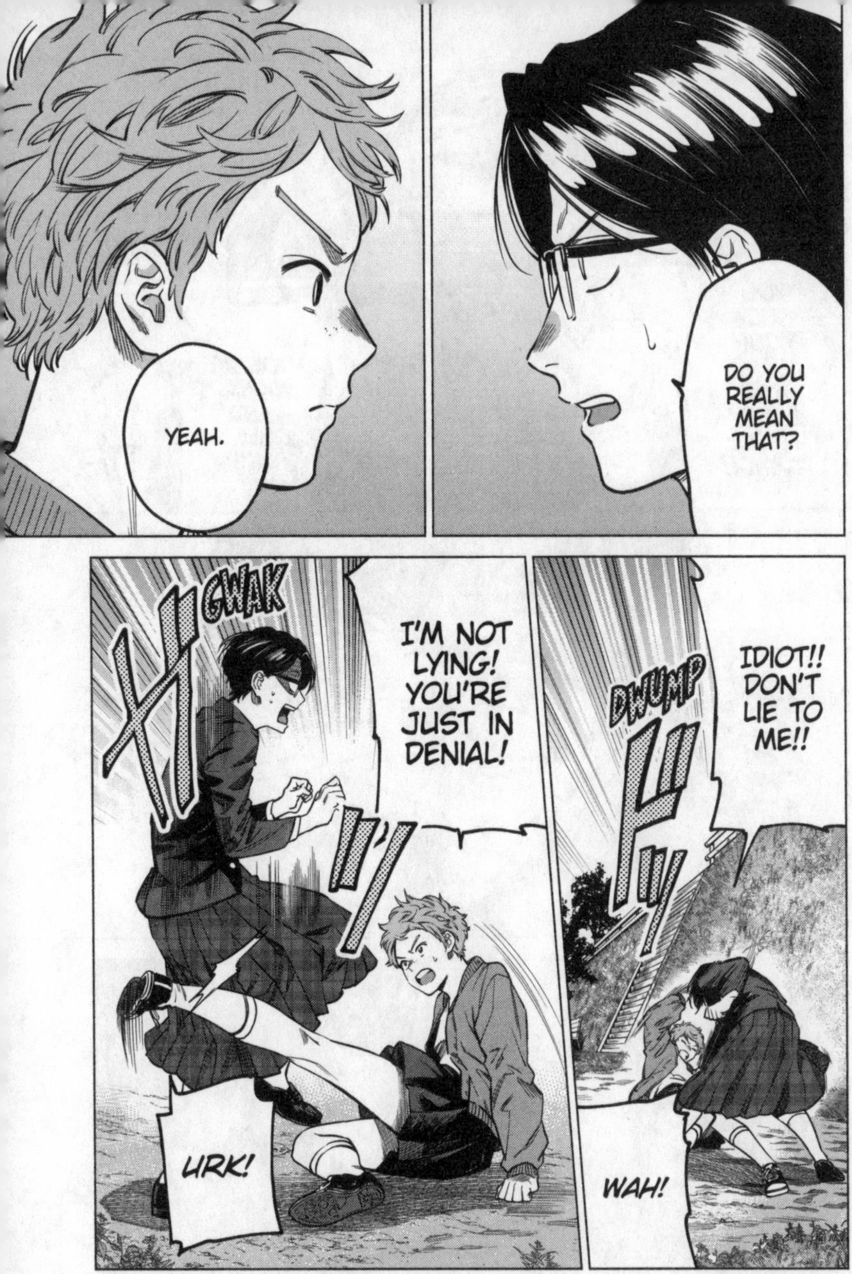
DO YOU REALLY MEAN THAT?
YEAH.
IDIOT!! DON'T LIE TO ME!!
DWUMP
WAH!
I'M NOT LYING! YOU'RE JUST IN DENIAL!
GWAK
URK!

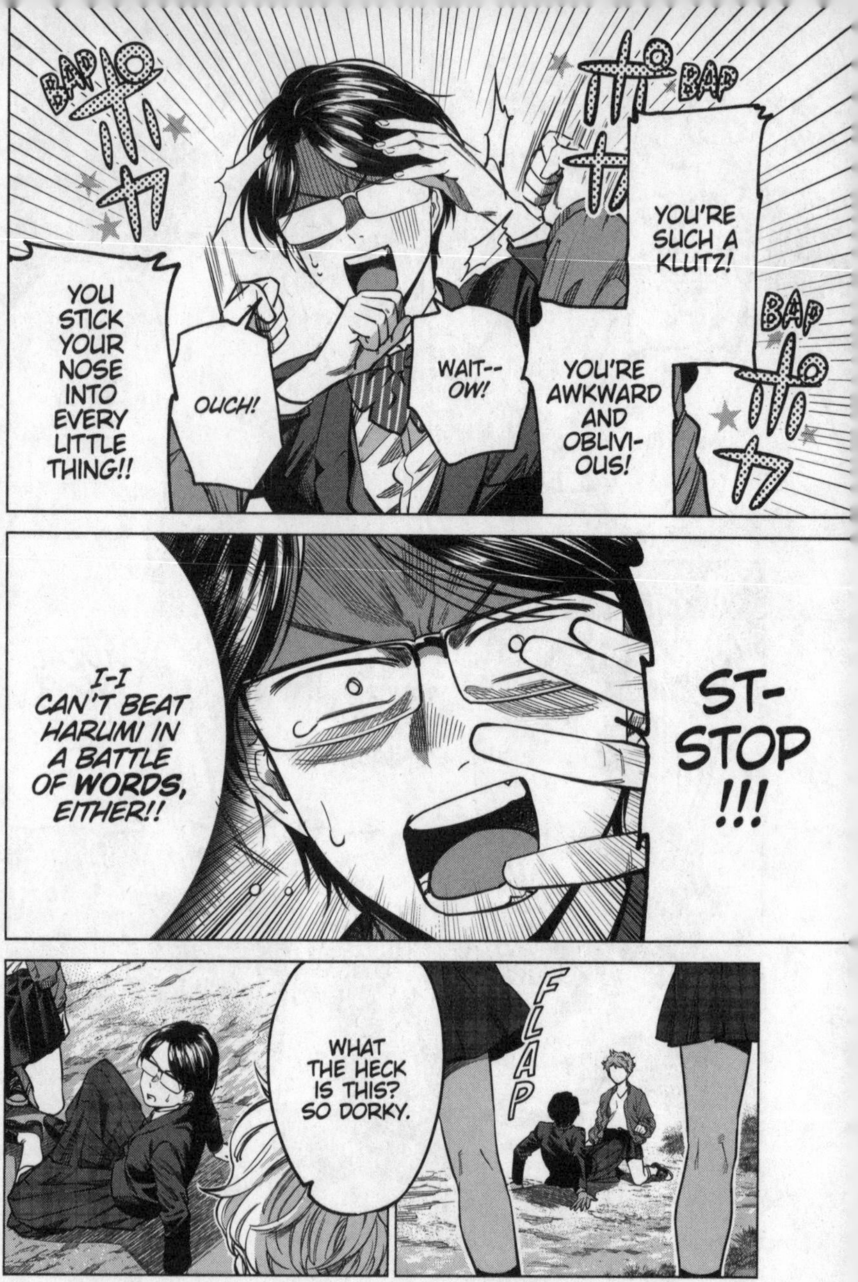
BAP
YOU'RE SUCH A KLUTZ!
BAP
YOU'RE AWKWARD AND OBLIVI-OUS!
WAIT-- OW!
OUCH!
BAP
YOU STICK YOUR NOSE INTO EVERY LITTLE THING!!
ST-STOP!!!
I-I CAN'T BEAT HARUMI IN A BATTLE OF WORDS, EITHER!!
FLAP
WHAT THE HECK IS THIS? SO DORKY.

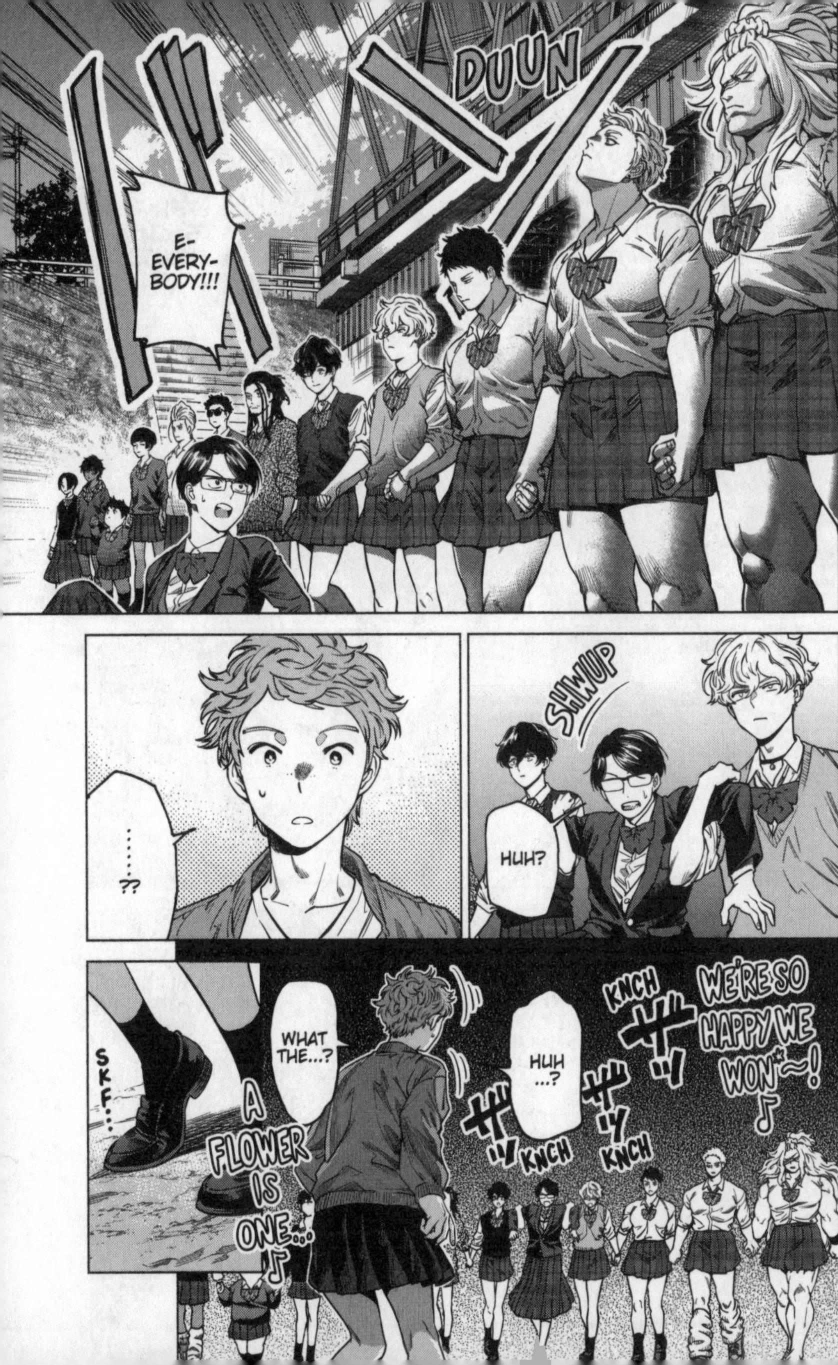
DUUN
E-EVERYBODY!!!
SHWUP
HUH?
......??
WE'RE SO HAPPY WE WON*~! ♪
KNCH
KNCH
KNCH
HUH...?
WHAT THE...?
A FLOWER IS ONE... ♪
SKF...

*This is a chant from the children's game "Hana Ichi Monme"/"A Flower Is One Monme" (a monme is an Edo-period coin). In the game, two teams line up and chant back and forth, pretending to charge and kick the other team. Then each team picks a player from the opposite team, and they play rock-paper-scissors to win the other team's player.

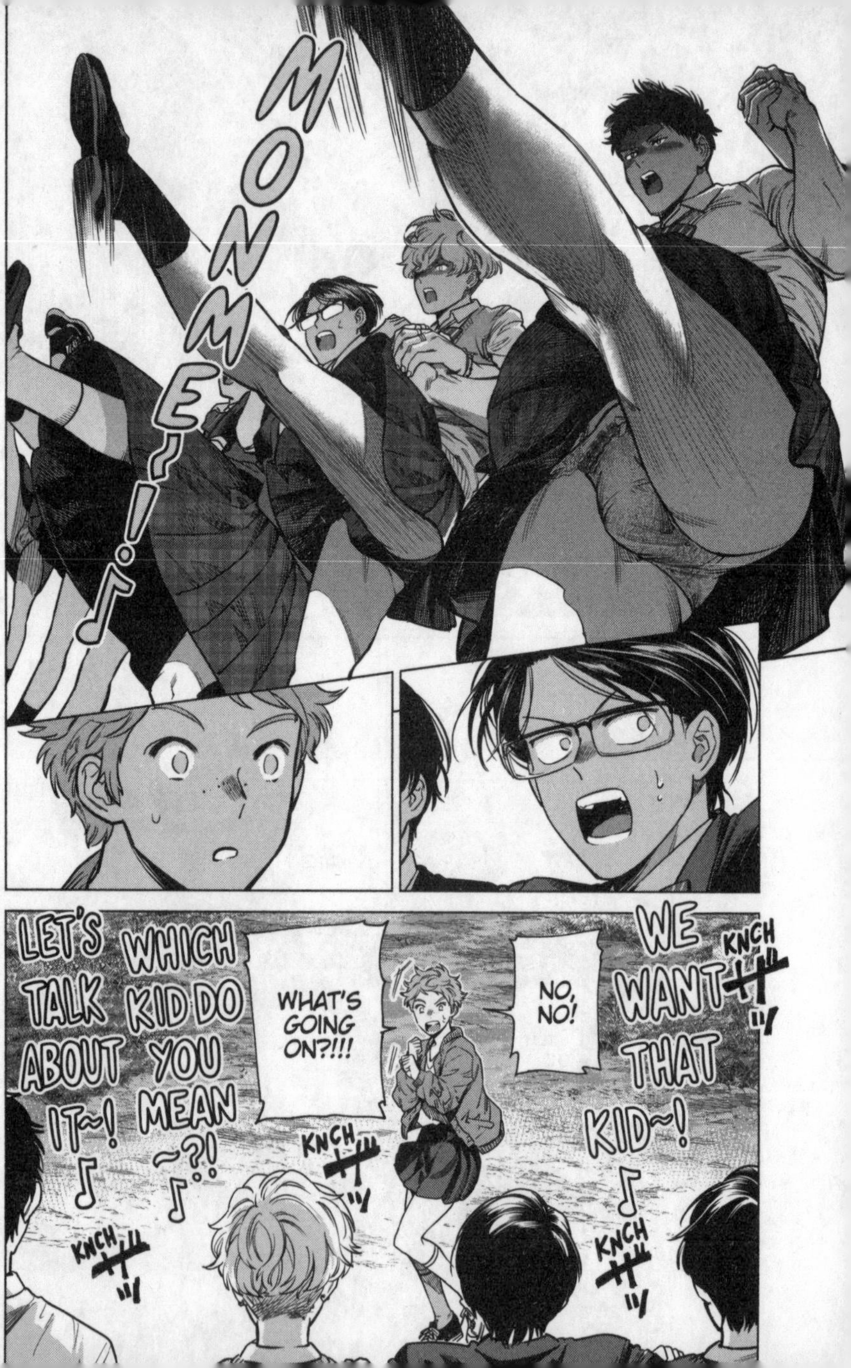
MONME~!♪
WE WANT THAT KID~! ♪
KNCH
NO, NO!
WHAT'S GOING ON?!!!!
KNCH
WHICH KID DO YOU MEAN ~?! ♪
LET'S TALK ABOUT IT~! ♪
KNCH
KNCH

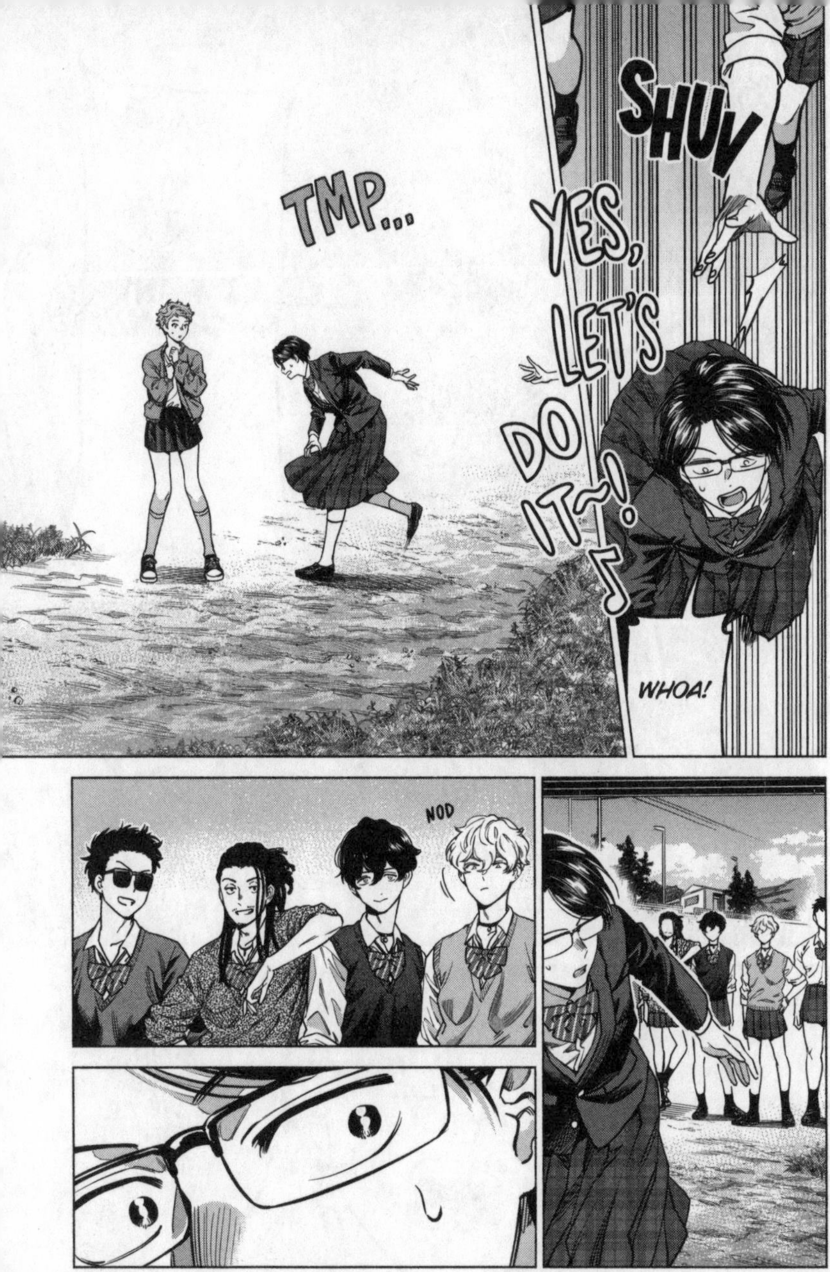
SHUV
YES, LET'S DO IT~! ♪
WHOA!
TMP...
NOD

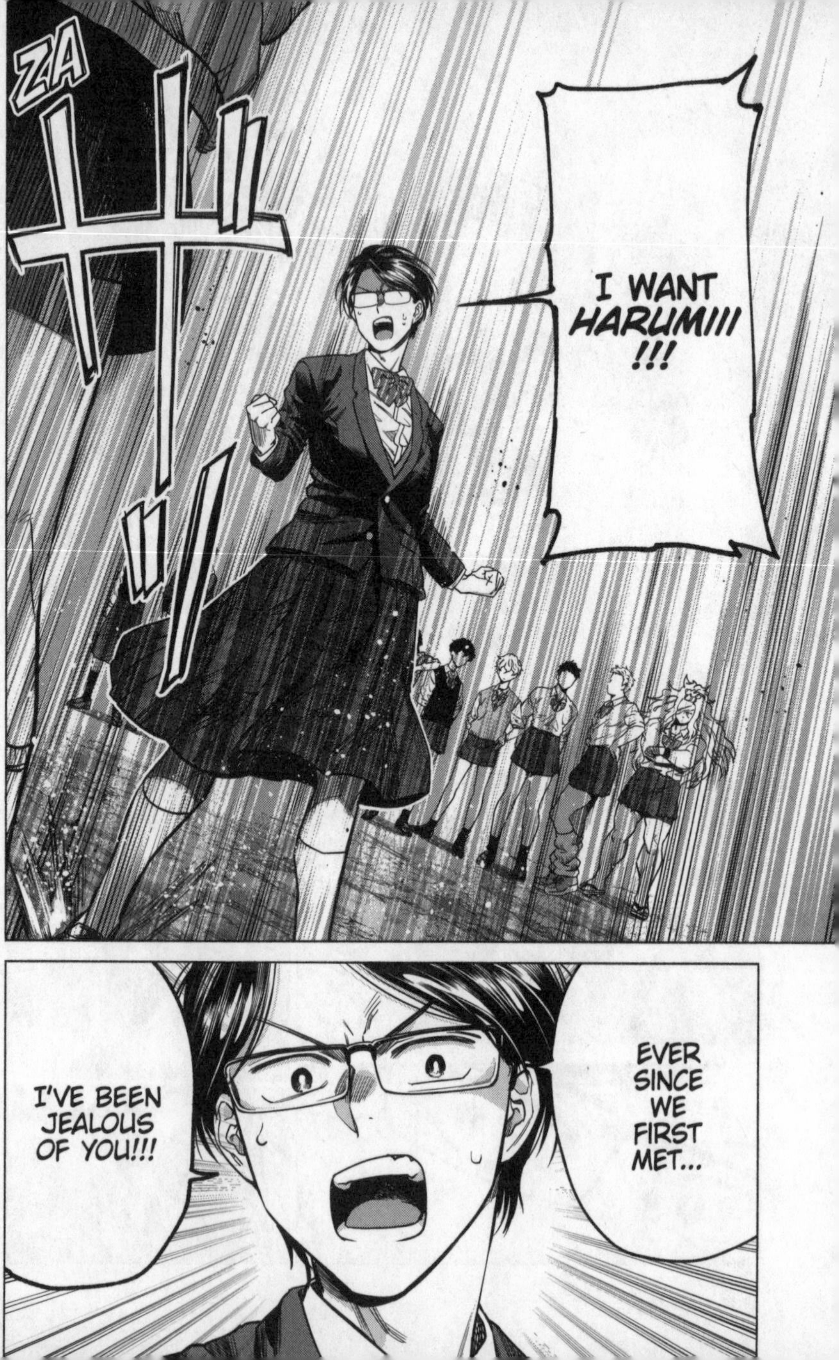
I WANT HARUMIIII !!!
ZA
EVER SINCE WE FIRST MET...
I'VE BEEN JEALOUS OF YOU!!!

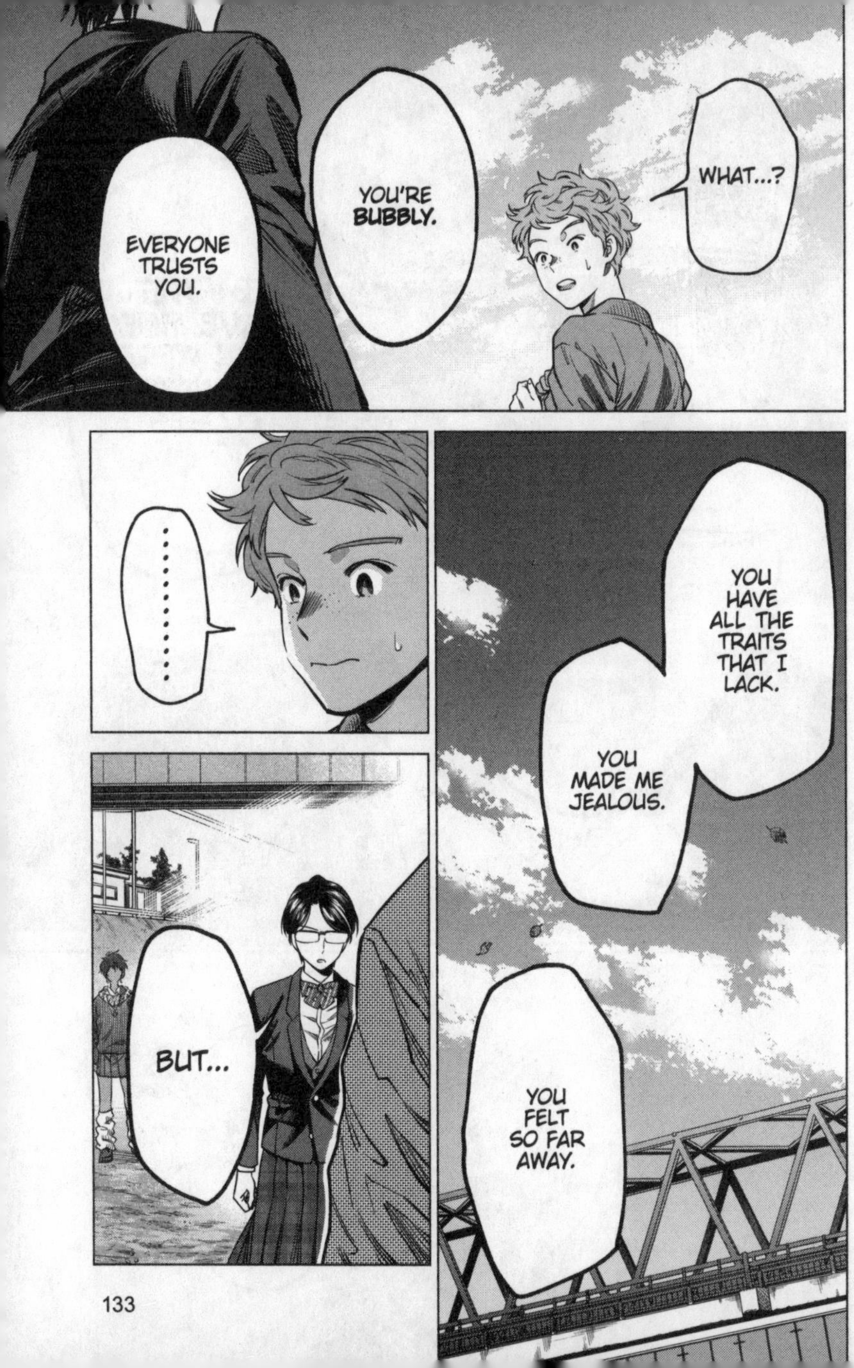
WHAT...?
YOU'RE BUBBLY.
EVERYONE TRUSTS YOU.
YOU HAVE ALL THE TRAITS THAT I LACK.
YOU MADE ME JEALOUS.
YOU FELT SO FAR AWAY.
......
BUT...

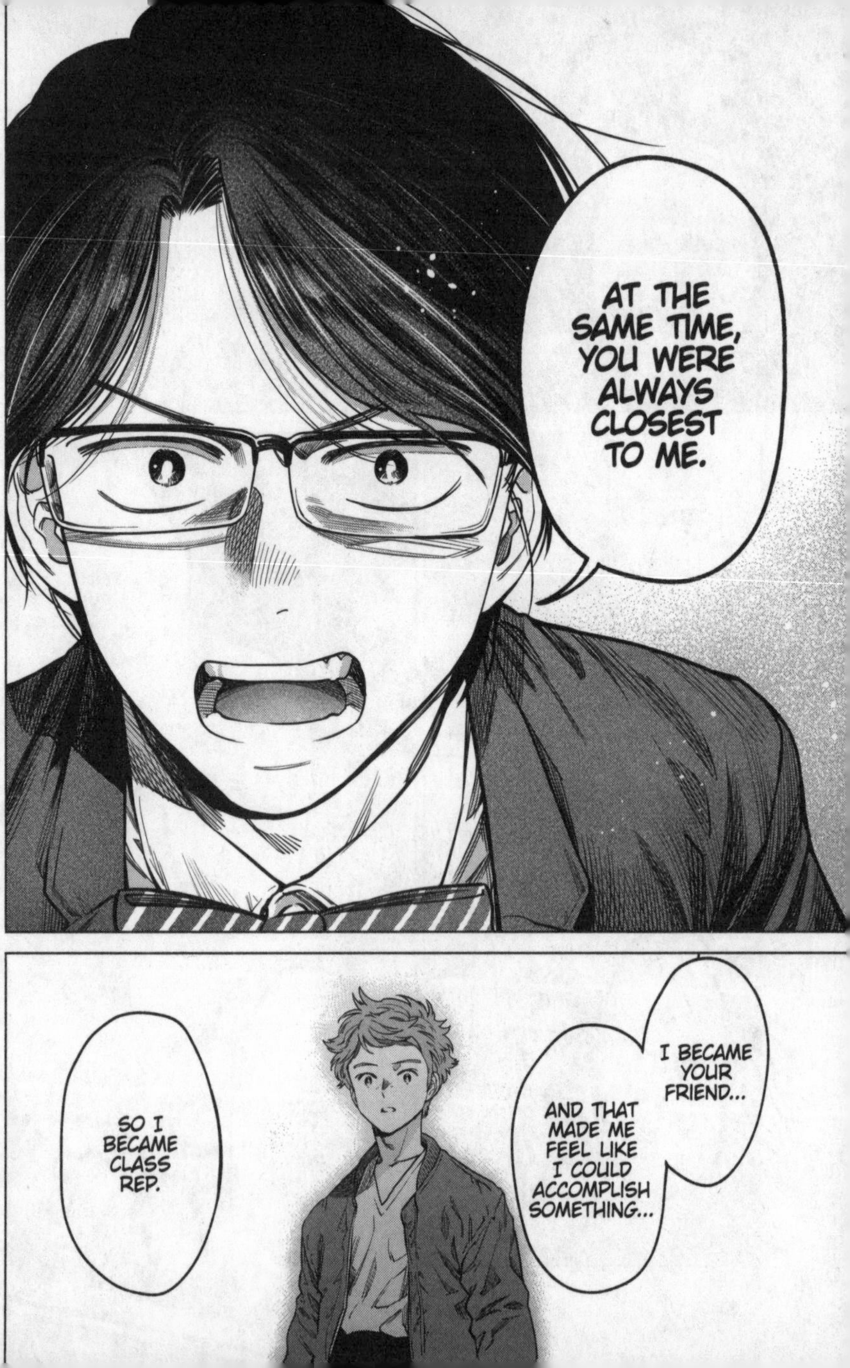
AT THE SAME TIME, YOU WERE ALWAYS CLOSEST TO ME.
I BECAME YOUR FRIEND...
AND THAT MADE ME FEEL LIKE I COULD ACCOMPLISH SOMETHING...
SO I BECAME CLASS REP.

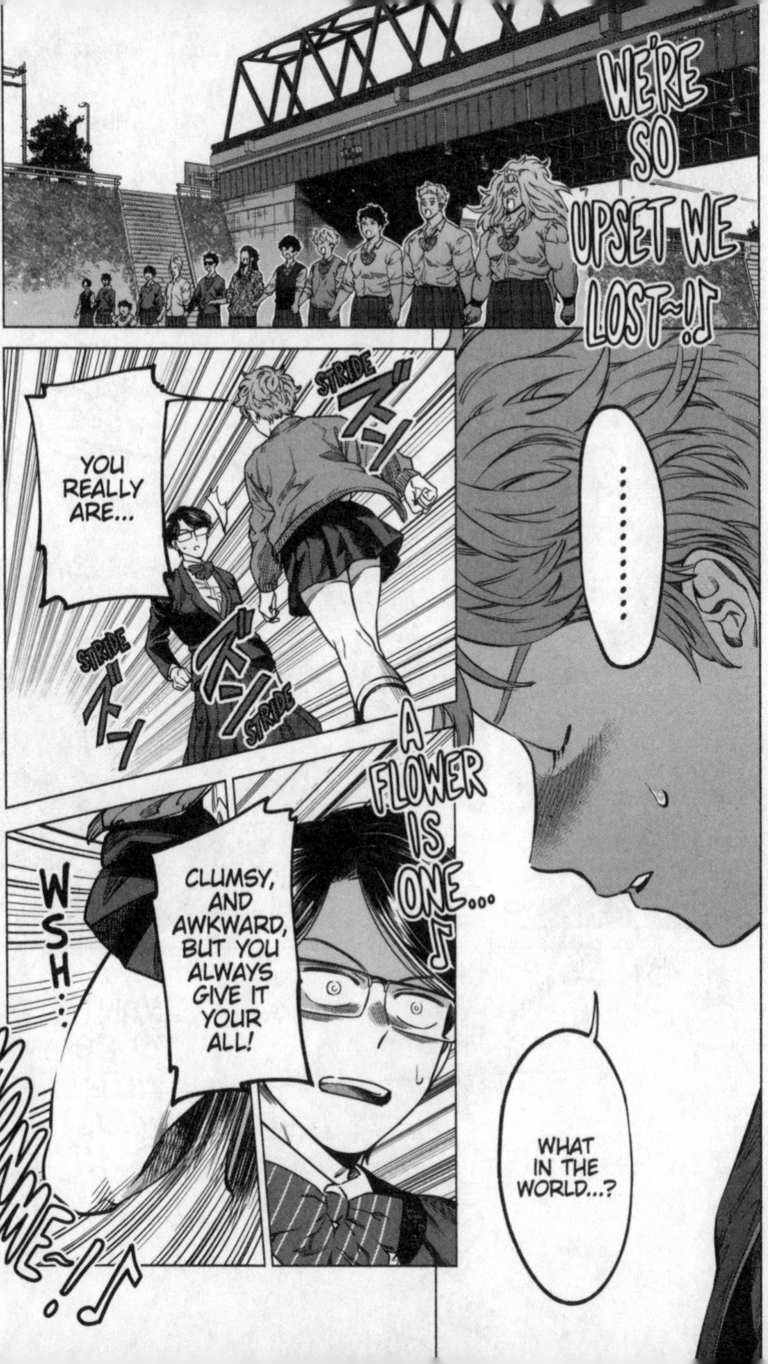
WE'RE SO UPSET WE LOST~!♪
......
WHAT IN THE WORLD...?
STRIDE
STRIDE
STRIDE
YOU REALLY ARE...
A FLOWER IS ONE...♪
CLUMSY, AND AWKWARD, BUT YOU ALWAYS GIVE IT YOUR ALL!
WSH...
MONME~!♪

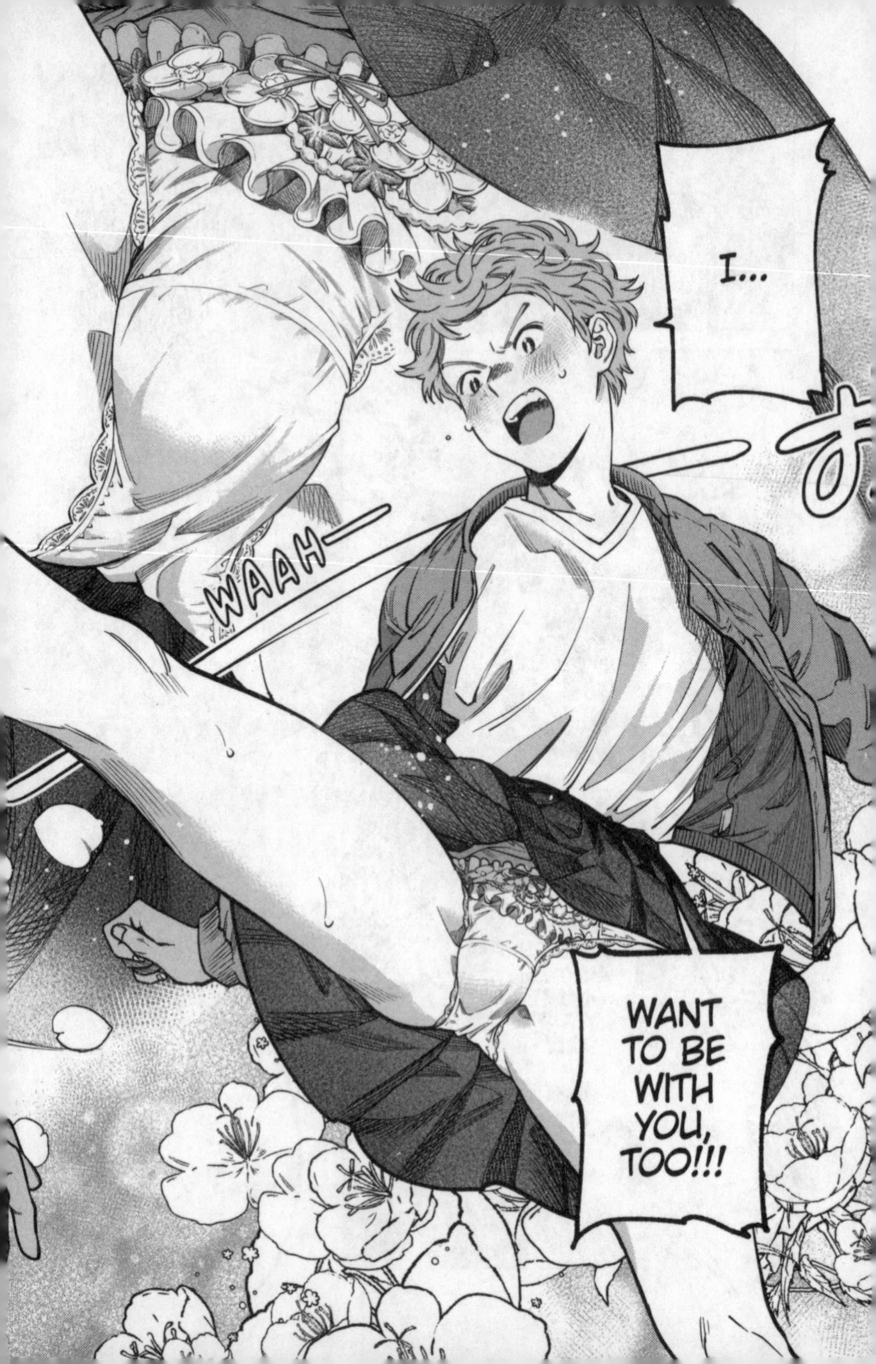
I...
お
WAAH—
WANT TO BE WITH YOU, TOO!!!

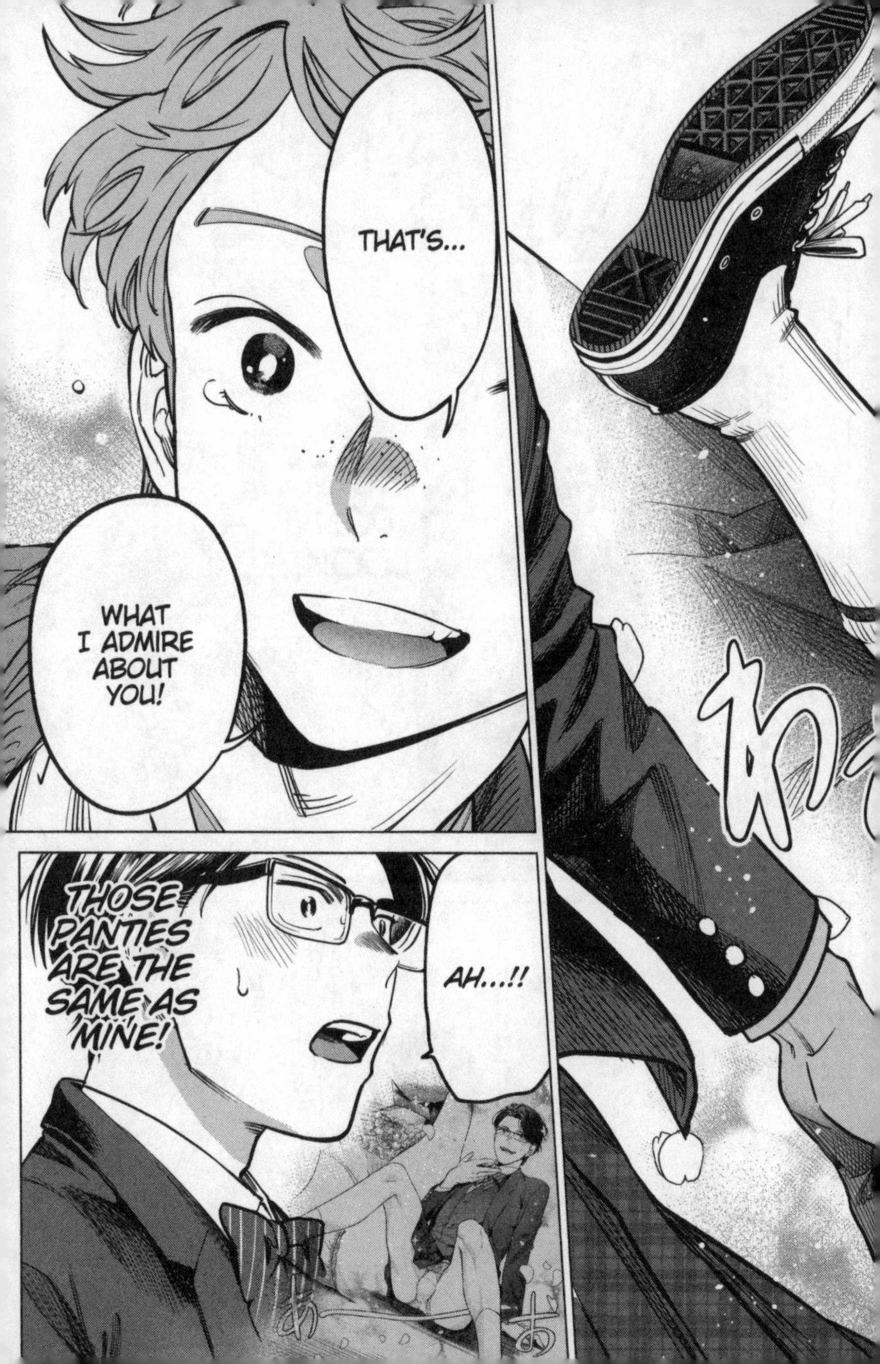
THAT'S...
WHAT I ADMIRE ABOUT YOU!
AH...!!
THOSE PANTIES ARE THE SAME AS MINE!

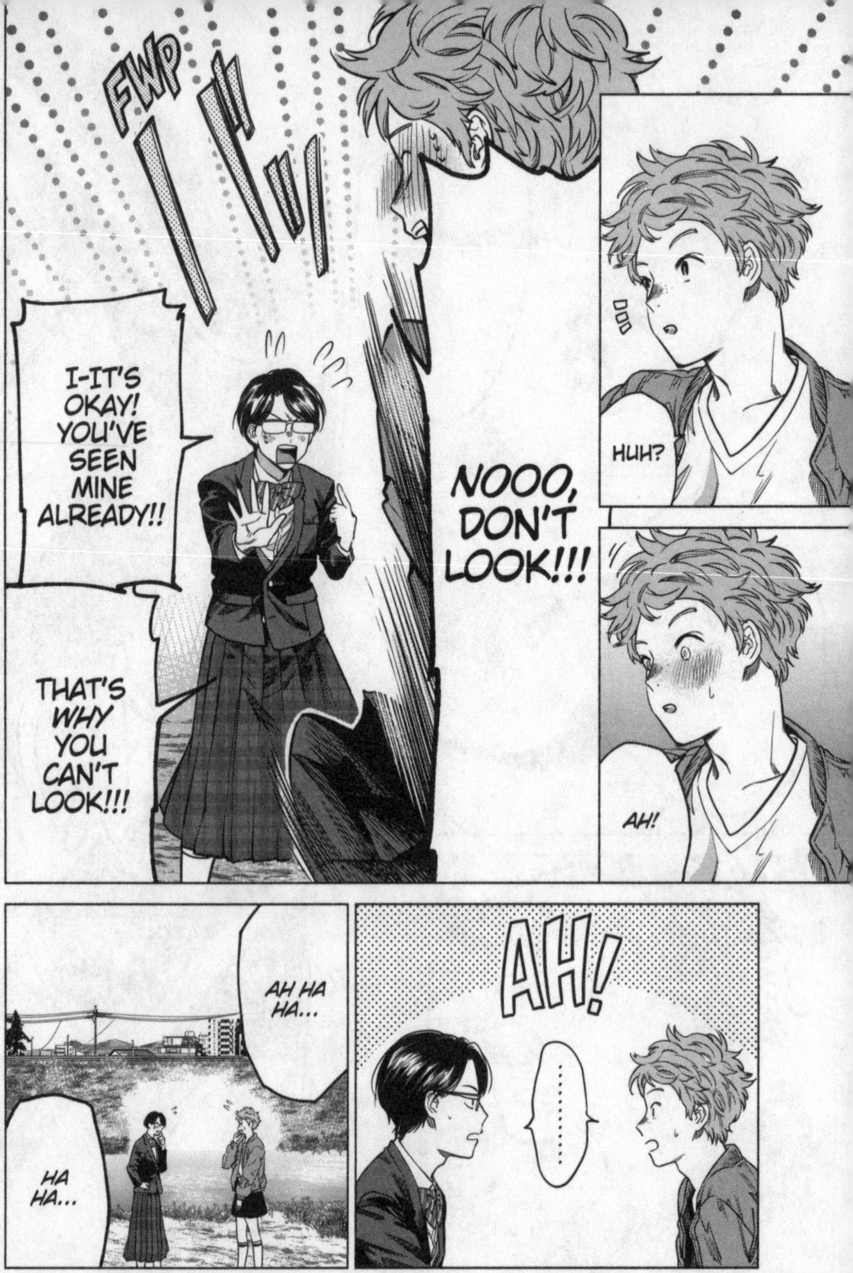
HUH?
AH!
FWP
NOOO, DON'T LOOK!!!
I-IT'S OKAY! YOU'VE SEEN MINE ALREADY!!
THAT'S WHY YOU CAN'T LOOK!!!
AH!
......
AH HA HA...
HA HA...

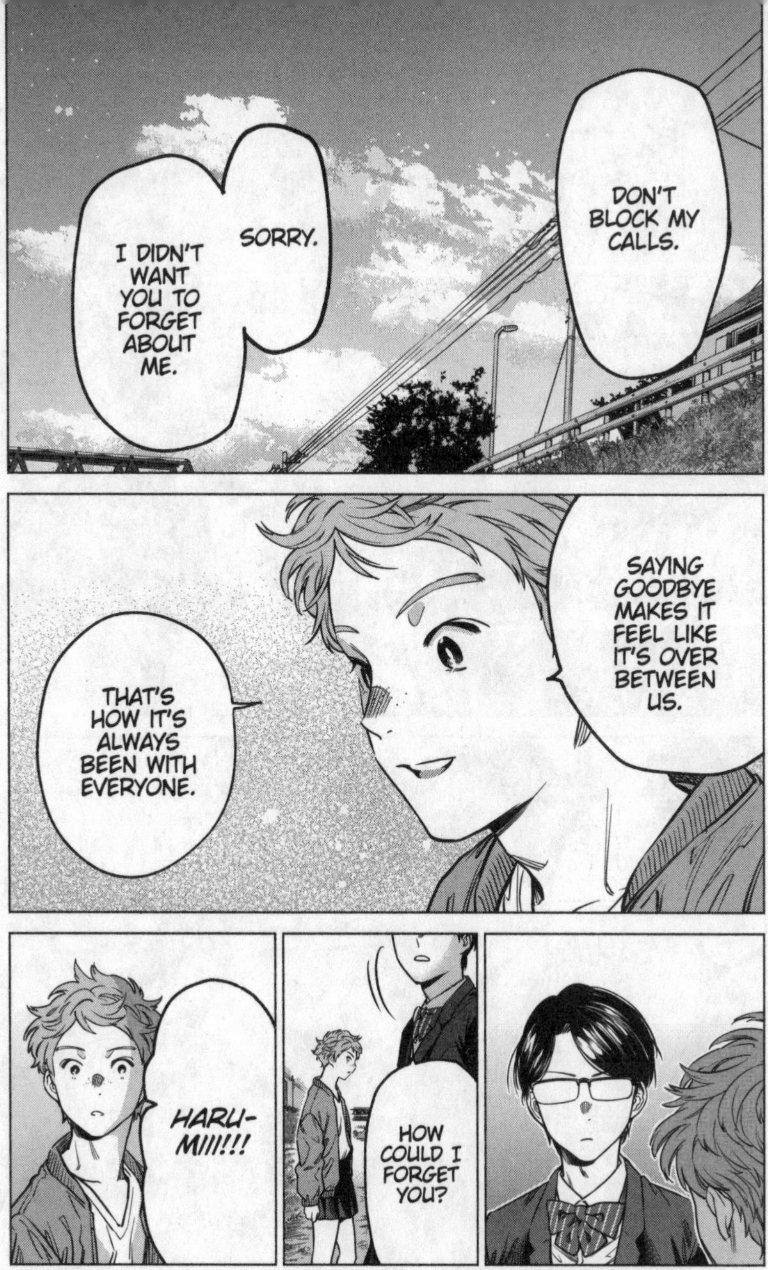
DON'T BLOCK MY CALLS.
SORRY.
I DIDN'T WANT YOU TO FORGET ABOUT ME.
SAYING GOODBYE MAKES IT FEEL LIKE IT'S OVER BETWEEN US.
THAT'S HOW IT'S ALWAYS BEEN WITH EVERYONE.
HOW COULD I FORGET YOU?
HARU-MIIII!!!

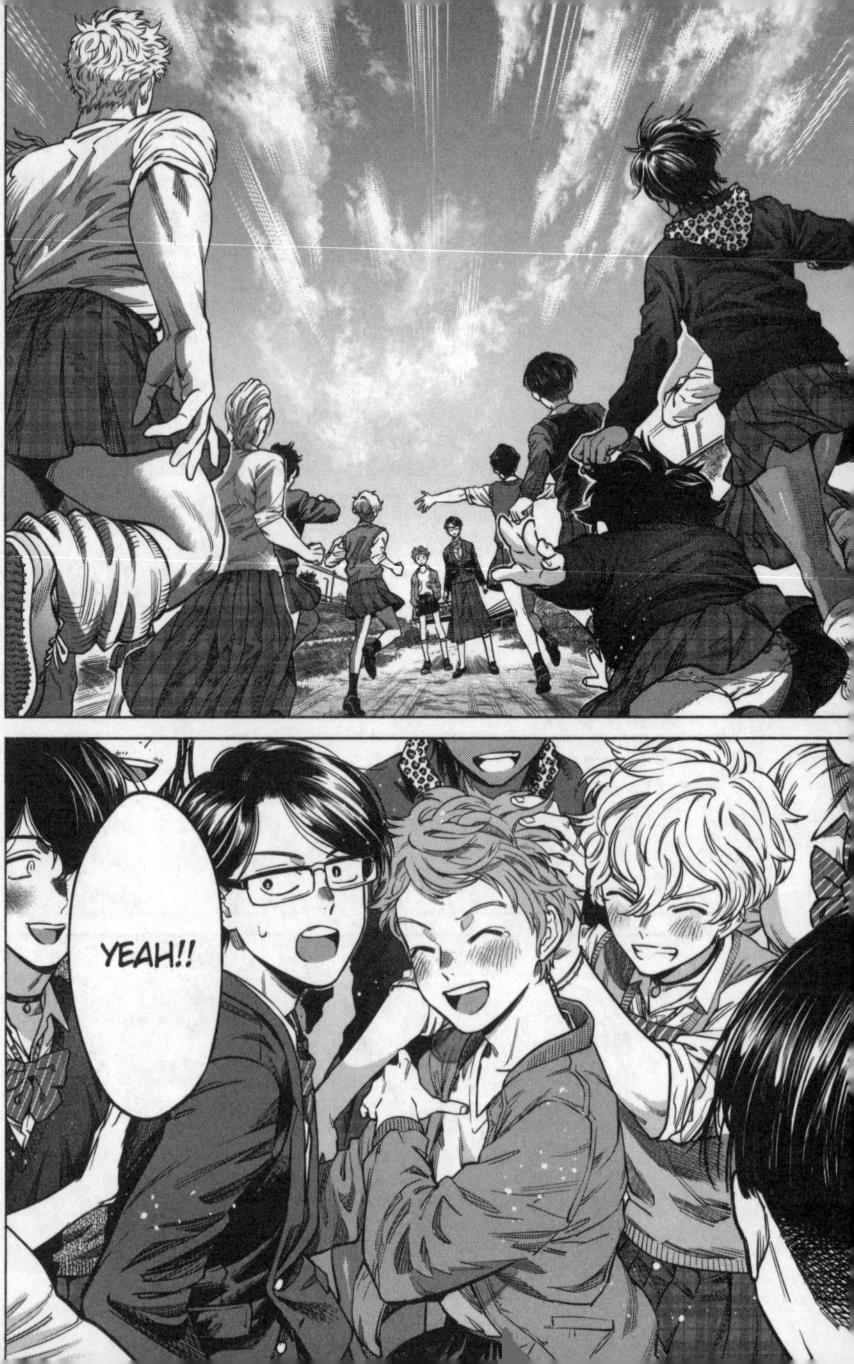
YEAH!!

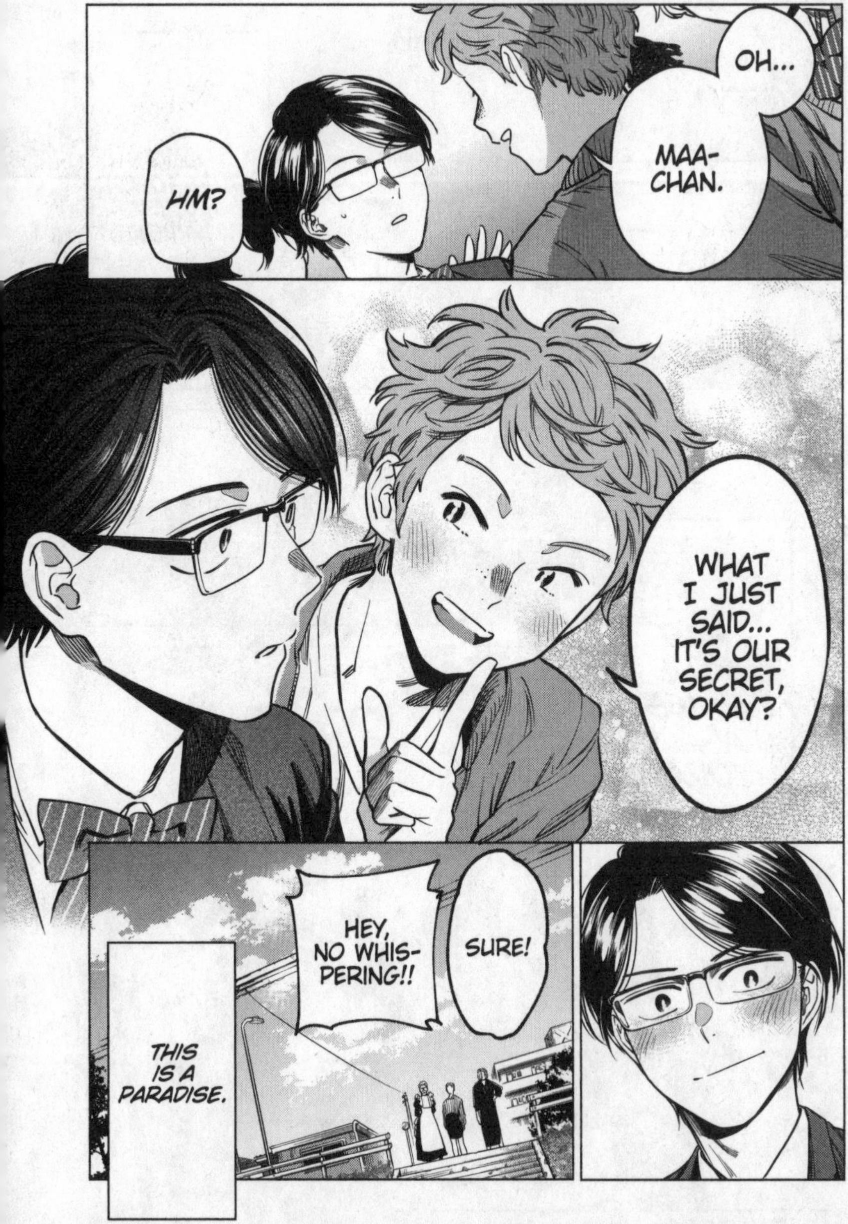
OH...
MAA-CHAN.
HM?
WHAT I JUST SAID... IT'S OUR SECRET, OKAY?
SURE!
HEY, NO WHIS-PERING!!
THIS IS A PARADISE.

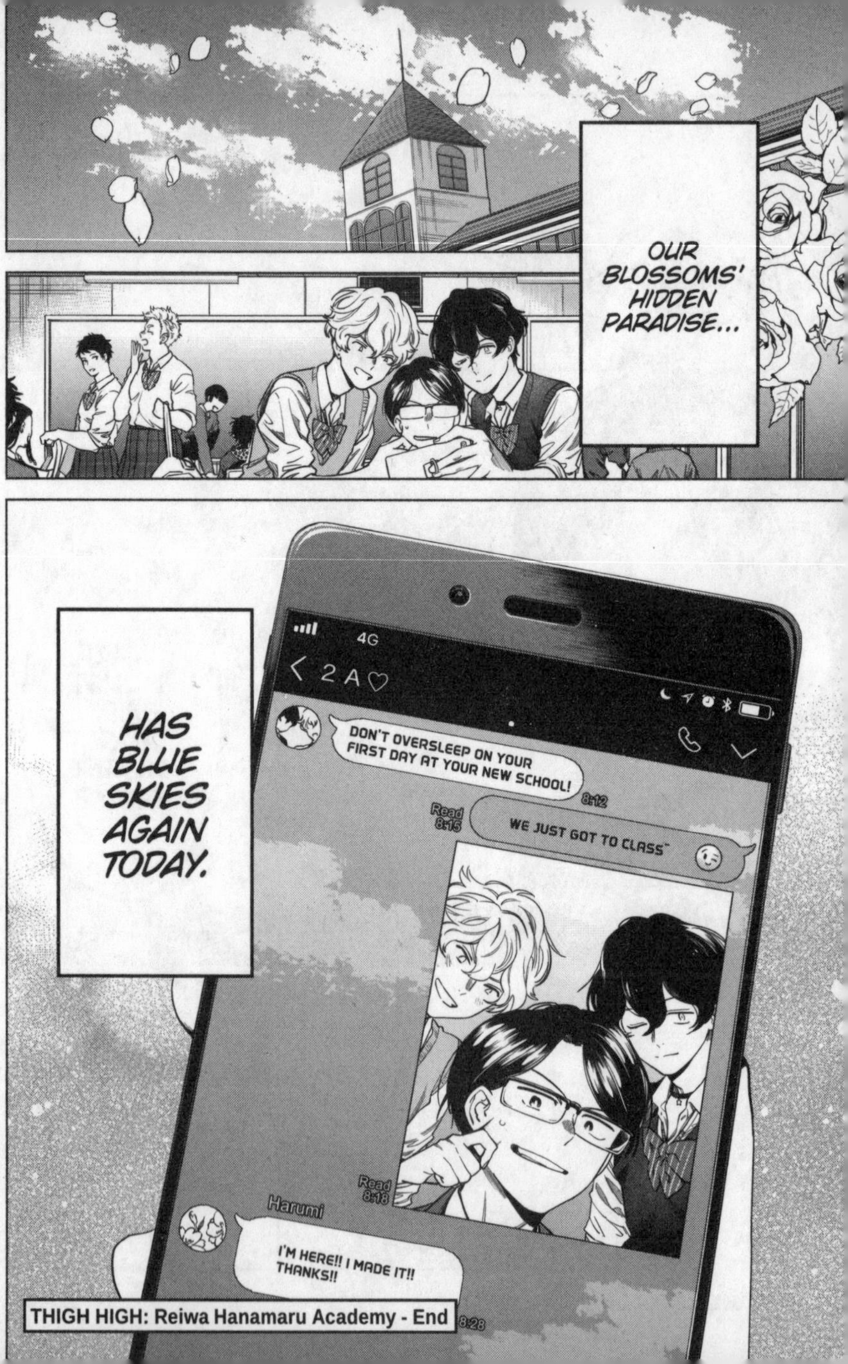
OUR BLOSSOMS' HIDDEN PARADISE...
HAS BLUE SKIES AGAIN TODAY.
4G
2 A♡
DON'T OVERSLEEP ON YOUR FIRST DAY AT YOUR NEW SCHOOL!
8:12
Read 8:15
WE JUST GOT TO CLASS~
Read 8:18
Harumi
I'M HERE!! I MADE IT!! THANKS!!
8:28
THIGH HIGH: Reiwa Hanamaru Academy - End

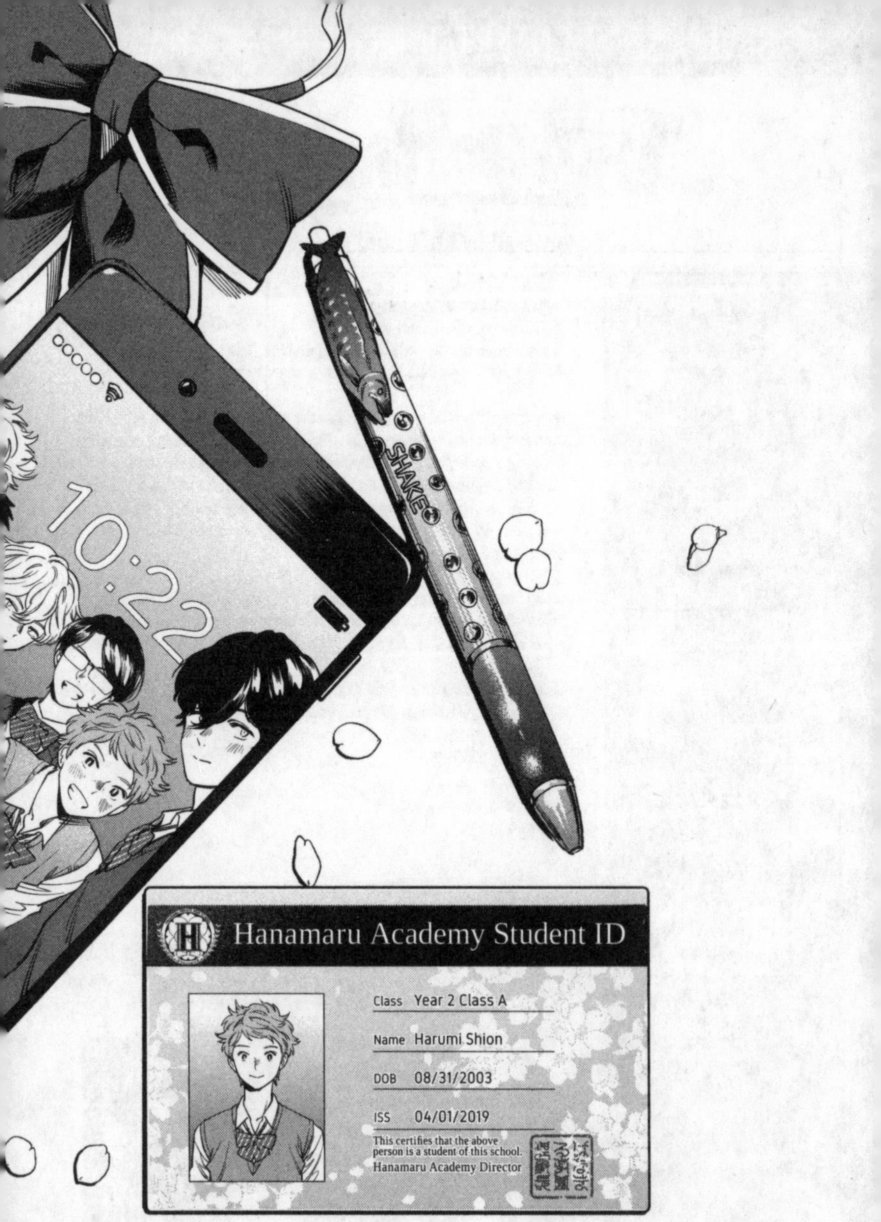
SHAKE
10:22
Hanamaru Academy Student ID
Class Year 2 Class A
Name Harumi Shion
DOB 08/31/2003
ISS 04/01/2019
This certifies that the above person is a student of this school.
Hanamaru Academy Director

Thank you for reading Thigh High: Reiwa Hanamaru Academy to the very end!! / Kotobuki

SEVEN SEAS ENTERTAINMENT PRESENTS

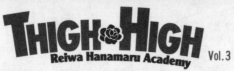

THIGH HIGH
Reiwa Hanamaru Academy Vol. 3

story & art by KOTOBUKI

TRANSLATION
Elina Ishikawa

ADAPTATION
Rebecca Scoble

LETTERING
Phil Christie

COVER DESIGN
Hanase Qi

LOGO DESIGN
George Panella

PROOFREADER
Leighanna DeRouen

EDITOR
Jenn Grunigen

PREPRESS TECHNICIAN
Melanie Ujimori

PRINT MANAGER
Rhiannon Rasmussen-Silverstein

PRODUCTION ASSOCIATE
Christa Miesner

PRODUCTION MANAGER
Lissa Pattillo

MANAGING EDITOR
Julie Davis

ASSOCIATE PUBLISHER
Adam Arnold

PUBLISHER
Jason DeAngelis

Seven Seas press and purchase enquiries can be sent to Marketing Manager Lianne Sentar at press@gomanga.com. Information regarding the distribution and purchase of digital editions is available from Digital Manager CK Russell at digital@gomanga.com.

ISBN: 978-1-63858-107-9
Printed in Canada
First Printing: February 2022
10 9 8 7 6 5 4 3 2 1

READING DIRECTIONS

This book reads from ***right to left***, Japanese style. If this is your first time reading manga, you start reading from the top right panel on each page and take it from there. If you get lost, just follow the numbered diagram here. It may seem backwards at first, but you'll get the hang of it! Have fun!!

1
2
3
4
5
6
7
8
9

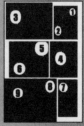

Follow us online: www.SevenSeasEntertainment.com